THE HORN OF AFRICA
IN CONTINUING CRISIS

THE HORN OF AFRICA
IN CONTINUING CRISIS

Colin Legum and Bill Lee

With
CUBA: THE NEW COMMUNIST
POWER IN AFRICA

Zdenek Cervenka and Colin Legum

AFRICANA PUBLISHING COMPANY
New York   London

A division of Holmes & Meier Publishers, Inc.

First published in the United States of America 1979 by
AFRICANA PUBLISHING COMPANY
A division of Holmes & Meier Publishers, Inc.
30 Irving Place
New York, N.Y. 10003

Great Britain:
Holmes & Meier Publishers, Ltd.
Hillview House
1, Hallswelle Parade, Finchley Road
London NW11 ODL

LIBRARY OF CONGRESS
CATALOGING IN PUBLICATION DATA

Main entry under title:

Legum, Colin.
The Horn of Africa in continuing crisis.

    Includes bibliographical references.
    1. Africa, Northeast—Politics and government—
Addresses, essays, lectures.   2. Africa, Northeast
—Foreign relations—Addresses, essays, lectures.
3. Africa, Northeast—Relations (general) with
Cuba—Addresses, essays, lectures.   4. Cuba—
Relations (general) with Northeast Africa—Addresses,
essays, lectures.   I. Lee, Bill, joint author.
II. Cervenka, Zdenek. Cuba, the new Communist
power in Africa.   III. Title.
DT 367.8.L44   1979   327'.0963'5   79-873

ISBN 0-8419-0491-X

Manufactured in the United States of America

089415

Contents

Introduction vii

I   International Dimensions of the Conflict in the Horn of Africa. 1
     Ethiopia 17
     Somali Democratic Republic 68
     Republic of Djibouti 96
     Democratic Republic of the Sudan. 109

II Cuba: The New Communist Power in Africa 137

III Documents 153

Introduction

PERSPECTIVES OF THE ETHIOPIAN REVOLUTION

When modern automatic weapons come into the hands of illiterate peasants, it is difficult to know who will give and who will take the orders—and this makes it impossible to predict with any confidence the direction of events—especially in a country like Ethiopia, where a minuscule power elite embarked on a 'progressive revolution' with literally only a few hundred Marxist–Leninist vanguard cadres on its side. Thoughts of this kind appear to have gone through the mind of the Polish journalist Jacek Kalawinski as he sat, in fear of his life, on a munition box watching military convoys—with arms provided by his own country and by other Warsaw-Pact members—roll by. In his own words:

> 'Behind me there stood two guys with Kalashnikov guns, safety catches back. I had already been told three times that if I reached for my pockets too suddenly, or made any sudden move at all, they would not warn me again. The fact was I was under arrest . . . Despite the sympathetic treatment from all the officers who had been handing me over to one another and who were very anxious to let me go, the decision rested with two illiterate peasants—but armed peasants—who had arrested me, who could not read my Government pass, and whom all the officers feared. The officers were saying: "We would let you go, but if we do, they will denounce us" '.

Kalawinski went on to tell Warsaw Radio listeners that he thought 'it would take a very long time for the revolution truly to transform that very backward country'. Then he added:

> 'Someone once said spitefully that after 3,000 years of independence—because, after all, it had never been conquered—Ethiopia now looks exactly the way Africa will look 3,000 years after decolonization. If it was a nasty thing to say about Africa, it was not nasty about Ethiopia perhaps—just a sad statement of fact. But I do think that despite what has taken place in Ethiopia—the suffering in the rural areas, the suffering of the intelligentsia, of those who live in towns, the various shortages, the consequences of political conflict—despite all that, the slow emergence from the many centuries of backwardness, which we find impossible to conceive, has begun. How many years more all this will last, I do not know'.[1]

Kalawinski offers one valuable perspective of the Ethiopian revolution as it headed unpredictably into its fifth year. A second complementary view was given by another Polish source:

> 'One of the greatest revolutions of the second half of the 20th century, and surely the biggest and most profound social revolution on the African continent, began in September 1974. The Dergue decree of 1975, which nationalized lands, was an act of both socio-economic and political importance. The peasants themselves carried out the agrarian reform and came out in favour of the revolution. Armed and formed into militia and self-defence units, they fought against the feudal units and then fought during the war with Somalia. The agrarian reform in Ethiopia was the most radical one in Africa. . . . The progress of the Ethiopian revolution, its authenticity and its scope, have made it a danger for the advocates of the old rule on the African continent. When the Dergue began a consistent implementation of its principles, Ethiopia became a victim of aggression. . . . The revolution has created the foundations for a peaceful coexistence of all nationalities living in Ethiopia. For this reason, feeding the fires of the Eritrea problem can be viewed as an anti-revolutionary act, with all Ethiopians having to pay the price for it. The reactionary centres in the Arab

world and the imperialist forces in the West do their best to halt the radical trends in Africa. Despite this, the Ethiopian revolution has entered the phase of consolidating the socio-economic transformation, the supreme goal of which is social justice. The Ethiopian just struggle is supported by the Soviet Union, Poland and other socialist States which, in line with their internationalist duty, render all kinds of assistance to all forces in the world struggling for social justice'.[2]

A third perspective—this time specifically about the situation in Eritrea—was provided by a Hungarian writer. 'One would be justified in thinking that, even in the event of the complete victory of the Ethiopian army, the bloodshed that has been going on in Eritrea for a decade and a half will *not* suddenly come to an end'.[3] [author's emphasis]

There is also a fourth perspective, as offered by a Russian commentator. Despite its contradictions, this helps to illustrate one of the many apparent paradoxes of the Ethiopian situation which even Marxist dialecticians find it difficult to resolve—and so end up by putting their complete faith in the invincibility of 'popular revolutionary forces'.

'Separatist trends can always be found in any multi-national State of national inequality and national oppression. In this respect the feudal and monarchist State of Ethiopia before the revolution was an excellent field for cultivating separatism. We must bear in mind that many nations, above all national minorities, suffered from the harsh national oppression when Ethiopia was an empire. The Government deliber- ately practised national inequality and discrimination. The superiority of one nation over another was claimed with the definite goal of winning the support of at least one privileged population group and prevent the working people from joint actions against the policy of exploitation in the country. National strife and inter-tribal hatred were kindled towards this end. Religious strife between the Muslim and Christians was fanned up. This explains why there were many movements against the Federal Government in pre-revolutionary Ethiopia. But today the situation is altogether different. First of all there is no feudalism and monarchy, from which all the working people, regardless of nationality, suffered to one degree or another. Irrespective of nationality or ethnic status, the working man has become a dominant figure in Ethiopian society. The revolutionary Government firmly stands guard to defend his vital interests and rights. . . . So, as you see, there is no nourishing media for separatism in Ethiopia today. It seems that all Ethiopians, without exception, should strive for a united, integral and consequently powerful State. But, regrettably, separatism does exist in Ethiopia and does damage to the revolutionary cause and the build-up of a new society. So where is separatism rooted today? First of all this [force] of separatism cannot be withered away easily. Secondly, separatism is maintained by the lust for power, selfish interest and adventurism of individuals. Thirdly, it is [fanned] by the outside forces hostile to the Ethiopian revolution seeking to impede Ethiopia's socialist development. These outside forces include imperialist circles and reactionary Arab regimes, Peking leadership and, finally, Ethiopian counter- revolutionaries in emigration. But the steady pace of the Ethiopian revolution reduces the influences of these factors to nil. Separatist ideas are getting less and less popular'.[4]

Thus, the composite picture presented by East European commentators is of an endlessly long revolutionary process bedevilled by local separatist (i.e., nationalist) and reactionary forces, as well as by reactionary external interventionist forces. In terms of their definition, 'reactionary' applies to all external forces which lie outside the Soviet camp (the NATO powers, China and the non-progressive Arab states) and to all internal forces opposed to the Dergue, including the bulk of Ethiopia's Marxists. In fact, the strongest centres of internal opposition to the Mengistu regime were all led by committed Marxist- Leninists. These included the Ethiopian People's Revolutionary Party (EPRP), the All- Ethiopia Socialist Movement *(Me'ison)*, *Ech'at*, WAZ (Labour) League, the Eritrean

People's Liberation Front (EPLF), the Eritrean Liberation Front (ELF) and the Tigre People's Liberation Front (TPLF). The feudal, liberal and social-democratic opposition forces turned out to be the least effective internal or external opposition in 1977–78.

The situation in Ethiopia in early 1979 might appear to have given the Ethiopian Provisional Military Administrative Council (PMAC, or the Dergue) cause for satisfaction. The war against Somalia in the Ogaden had been won, and the ethnic Somali insurgent movement appeared to have been smashed. The closest thing to a military victory seemed to have been achieved in Eritrea, with the main towns back under central government control and the guerrilla movements driven to rely on their earlier tactics of holding only the countryside. In the towns and cities of Ethiopia, the militant opposition groups which had waged a campaign of 'white terror' against the regime's 'red terror' throughout 1977 and in much of 1978 had disappeared. The regime, now purged of all but those dedicated to Mengistu's ideas about how the revolution should be waged, had seemed to gain both in self-confidence and in the esteem of Africa because of the determination of its struggle for 'national unity' and 'territorial integrity'. It had formed the strongest possible alliance with the Soviet Union and its Warsaw-Pact allies—even to the extent of acquiring associate membership in the Council for Mutual Economic Assistance (COMECON)—and had put out the first tentative feelers towards normalizing relations with the West as well.

According to this view of the situation, the ruling military committee, under Lt. Col. Mengistu Haile Mariam, seemed—for all the turmoil of the preceding five years—to have played its cards right. But this confident assessment not only failed to take into account certain less palatable facts but also ignored the critical failure of the Dergue to transform itself from a military regime into a truly Marxist vanguard organization and its almost total dependence on foreign support—both to repel external enemies and to sustain itself in power. In other words, the regime completely lacked revolutionary legitimacy.

The basic problems in both the Ogaden and Eritrea still remained unresolved. Neither war could truly be said to be over; nor were the revolutionary forces in control of important parts of Oromo territory or Tigre. The toll of damage, dislocation and economic destruction in Eritrea and the Ogaden was so vast that it could scarcely be realized, much less remedied.

Nor did the Dergue's apparent suppression of the opposition and secessionist movements on the fringes of the decaying empire—the Ethiopian Democratic Union (EDU) in the northwest, the Tigre People's Liberation Front (TPLF) in the key northern province just below Eritrea, the Afars in the east and the Oromos (Gallas) in the south and southeast—really appear to signal the end of what the regime euphemistically, but accurately, called Ethiopia's nationality problem'.

The EDU, to be sure, crumbled in the face of its own disunity rather than as a result of the Dergue's campaigns against its guerrillas in Gondar, Gojjam and Tigre. The TPLF, which had grown steadily closer to the EPLF as the latter consolidated and expanded its gains in the north, continued to harass the considerable Ethiopian military build-up in Tigre prior to the Dergue's final onslaught on Eritrea. The Dergue had some success in 'rehabilitating' and resettling some Afar tribesmen, and had enlisted some of these once violent opponents into a special unit charged with protecting traffic on the newly reopened Addis Ababa–Djibouti rail line, which passes through Afar territory. But, like many other distinctive nationalities (and religious minorities) within Ethiopia, the intensely proud Muslim Afar still felt unfulfilled by either the Dergue's programmes or its promises of regional autonomy. As for the Oromo, who saw the Dergue as a continuation of Amhara-Tigre domination, there were few signs that they were ready to abandon their traditional resistance to central authority. If anything, they had gained in numbers, in strength and in organization since 1974 revolution. Moreover, their movement had taken on a much greater military character as a result of collaboration with their Hamitic cousins, the Somalis in the Abo Somali Liberation Front (ASLF), which was active in the Bale, Sidamo and Arussi regions.

The debate within the Dergue, and the small elite surrounding it, over what type of 'mass party' to establish to guide the revolution continued indecisively. Although Mengistu kept reassuring the Russians and Cubans—who were prodding him to establish a revolutionary mass organization—that he 'realized that the development of the revolutionary process can be guaranteed success only when guided by a vanguard party of the working people',[5] he claimed that the projected Ethiopian Marxist-Leninist Organization (EMLO) could not be established until he was sure that the 'enemies of the revolution' would not be able to capture it—a clear confession of the narrow base of his regime's support. Meanwhile, as Mengistu cultivated an image of personal invincibility, the direction of the revolution was centralized in his own hands—without even the pretence of a dictatorship of the proletariat.

The only contender for the mass party was a grouping called *Abyot Seded* (Revolutionary Flame), which Mengistu himself had created and whose members were drawn mainly from the military. His Marxist critics taunted him of wishing to become the first military leader in history to produce a communist revolution without the help of a revolutionary vanguard—apart from foreign communist forces.

Meanwhile, in the absence of a popular party, the Dergue continued to rule by fiat and by terror through the use of military proclamations, martial law, the East German–trained secret police and the armed vigilantes of the *kebelles* (urban dwellers' associations). The prisons were full to overflowing with thousands of youths who had dared to challenge the military's assumption of the revolutionary mantle, and who had been subjected to unspeakable cruelty for their audacity. No one knew what would be the end result of the Dergue's attempt to 'rehabilitate' these thousands of 'counter-revolutionaries'.

On the other hand, there were ways around some of the less successful aspects of the regime's rule. Skillful groundwork could be employed to ensure that pro-Russian elements were strengthened within the Dergue and its political apparatus, and the nationalist tone of the revolution could be tempered. (When Mengistu's deputy and rival, Atnafu Abate, was purged and killed, in November 1977, he was accused of 'putting the interests of Ethiopia above the revolution'.) Once the revolutionary credentials of the Dergue were firmly established, ways could also be found of portraying the Somali and Eritrean insurgencies as 'counter-revolutionary'. Moreover, the Russians' long experience with the Eritreans afforded them the possibility of infiltrating the guerrilla movements to identify and encourage pro-Russian elements who could promote a negotiated settlement with the Dergue. At the very least, there was the prospect of dividing the rival guerrilla movements even further as a means of speeding their capitulation.

National sensibilities could best be assuaged by using Cuban troops and advisers whose temperament and background were closer to those of the Ethiopians. This, of course, was effected with great success in the Ogaden war of 1977–78, when Cubans fought in the front lines and were instrumental in the Ethiopian victory. By the end of 1978, there were c. 13,000 Cubans in the country.

An even more decisive factor in Ethiopia's Ogaden victory was the massive Soviet infusion of c. $1 bn worth of military equipment—from small arms and ammunition to MiG fighters and heavy tanks—which transformed the Ethiopian army overnight. There were a few alarums raised in Africa (though many in Washington) about the Soviet re-arming of Ethiopia; the Africans, for the most part, saw this as a necessary feature of a good cause (African states were virtually unanimous in supporting Ethiopia against Somali 'aggression')—and the Americans were not really in a position to condemn or prevent it.

ERITREA: REVOLUTIONARIES AT WAR

Throughout the revolution in Ethiopia, one thing has remained absolutely clear: the military regime could not survive, and the revolution could not succeed, without a satisfactory settlement in Eritrea.

As the post–Haile Selassie era has lengthened, the criteria for such a settlement have changed. Early hopes of negotiations with the Eritreans on some form of autonomy were dissipated with the ascendancy of Mengistu's hard-line faction of the Dergue over the moderate approach, personified by Aman Andom (the first Dergue leader, killed in November 1974), and by the subsequent Ethiopian offensives in Eritrea in 1975 and 1976. Prospects for a Soviet-Cuban–sponsored plan for a Federation of Marxist-Leninist Ethiopian and Eritrean States faded away against the intractability of centuries-old irreconcilable nationalisms. Expectations that the 'Marxist' Dergue and the 'Marxist' Eritrean fronts might 'resolve their contradictions' in the name of Marxism alone were shattered as the Dergue set out to liquidate all those whom the Eritrean leaders had regarded as the true Ethiopian Marxists (i.e., the EPRP). The Russians contributed heavily to alienating the Eritrean Marxists by giving massive military support to the Ethiopian army's effort to crush the 'rebels' by superior force.

To be fair, the Russians did not favour the use of military force to suppress the Eritreans. They preferred a political solution to the problem and worked hard to persuade both sides to reach an acceptable constitutional compromise. But, at the same time as working for a settlement, they continued to allow their military supplies, their technicians and even their generals to be used in Eritrea. To the Eritreans—and particularly to their Marxist leaders—this could only be seen as a betrayal of their 'strategic allies', whereas to Mengistu's supporters, Russian backing for their campaign in Eritrea was the acid test of friendship. Since the Russians were more concerned with their Ethiopian than their Eritrean relations, they pleaded with Mengistu; however, against their own better judgment, they joined in the massacre of Eritrea.

Mengistu admitted, in private conversations with diplomatic friends, that in discussions with the Russians he had been teased with being 'too much of an Ethiopian nationalist'—a comment which he properly understood to imply criticism. But if Mengistu was intransigent in not making concessions to the Eritreans—beyond recognizing their right to a limited form of autonomy—the Eritreans were no less so. For them the only basis of any possible compromise was a recognition of their independence; only after such recognition would they consider conditions for a future constitutional relationship.

The Soviet Union's difficulties over Eritrea were not simply confined to trying to balance their relations with both the Ethiopians and Eritreans; they also had to contend with the publicly expressed opposition to the use of force against the Eritreans from their other close allies in the Ethiopian enterprise—the Cubans, South Yemenis and Libyans. All three had insisted that there should be no 'Ogadeni solution' of the Eritrean problem. Libya's foreign secretary repeated the Jamahiriya's strong support for the revolution in July 1978.[6] Although South Yemen and Cuba both announced that they would not allow their forces to be used in Eritrea, the latter's refusal seems only to have applied to combat troops, since Cuban technicians remained on station in Asmara throughout the 1978 campaign. Cubans also trained Ethiopian troops, who were flown into Eritrea and were engaged in Tigre in helping to open up the highway into the northern province.

The Russians, in fact, skilfully exploited the stand of the Cubans, Libyans and South Yemenis in two ways: first, they used their reluctance to become militarily involved in Eritrea to try and persuade Mengistu to adopt a less obdurate position; second, they encouraged the Cubans and Libyans to play an active mediatory role with the Eritreans to try and soften their stand. The Russians also used the Palestinians to promote these mediation efforts.

The Palestinians and Eritreans were old comrades-in-arms, having shared a common enemy in Haile Selassie and his Israeli ally, which had been involved in counter-insurgency operations in Eritrea. Both the ELF and EPLF had developed particularly close relations with the Popular Democratic Front for the Liberation of Palestine (PDFLP), whose leader, Naif Hawatima, played a major part in trying to bring the Eritreans and Russians closer together. PLO leader Yasir Arafat was also brought into the negotiations by the Russians, but in his case mainly in the effort to persuade Mengistu to accept the need for compromise. The Popular Front for the Liberation of Palestine (PFLP), led by Dr George Habash, also played a part; it was the Palestinian faction most favoured by the Dergue.

Negotiations were hampered, to some extent, by the continuing divisions between the ELF and EPLF. Despite a unity agreement, they continued to operate as two separate political entities abroad, as well as to maintain separate military forces inside Eritrea. After suffering serious setbacks in mid-1978 (see below), the ELF began to disintegrate; its Soviet-oriented Marxist leaders began to show a greater responsiveness towards the federal idea promoted by the Soviets and Cubans. The EPLF, however, remained firmly resistant to these overtures. After the heavy onslaught against them in the latter part of 1978, they strongly denounced both the Russians and Cubans for their role in the Ethiopian military offensive. As of early 1979, there was no visible evidence of any weakening of opposition by the EPLF to the Soviets' plan, although there were suspicions that some of its top Marxist leaders had begun to see a possible tactical advantage in accepting a federal solution under certain conditions.

The serious weakening of the ELF and the heavy involvement of the Russians in Eritrea worked in favour of the third Eritrean force—the ELF-Revolutionary Command, led by Osman Sabbe. The ELF-APLF stuck closely to Sabbe's original position of regarding the neighboring Arab states as the Eritreans' 'strategic ally'. Although he became more closely identified with the Saudi Arabians and the Gulf State sheikhs after 1977, he nevertheless still managed to retain the confidence of his earlier backers—the Libyans, Syrians and Lebanese. Many of the dispirited ELF cadres elected to join the ELF-APLF after their military defeat, although Sabbe's forces remained much less significant than those of the EPLF.

In the new Ethiopian offensive against Eritrea, six months passed before a premature victory could be claimed at the end of 1978. After the end of the war on the Somali front in March (Cuban combat forces were left to mop up in the Ogaden), the Dergue was free to transfer its now battle-hardened forces and its impressive array of Russian weaponry to the northern front. Despite the disastrous failure of two previous attempts to deploy a 'peasant army' against the Eritrean guerrillas, the Dergue once again turned to its 'people's militia'. By this time it was no longer a motley collection of farmers but a crack force of some 200,000 well-armed men who had undergone months of hard training by Russians, Cubans and East Germans.

The offensive was launched, in June 1978, from a Soviet-built base near Axum, in Tigre. It was aimed primarily at positions in western Eritrea controlled by the ELF. The fighting that followed, at the height of the rainy season, was apparently the bloodiest in the entire seventeen-year history of the Eritrean rebellion. The new campaign succeeded in destroying most of the ELF's positions along the border with Sudan and largely crippled it as an effective organization. But by September the offensive had stalled due to determined EPLF resistance.

During a two-month lull in the fighting, a Russian *Antonov* aircraft ferried more men and supplies, including an estimated 100,000 militiamen, into Asmara, where Cuban experts were reported to be engaged in such operations as air-traffic control. The EPLF alleged that Russian officers were 'commanding the battles' on the Eritrean front and claimed to have proof of this.

The new offensive, launched in mid-November, did succeed in reopening the road up from the coast. Ethiopian troops entered Asmara from the direction of Massawa on 22 November. Within a week the Ethiopians had marched into Keren, now virtually denuded of its usual 40,000 inhabitants. With a few more towns and villages still to be recaptured, the EPLF guerrillas withdrew into the mountains to carry on the type of 'people's war' which they had waged during the first fifteen years of their independence struggle.

THE SITUATION ON THE SOMALI FRONT

Meanwhile, a year and a half after the start of hostilities, the Ogaden front with Somalia was anything but quiescent. Cuban and Ethiopian troops were manning outposts across the vast desert landscape, while much of the government's activity was directed towards housing, feeding and resettling the tens of thousands of refugees displaced by the war. Many of the Somali-speaking inhabitants of the Ogaden had not returned to their homes, however; they lived in pathetic conditions in refugees camps in Djibouti and Somalia.

After months of inactivity, the Western Somali Liberation Front (WSLF) offices in Mogadishu sprang back to life in December 1978, and again began to recruit young men for the movement's guerrilla forces. There was also unconfirmed reports about Somali regular soldiers being infiltrated back into the Ogaden. The related Abo Somali Liberation Front was still vigorously active in remote parts of the southern Ethiopian provinces of Bale, Sidamo and Arssi.

Somalia itself had settled into a barely penetrable gloom since its withdrawal from the Ogaden in March 1978. Its army was shattered—perhaps half its equipment lost or captured, perhaps a quarter of its men killed. Having thrown out the Russians and Cubans, President Siyad Barre had failed to entice any other power to take their place as Somalia's chief foreign benefactor and arms supplier. Lacking supplies for the replenishment of his restive army, Barre had to content himself with second- or third-hand consignments of arms made available to him by Egypt, Saudi Arabia and Iran. Although China showed considerable interest in helping Mogadishu, it was similarly unwilling to do much in the way of supplying arms. On the other hand, Saudi Arabia and some of the Gulf States increased their financial aid to rescue the sinking Somali economy. Western economic aid increased to the point where the country could not, under existing conditions, absorb it effectively. While the Western countries—especially the United States—was ready to help with economic aid, none was willing to supply Somalia with arms. After visits to West Germany and Britain in June 1978, President Barre complained: 'All I got were hesitant and ambiguous replies'.

Siyad Barre survived an attempted coup, in April 1978, by soldiers disgruntled at the handling of the Ogaden campaign; several dozen conspirators were tried and executed for the attempt. Above all, there remained the constant threat of renewed hostilities with Ethiopia, which Somalia continued to accuse of planning an 'invasion'. It also railed unavailingly in world forums against the Cuban presence in Ethiopia.

THE ETHIOPIAN REVOLUTION IN ITS AFRICAN CONTEXT

The Dergue's improved standing in Africa seemed as much the result of the passage of time as a sign of other African countries' approval of its successful fight for those two sacred African desiderata: territorial integrity and national unity. But Ethiopia's new role in Africa (it remains the seat of the Organization of African Unity and of many other continental institutions) was now very much a function of the Soviet Union's activist policy in the continent. Whereas Ethiopia, like the emperor himself, was once the 'grand old man' of Africa—a ready mediator in disputes, a reconciler of opposites, a symbol of stately longevity in a continent of hot, young passions—it was now one of the young militants, an eager link in a chain of 'progressive' states with which the 'reactionary' regimes of the continent could be encircled. The victory of Ethiopia's revolution had 'strengthened the position of communism in Africa', Mengistu boasted in December 1978. It was far from clear whether that achievement was something which even the leaders of the more progressive regimes in Africa could take comfort from. And it was hardly a tribute to the Dergue's African diplomacy that Ethiopia should remain on very bad terms with almost all its immediate neighbours; even Kenya's pledges of friendship, strongly voiced in 1977 and early 1978, appeared more clearly as a tactical response to the common threat posed by the expansionism implicit in the idea of a 'Greater Somalia'. Kenya's foreign minister, Munyua Waiyaki, predicting a short run for the Russians in Ethiopia, said, in January 1979: 'You will find that the African mind is not likely to swallow this stuff about scientific socialism. . . . We know the Ethiopians pretty well. They are the most nationalistic people in Africa. If the Soviets start telling them to do things they do not want, they will be told it's time to depart. It will not stick'.[7]

Indeed, Ethiopia's evolution from being Africa's historically most independent-minded (many would say xenophobic) nation to one of the loyal adherents of the Soviets' system of 'progressive nations' was one of the more remarkable results of the Dergue's revolution. And it was certainly the one factor with the greatest potential influence on future developments in the Horn of Africa.

Just as 'Ethiopian socialism' comes complete with all the trappings of Moscow-style Marxism-Leninism—red hammer-and-sickle flags, posters of Marx and Engels—so does Ethiopia's foreign policy faithfully echo the position of Moscow on all world issues: from support for the overthrow of the Pol Pot regime in Kampuchia and for the new Afghanistan regime to denunciation of Chinese policies in Vietnam. In September 1978 Mengistu branded China as 'one of the 13 reactionary countries that had directly or indirectly launched a concerted assault against us'. Having co-operated closely with Israel in the military and economic fields until as late as February 1978, he rounded on Israel as 'a stooge of imperialism' at the Afro-Arab Anti-Imperialist Solidarity Conference, held in Addis Ababa in September 1978.

THE EXPANDING ETHIOPIAN-SOVIET CONNECTION

The Soviet-Ethiopian relationship was based on a series of agreements and treaties signed by Mengistu during visits to Moscow in November 1977, April 1978 and November 1978, culminating in a 'Treaty of Frienship and Co-operation' signed by Mengistu and Brezhnev in Moscow on 20 November 1978. That date was just a year, almost to the day, after the Soviet Union's erstwhile main ally in the region, Somalia, had unilaterally abrogated an identical friendship and co-operation pact. But the Soviet-Somali relationship had always been a fairly tepid affair based on mutual national interest. The Russians never seemed to have held high hopes of winning the Somalis over to the cause of 'international socialism'. They were always prepared to concede their incapability of diverting the Somalis from their fervent devotion to Islam, or of quelling their equally fervent determination to create a 'Greater Somalia'. Somalia, a vast, barren, individualistic country with a small population and almost no natural resources, was, in the Soviet view, convenient but dispensable.

Ethiopia, by contrast, was the choice prize of all of northeastern Africa, particularly for a country seeking facilities for its navy and means to influence events in the huge arc extending from East Africa, through the Red Sea and the Persian/Arabian Gulf to Southeast Asia. Here, also, was a country with a struggling infant revolution desperately in need of a benefactor; an army faced with half a dozen insurgencies and badly in need of the military power with which to suppress them; and a regime frantically seeking to impose its control on a fractious and politically awakening population, one which had chosen communism as the instrument by which to do this.

It is doubtful whether, in the early days of the revolution, even the Soviet Union could have expected conditions to turn so singularly in its favour. There was much in the agrarian nature of Ethiopian society and in the Ethiopian termperament to commend the young revolution to the Chinese example. The age-old enmity between Ethiopia and Somalia, which, until 1977, was Moscow's strongest ally in Africa, would have seemed to militate against the early formation of an equally strong relationship between the Soviet Union and Ethiopia. But it appears in retrospect that the Russians must have been looking for ways to dilute their Somali connection at just about the time when the Dergue had decided to replace the network of relationships with the West which they had inherited from Haile Selassie.

But there were other, perhaps not so coincidental, factors. Somalia had already begun edging away from its Soviet connection in favour of stronger ties with its Arab neighbours. (It had been accepted into the Arab League in 1977.) The Somalis were also increasingly tempted to take advantage of the unsettled security situation in Ethiopia to launch an all-out attempt to 'recapture' the Ogaden region to which they had long laid claim as one of the 'lost' territories of the Somali-speaking nation. It is doubtful that the Soviets would have wanted to be identified directly with an act likely to be seen elsewhere in Africa as one of blatant aggression—even though they had for years been lavishly building up a Somali army which could conceivably only have the reconquest of the Ogaden as its principal military function.

THE ECONOMIC AND SOCIAL COSTS OF REVOLUTION

Whatever the external and international factors, an essential cause of continuing conflict in the Horn of Africa has been the failure of the Ethiopian revolution to ameliorate the country's pressing problems of poverty and economic backwardness; to usher in the new era of justice and equality—in whose name the revolution was launched; to contain the centrifugal forces within the former empire which have drawn many Ethiopians even further from the grasp of central authority; and to resolve the conflicting and long-standing nationalisms which for centuries have vied for supremacy in the region.

Economically, Ethiopia's position throughout 1977 and 1978 drew closer to disaster. The balance of payments went into deficit in 1977 for the first time since 1971, this despite record world prices for coffee, which is Ethiopia's principal export commodity. Export earnings have kept growing thanks to the world coffee boom, but they have been consistently outpaced by imports. Capital investment in the country, both private and official, has virtually dried up. The volume of coffee and other commodities exported continued to fall off due to internal production and distribution difficulties, and the precious foreign exchange and gold reserves carefully built up over the years declined sharply as a result of heavy spending on arms.

Even more alarming were chronic food shortages caused by a combination of natural and man-made factors. By late 1978 these shortages had created the threat of famine conditions similar to those of 1972–73, which had sparked the first protests against the Haile Selassie regime. Drought had hit Wollo, Tigre, Shoa and Gondar, the same regions devastated by the 1973 disaster. To add to this bleak situation, one of the worse locust plagues in years devastated the drought-hit parts of Ethiopia and Eritrea in mid-1978. The locust plague was a direct result of the hostile environment in the Horn, which had wrecked the international locust control organization. These setbacks occurred as Ethiopia's food-supply position was already deteriorating and the country was having to import large quantities of grain just to meet everyday needs. Crop production had been inhibited by uncertainty over the course of the land-reform programme. The merchants, who had once brought the crops to market, had been intimidated by the campaign against 'profiteers'. Their truck fleets had, in any case, been requisitioned for use as transporters of men and material to the war fronts. Ethiopia's main ports—Massawa, Assab and Djibouti—were either cut off by war or heavily congested, particularly during the great influx of Soviet arms. Millions of people, especially in the Ogaden and Eritrea, were dislocated by war. Foreign aid, on which Ethiopia traditionally depended, had declined. Offers of economic aid from Western countries were being turned down on ideological grounds, while aid from the East-bloc countries either failed to make up the difference or went for different purposes.

In response to all of these crises, in October 1978 the Dergue proclaimed the launching of a 'national revolutionary economic development campaign' and the setting up of a Supreme Council for Development and Central Planning, which was comprised of all sixteen members of the Dergue's standing committee as well as other officials. But this still left millions of Ethiopians living in subsistence conditions outside the mainstream of the economy—the very situation which the revolution had been designed to alleviate. The government's confident assessment of the gains of the revolution—a 30 per cent increase in the number of factory workers, the spending of $28m on improved housing, the building of as many kilometres of road in four years as in the previous twenty-five, the freeing of 'over 85% of the country's rural manpower from exploitation'—took a hard knock.

A SUMMING UP

If anyone had profited from the manifold troubles of the Horn of Africa during 1978, it was clearly the Soviet Union. It was a year of which Lenin would have approved: there was trouble everywhere, and conditions were 'very favourable'. Western strategists had got out their world maps and sketched in a 'triangle of tension' linking Ethiopia, Afghanistan and South Yemen, three countries where the Soviet Union had made remarkable gains in 1978. Within this triangle lay Iran—and by early 1979 the Shah had fallen.

It is quite possible that much of the West's concern over the vital Gulf and Red Sea lifelines of its oil trade and, at the centre, the Arabian peninsula itself—whose kingdoms and sheikhdoms were thought to be particularly vulnerable to communist subversion—was misplaced. It could be said that the Ethiopians, Afghans, Yemenis and Iranians should not be stopped from evolving political systems of their own choosing; that the West was paying the price for decades of support given to unrepresentative and repressive regimes in inherently unstable settings. Much also depended on events beyond the edges of this triangle: on the outcome of the Camp David approach to peace in the Middle East and the negotiations between Egypt and Israel; on the ramifications of political turmoil in Southern Africa, Turkey, Pakistan and India; on the development of new diplomatic relations between the United States and China; on the SALT-II negotiations between the United States and the Soviet Union.

The Horn of Africa was merely a piece in this geopolitical jigsaw. But the almost pre-ordained events which unfolded there since 1974 contained the seeds of continuing, and seemingly unresolvable, conflict. None of the basic problems in the Horn had been eliminated by early 1979. The nationalist conflicts inherited from the old Ethiopian empire were still proving stronger than the communist revolutionary forces directed against them, with Eritrea remaining the greatest obstacle in the latter's path. The Ethiopian/Somali conflict had not ended with the defeat of the Somali forces in the Ogaden; relations with Ethiopia's other neighbours—Kenya, Sudan and Saudi Arabia—remained hostile or suspicious; the competition over control of the Red Sea ports on the African littoral continued; and the Ethiopian revolution was still being directed not by a structured, mass political organization but by only one man—the exceedingly though, ruthless, determined, young and very able Colonel Mengistu Haile Mariam. He was being advised by Russians, Cubans and East Germans on how to evolve a thoroughgoing communist revolution.

Among many unresolved questions, two most crucial ones are whether Mengistu will survive and whether, in the end, he may turn out to be more of an Ethiopian nationalist than an international communist (in the mould of Fidel Castro). One thing seems perfectly clear: the Soviets are committed to turning Ethiopia into a major triumph for international communism. They have sought to justify their military role in Ethiopia on three grounds: their 'international duty' to assist an African country against aggression across its borders (i.e., against Somalia); their international right to supply arms to a sovereign state which had turned to it for help; and their support for world revolution. This last justification—which would make the martyred Trotsky turn in his grave—was formally incorporated into a joint communiqué, signed by Mengistu Haile Mariam and Vasiliy Kuznetsov, the First Vice-President of the Presidium of the USSR Supreme Soviet, in Addis Ababa on 20 September 1978, which declared: 'In the USSR, the Ethiopian revolution is regarded as a component part of the world revolutionary process. . . . The Soviet Union will continue giving all-round assistance to the friendly people of Ethiopia in attaining the [*sic*] noble aims'.[8]

Colin Legum, London
Bill Lee, Amman
February 1979

NOTES

1. Radio Warsaw home service, 'Hour of Reflection programme', 26 March 1978.
2. Zycie Warzawy, 'Ethiopian Transformations', *PAP*, 13 October 1978.
3. Laszlo Benda, Radio Budapest; 11 August 1978.
4. 'An Observer' (which usually means an official source); Radio Moscow, 16 October 1978.
5. Statement reported by Radio Moscow, 17 November 1978.
6. Sudan News Agency, 11 July 1978.
7. Interview with *International Letter* [Paris]; quoted by Reuter, 2 January 1979.
8. *Tass*, 20 September 1978.

PART ONE

International Dimensions
of the Conflict in
the Horn of Africa

International Dimensions of the Somali-Ethiopian Conflict

Although international involvement in the Red Sea-Horn region achieved its sharpest focus yet in 1977-78, it actually predates the present crisis by a century. It was after the opening of the Suez Canal in 1869 that the colonial powers moved into the area to secure their shipping routes.[1] African independence and the British withdrawal from east of Suez ended the colonial period, while the closure of the Canal from 1967-75 turned the Red Sea into a cul-de-sac of concern mainly to those living along its shores.

During this period, the littoral States of the Red Sea and Gulf of Aden evolved policies based more on their own interests than on any pattern of international inter-relationships. Thus Israel, for example, sought every way of ensuring passage along the Red Sea for her shipping and her oil supplies from the Gulf which meant running a gauntlet of hostile Arab States and forming a close relationship with the only non-Arab littoral State, Ethiopia. Egyptian naval vessels shadowed Israeli craft patrolling the Red Sea from bases in occupied Sinai, while President Sadat, between 1972-75, threw off the Russian influence that was draining his treasury and his credibility, launched a war with Israel to regain Sinai and reopen Suez, and brought in the US as the Middle East mediator. With the considerable natural and financial resources as well as moral authority at its disposal, Saudi Arabia sharpened its relationship with the US to the point of virtual interdependence. Sudan, stung by Communist involvement in its politics, disillusioned by its brief essay at large-scale nationalization and seeking help in exploiting its vast untapped resources, was drawn into the Egyptian and Saudi orbit (which circles the US sphere of influence). North and South Yemen, after a failed attempt at unification under a Soviet patronage briefly shared in the mid-1970s, saw their interests as diverging: North Yemen drew closer to Saudi Arabia and opened up to the West; South Yemen (while ending overt subversion of its conservative neighbour Oman) shied away from the Saudis—despite substantial financial inducements—and hardened its solidarity with the Soviet Union, a position strengthened in July 1978 by the coup against the Head of State by his pro-Moscow deputy. Across the Strait of Bab el-Mandeb, the tiny Republic of Djibouti won an independence imperilled by ethnic division and guaranteed only by the continuing presence of a garrison of 3,500 French legionnaires. Meanwhile, the Arab States continued to support the Eritrean independence movement as a means of strengthening their own positions and of securing the last stretch of 'non-Arab' Red Sea coastline; they also worked to undermine Ethiopia's close links with Israel.

Ethiopia's regional interests—retaining access to the sea through Massawa, Assab and Djibouti and preserving its territorial integrity in the face of 'Muslim encirclement'—did not change with the otherwise drastic convolutions following the 1974 coup. If anything, hostility to its Arab neighbours, as well as to its biggest African neighbour—Sudan—increased under the new ultra-nationalist ('Ethiopia First') military regime. The Dergue thus maintained its American (and Israeli) connections for a surprisingly long time after committing itself to the path of Marxism-Leninism.

Likewise, Somalia's priorities remained steadfast: national development and the

3

reunification of the Somali-speaking peoples under one flag. The disintegration of Ethiopia under the Dergue and the passage of Djibouti to a vulnerable independence seemed to provide the optimum conditions for pressing the Somali claim.

Thus it was in the pursuit of their own local interests (often parochial and mutually inconsistent) that the local contenders in the struggle to reshape the political contours of the Red Sea-Horn of Africa region sought foreign allies to buttress their perceived strategic and economic needs.

While the sands thus shifted on the periphery, there were seismic upheavals in the political landscape at the Horn's epicentre, in Ethiopia and Somalia. The Dergue ended 25 years of military and economic dependence on US 'imperialists' in favour of a much more fruitful—and much more demanding—relationship with the Soviet Union. Somalia tore up Black Africa's first friendship and co-operation treaty with Moscow and sought alternative military (as well as political, economic and moral) backing from the West and from both the conservative and radical Arab States.

Both Ethiopia and Somalia made these dramatic breaks with the past without really securing the degree of alternative support which their equally vulnerable regimes might have required to survive. Before the end of US military assistance to Ethiopia in April-May 1977, the Dergue had arrived at an understanding—no more—with Moscow for some $350m worth of military assistance. The Americans had supplied and trained what was essentially a 'peacetime' Ethiopian army (though it had seen action as part of a UN force in Korea and the Congo and, of course, against the Eritreans and other insurgents over the years); now a very real war was under way in Eritrea and another was threatening in the Ogaden, while the countryside seethed with rebellion. The changeover from American to Russian equipment and training strained the absorptive capacity of an already overstretched and demoralized Ethiopian army. Moreover, while the US had supplied weapons under a mixture of grants and sales credits, the Ethiopians had to pay for their Russian supplies on commercial terms—in the process draining their national treasury of its surplus coffee earnings.

What the Russians expected in return was equally far-reaching. American military aid had been exchanged for a lease on the Kagnew communications station near Asmara and in the Emperor's day had coincided with a pro-Western bias in the government, civil service and armed forces. But the USSR wanted to ensure that the Dergue's socialist policies would evolve along lines it could approve. Russian and East European advisers and technicians quickly moved into influential positions previously held by Westerners; Cuban troops moved into houses recently vacated by American military personnel. Insofar as the Russians were motivated by hopes of gaining larger strategic interests, such as securing access for their navy to the ports of Assab and Massawa, they were to discover that this was the one condition that the Ethiopians could not guarantee to provide—with or without the help of Soviet military support—since those ports lie in the rebellious lands of the Eritreans and the Afars. Massawa was already under siege, while Assab was only intermittently accessible.

The Dergue's two principal interests in enlisting Russian help were to re-establish its control over the Ogaden and to reassert Ethiopian sovereignty over its Red Sea coast. The Russians therefore must have known that unless a negotiated agreement became possible, they would be engaged in building up an Ethiopian military machine to crush the Eritreans—just as they must have known that their substantial military aid to the Somalis in turning an almost scratch army into one of Africa's finest fighting forces could have only one purpose: the 'reunification', by force if necessary, of the Somali-speaking areas of Ethiopia and Kenya. Once the Somali

4

army was trained and equipped and the Americans were no longer willing to commit themselves to an undependable and weak revolutionary regime in Addis Ababa, the Russians no doubt realized that if they stayed in Mogadishu they would willy nilly be involved in the Somali adventure in the Ogaden. This was doubtless a crucial factor in their decision to abandon their efforts to mould Somali socialism and their big investment in Berbera for the offer of an even bigger (though very risky) prize in Ethiopia—a nation with ten times the population of Somalia, with untold potential resources and the beginning of an as yet inchoate revolution.

Whereas pro-Western (but not necessarily anti-revolutionary) Ethiopians took to angrily denouncing the Americans for having 'abandoned' them to the Russians, the Somalis had been abandoned totally. Before being hustled out of the country in November 1977, Russian technicians sabotaged projects they were working on, taking away plans for uncompleted construction work and scuttling boats used in a fisheries scheme—much as the French behaved under de Gaulle in Guinea in 1960. Russian prestige was at an all-time low in Somalia.

In severing their Russian connection, the Somalis burnt their bridges even more thoroughly than the Ethiopians had done with the Americans—and with even less prospect of an alternative lifeline. The West's attitude toward Somalia after 1960 was made uncomfortable by the country's 'scientific socialism' and by Siyad Barre's erratic flirting with the Russians and the Arab League. Nor was the country's strategic position considered by the West to be of any great value, particularly with the development of the US-UK base at Diego Garcia. Eager as the West might have been to counter Soviet influence in the Red Sea, it could not reconcile its wider interests with Somali irredentist ambitions: to endorse them would not only antagonize Kenya but also flout one of the fundamental OAU principles, thereby alienating African sensibilities (see below). Even the West Germans, who owed Siyad Barre a favour for his acquiescence in the 1977 commando hijack rescue raid at Mogadishu, could not bring themselves to extend any meaningful military aid to Somalia.

Nor did Siyad Barre's Arab option prove as fruitful as he had undoubtedly been led to believe. At the height of the Ogaden war, Somalia failed to win the blanket endorsement it sought from its fellow Arab League members at a meeting in Cairo; nor did it obtain the level of military aid required from the Arab States, including Saudi Arabia, to resist the final Ethiopian offensive. In fact, the Russian-backed Ethiopian war machine simply ground up the Somalis in the battle of Jijiga; there cannot have been a Somali family that did not have someone killed or wounded.

Yet, having been let down by his Arab 'brothers' and by the Western nations (who had encouraged him to break with Moscow and then failed to replace Russian military support), and having failed to put together a Saudi-Iranian-Western alliance to cushion him from the repercussions of the Ogaden defeat, Siyad Barre still retained a Soviet option. Whereas in the first half of 1978, the Americans were offering him 'defensive' weapons and only on condition that he renounce any designs on Ethiopian or Kenyan territory, the Russians had actually come up with a package in the closing stages of the war offering him peace—and aid—with honour. Siyad Barre went to Libya to hear the Russian terms, which included a formula for Somali autonomy in the Ogaden. The attempt by disgruntled officers to overthrow Siyad Barre in April 1978 underscored his vulnerability, and there are still some factions within his ruling group who, despite all, continue to believe that Somalia's future lies in working within the context of *Pax Sovietica*.

Mengistu Haile Mariam, though no less susceptible to offers of Russian aid, has not shown himself willing to accept Moscow's or Havana's terms. Yet the concessions of territory and sovereignty which the Dergue is even less willing to make in

5

Eritrea than in the Ogaden may be resolvable only under some Russian formula. Thus, nearly a year and a half after it was first broached at the Cuban-sponsored talks in Aden, the plan for a federation—or 'progressive front'—at the mouth of the Red Sea was more alive than ever, despite the bitterness and ravages of the Ogaden and Eritrean wars.

To the West, such a plan amounted to a Russian 'strategy' for building a strong citadel in north-eastern Africa from which it would be possible to: (1) link up with the Russian-backed liberation wars of central and southern Africa and direct the final confrontation over the greatest prize of all, South Africa; (2) undermine unstable, or potentially unstable, pro-Western regimes in places like Kenya, Sudan and Egypt; (3) extend Russian control over the shipping lanes of the Red Sea, Indian Ocean and the Cape, and (4) spread subversion across the Arabian peninsula to the Gulf and, beyond, to Iran (the pro-Soviet coups in Afghanistan and South Yemen having added force to this prospect).

None of these eventualities is beyond the bounds of possibility, although they do tend to leave aside such factors as: (1) the steady erosion of Soviet influence in the Middle East, even among such formerly staunch friends as Iraq and Syria; (2) the resistance of African States, even those who accept Soviet military aid, to the extension of Russian influence and interference in their affairs, perceived by many as 'Russian imperialism'; (3) the extent to which the Third World raw-material-producing countries are, to their own advantage, intertwined with the West through the world economic system, to an extent that the Soviets can hardly hope to match, and (4) the so-far untested response of China to a major Soviet challenge, particularly in the Third World.

There also remain serious questions about the durability of any alliance forged between Russia and her existing and erstwhile allies, Ethiopia and Somalia. Both countries are fiercely independent-minded, with atavistic nationalisms. Soviet attempts to interfere with the teaching of Islam in schools earned it outright hatred from many Somalis, and any similar attempt to promote atheism among Orthodox Christians in Ethiopia would also be staunchly resisted. Somali 'socialism' is eccentric, shaped by the mores and folkways of a nation of pastoralists in which the delicate ties of tribal lineage remain all-important. Ethiopia's kaleidoscope of nationalities, complex hierarchies and its miniscule industrial base likewise inhibit the spread of proletarian egalitarianism. Ethiopians have resisted foreign domination for centuries and are unlikely to surrender their sovereignty now. There was also a more basic clash in temperament and outlook between the African and the dour, authoritarian Russian personality.

Nevertheless, by mid-1978, the Soviet Union and Cuba could look with some satisfaction on the immediate results of their adventurous decision to move from Somalia to Ethiopia. Though success was far from being assured, they had established a strong initiative in the Horn and had strengthened their position across the sea in South Yemen, with its very desirable port of Aden. They were able to make an impressive display of their commitment to 'progressive' African forces threatened with aggression; Soviet generals had a marvellous opportunity to test their capability of establishing a forward military command in a global crisis; and Soviet diplomats had a chance to act as mediators and reconcilers of several deep-seated African disputes (helped by the Cubans when they looked like possibly failing in Eritrea). The Soviet leadership was thus able to take on the West in a situation where it knew the West had no real capacity to respond without taking the undesirable step of 'linking' Soviet behaviour in Africa to sensitive East-West issues elsewhere.

It will be of no comfort to those who have died in the Ogaden and Eritrea, in the streets of Addis Ababa and a thousand villages in Tigre, Bale, Sidamo, Wollo, Wollega and Gondar, or on the Danakil plains, if these turn out to be 'short-term' Soviet gains.

INTERNATIONAL ATTITUDES TO THE CONFLICT IN THE OGADEN

External intervention was decisive in shaping the emergent pattern of political forces and the balance of power in the Horn of Africa in 1977 and the first half of 1978—the period covered in this review. Until September 1977, the balance was heavily in favour of the Somalis, Eritreans and to a lesser extent of those opposed to the Ethiopian Provisional Military Administrative Council (PMAC), more widely known from its earliest history as the Dergue. By early 1978, however, the balance had begun to move heavily in favour of the Dergue, due entirely to its foreign military allies—the Soviet bloc, Cuba, Libya, South Yemen and, to a much lesser extent, Israel. The Dergue's only active African ally was Kenya, which shares Ethiopia's interest in resisting pan-Somali ambitions.

The heaviest loser in this period was the Somali Republic, whose allies (mainly the Arab States, Sudan and Iran) failed to match the military assistance supplied to the Dergue. Having come to the brink of victory in the Ogaden in September 1977, the Somali forces were unable to consolidate their position by capturing the two remaining Ethiopian strongholds of Harar and Dire Dawa. Just when their military and economic resources were stretched to the limit, the help which they expected from the Arab League countries and the Western powers failed to arrive. The war then stalled in the Ogaden, giving the Soviet bloc (not just the Russians) and the Cubans time between October 1977 and February 1978 to deliver substantial quantities of war materiel, trained combatants and technicians to Addis Ababa. This impressive military operation turned the tide in favour of the Ethiopian forces and forced the Somali army regulars to retreat from the Ogaden. But military defeat by no means ended the dream of a Greater Somalia, kept alive by Ogadeni irregulars led by the West Somali Liberation Front (WSLF). Helped on their flanks by the still undefeated Oromo and Abo forces in Bale and Sidamo, WSLF activity has kept the province militarily insecure.

However, by April 1978, the situation on the eastern front was sufficiently under control to allow the Dergue and its allies to turn their attention to the other major war zone—Eritrea in the north. But in that dissident 'province', there was to be no quick repetition of victory; firstly because the Eritreans' prolonged struggle had enabled them to establish a much firmer hold on their territory than the Somalis in the Ogaden; and secondly, because the Dergue's allies disagreed about how to confront the Eritrean problem.

Foreign involvement on the side of Ethiopia in the Ogaden could be justified on the grounds that its border had been transgressed. The Somali Republic's protestations that its regular forces were not actively engaged in the fighting but simply 'supporting' the WSLF were never seriously believed.[2] Until Mogadishu's formal announcement on 11 February 1978 that it was sending its regular forces into the Ogaden, the official position was that a war of liberation was being waged by local Ogadeni guerrillas.[3] But the crux of the Somali case was that the border itself lacked international validity, having been arbitrarily determined, not by the former colonial powers, but by Ethiopia's 'imperialist expansionism'. However, this Somali claim was not upheld by the OAU: not a single Black African member-state supported Somalia's use of force to seek redress. The overwhelming opinion was that the Somalis were the aggressors and that the regime in Addis Ababa had the right to invite any allies it chose to help defend its territory—an African stand which legitimized Soviet-Cuban involvement in the Ogaden fighting.

The Western powers, too, were unanimous in upholding the OAU position, though not in accepting the role played by the interventionist forces. Accepting that Somalia was the aggressor, the West refused to assist it militarily after its break with Moscow on 13 November 1977. This left Mogadishu with the active support of a mainly Islamic coalition of regional powers, some of which had military ties with the West (Saudi Arabia, Egypt, Sudan and Iran), and others with the USSR (Iraq and Syria). Although the terms under which these countries obtain arms from Moscow and Washington preclude passing them on to third parties, this did not prevent Iraq from showing a considerable degree of independence and delivering some spare parts for Somalia's Soviet aircraft and tanks. Nor were Saudi Arabia and Iran prevented from financing the purchase of arms on the open market. Yet the total extent of this joint military assistance could not begin to match the quantity of Communist weapons and manpower poured into Ethiopia.

Two additional constraints inhibited Somalia's allies from active military intervention: unwillingness to defy the OAU openly, and direct opposition (especially by the US) to increasing the number of countries involved in the conflict. Despite this Western stand, the leitmotiv of Russian propaganda was that the war in the Horn was entirely due to the policy of the NATO powers in wishing to establish a 'Red Sea bloc' to perpetuate the split between the Arab and non-Arab States of the region and to gain control over the countries bordering the Red Sea.[4]

While the Western governments refused to help Somalia in the Ogaden, both they and the Arab grouping accepted that if the Ethiopians were to cross into Somalia, a completely different situation would obtain. Mogadishu would then be entitled to military support to protect its sovereignty. Egypt put some of its forces into Somalia to prepare for such an eventuality, but when Iran announced that it was also prepared to send air and other units for the same purpose, the OAU reacted sharply, strongly advising the Shah to refrain from interfering in this African conflict.[5] That no similar warning was given to the Russians and Cubans was because the OAU considered that they were legitimately engaged in helping Ethiopia repel 'a hostile attack' across its borders. Iran was also a special target for OAU criticism because of its role as South Africa's major oil supplier.

INTERNATIONAL ATTITUDES TO THE ERITREAN CONFLICT

The shift of the war front to Eritrea raised quite different issues. Nobody could accuse the Eritreans of being 'foreign aggressors', as their liberation struggle aimed at regaining the country's independence. Under an agreement approved by the UN, Eritrea was joined to Ethiopia as a federal state in 1952—a status unilaterally abrogated by Emperor Haile Selassie in 1962 with no protest from the world body. The resulting liberation struggle intensified over the succeeding 16 years, as the Eritreans slowly moved away from their original demand for the restoration of their federal status to one for complete independence. However, this aim conflicted with another OAU principle; namely, to preserve the internal unity of member-states (the stand against secessionism having been tested to the limit when the Ibos attempted to establish their breakaway Biafran republic in 1967). The Eritreans could therefore not hope for OAU support in their claim to independence, although they might expect considerable backing for a new federal relationship with Ethiopia such as was established in the Sudan after the prolonged struggle by the Anyanya who had also aimed for the secession of the three southern Sudanese provinces at one time, but had been persuaded to participate in a federal structure instead.

Throughout their long struggle, the Eritreans' strongest support has come from the Arab States who saw their bid for freedom from Haile Selassie's rule as a Muslim cause, even though Christians are probably in a slight majority in the

8

region. But the Eritreans also attracted Soviet, Cuban and, for a brief period, Chinese support, the Cubans in particular having been identified with the training of Eritrean guerrillas. The support of radical Arab States, the PLO and Marxist regimes, together with the deepening political experience of the struggle, resulted in both the major Eritrean liberation groups—the EPLF and ELF—coming under revolutionary Marxist leaders; this in turn brought wider support from Leftist regimes and movements. While this Marxist direction of the Eritrean leadership lost it some direct financial backing from a few of the more conservative Arab States who preferred the breakaway ELF-PLF of Osman Sabbe, it did not significantly reduce Arab support. In May of 1976, however, Moscow endorsed the Dergue's proposal to give Eritrea a limited form of autonomy—a proposal which did not even match the minimal federal demands originally put forward by the Eritreans.[6] The EPLF and ELF saw this as a betrayal of their position, but still continued to hope that their 'strategic allies' would come round to the 'correct line'. But in the following two years, when the Russians poured into Ethiopia arms they had once provided to the Eritreans, while also endorsing the Dergue's settlement proposals, the Eritreans grew increasingly disillusioned.

When the Russian military team which had planned the Ogaden campaign arrived in Asmara, the Dergue began to speak boastfully about smashing the Eritrean resistance. But even as the new campaign got under way, it was clear that the Dergue's allies were reluctant to try to impose a military solution. First the Libyans, then the South Yemenis and Cubans, began to make it clear that they favoured a political solution—a position clearly expressed by Cuba's Vice-President Rodriguez who recalled his country's role in supporting the Eritrean cause.[7]

The Cubans took the initiative in trying to establish a basis for agreement over Eritrea by inviting the Dergue's chairman, Col Mengistu Haile-Mariam, to Havana in April 1978. His ten-day visit coincided with the opening of the new offensive in Eritrea. George Habash, the leader of the Popular Front for the Liberation of Palestine, who enjoys good relations with both the ELF and EPLF, was in Cuba at the same time. To judge from the speeches made by Mengistu on his return home, however, Castro failed to persuade him to co-operate.

Further disagreements emerged when the South Yemeni and Cuban ambassadors left Addis Ababa for a time after having tried to strengthen the position of the Dergue's civilian Leftist opponents.[8] In fact, while Col Mengistu was visiting Havana in May 1978, Cuban and South Yemeni diplomats in Addis Ababa had helped pro-Moscow members of the Dergue to smuggle into Ethiopia a prominent Marxist civilian, Negede Gobezie. A founder of the anti-Mengistu Me'ison party, Negede travelled from Paris on a South Yemeni passport and took refuge in the Cuban embassy. From there—according to the plan—he would engineer the revival of Me'ison which had been weakened and driven underground by the Dergue's 'red terror' purges. The aim was to prepare Me'ison to form the core of the 'proletarian party' which the Dergue intended to form later in the year. Mengistu's discovery of the plot and the connivance of his main foreign allies in it cooled his relations with Havana, Moscow and Aden and led to further purges within the Dergue and civil service; Negede himself managed to get out of the country.

The Cubans, meanwhile, were busy assuring the Eritreans that their forces would not be sent to fight them, explaining that the 3,500 Cuban soldiers in Asmara were engaged in a purely defensive role—an explanation that did not satisfy the Eritreans. Habash confirmed in Beirut in late April that Castro was working for a negotiated settlement.[9] The Cuban Foreign Minister, Isidoro Malmierca Peoli, went to Moscow for talks from 18-24 April, but the joint communiqué issued at the end of the visit gave no hint of discussions on Eritrea, referring only in general terms to the situation in the Horn.[10] In June, Castro told US journalists that the Eritrean problem was Ethiopia's 'and not ours'. He added: 'The Ethiopian government knows our position. It is aware of it and respects it.'[11] In the same month, the EPLF spokesman in Paris announced that the Cuban soldiers in Eritrea had stopped fighting.[12]

There is no publicly recorded statement expressing Moscow's view of this Cuban-led initiative, or of the Cuban and South Yemeni decision not to lend military support to Ethiopia in Eritrea. (In June 1978, the South Yemenis, close Cuban allies, withdrew the 1,000 combat personnel they had lent to Ethiopia during the Ogaden campaign. The Eritrean guerrillas had previously claimed to have shot down and captured a South Yemeni pilot flying for the Dergue.) Thus the Russians were isolated in their apparent commitment both to the Dergue's internal policies and to its new campaign in Eritrea, where it continued to reinforce the Ethiopian army's position from April to June 1978. However, in July, the Russians joined with the Cubans, South Yemenis and the PLO in secret talks in Aden with leaders of the EPLF and ELF. Although this conclave produced terms for a settlement acceptable to the Eritrean leaders, it is not yet known if they can be sold to the Dergue.

THE SOVIET-WESTERN CONFRONTATION IN THE HORN

A majority of African States accepted that Soviet-Cuban military intervention had been justified in Angola in stopping South Africa's military invasion in support of Unita. However, since Moscow and Havana had planned to intervene on behalf of the MPLA well before the South Africans crossed the border, this was a *post facto* rationalization.[13] The South African factor was a piece of luck which turned initial OAU hostility to external interference in an African conflict into approval. The result of that intervention, in what was essentially a civil war, was that the communist-backed party won power and that a Marxist-Leninist regime was established, initially dependent on the Russians and Cubans.

In Ethiopia, Soviet-Cuban military intervention was once again accepted by the majority of African States as necessary in resisting the aggression of one OAU member-state against another—a sad admission of the powerlessness of the OAU to settle conflicts in the continent without foreign interference. As in Angola, the Soviet-Cuban decision to give military support to the Dergue was taken almost a year before Ethiopia's border was crossed by regular Somali forces—another instance of *post facto* rationalization. Also, as in Angola, the result of that intervention was to buttress an insecure Marxist-Leninist regime dependent for immediate survival on the Russians and Cubans. Again foreign intervention was decisive—at least in the short term—in determining the result of the power struggle.

Three of the movements engaged in this power struggle were already receiving external assistance before the arrival of the Russians and Cubans on the scene: the Eritreans from Arab and Communist countries; the Ogadeni Somalis from Somalia; and the Ethiopian Democratic Union from Sudan. However, except for the relatively minor direct Communist input into the Eritrean struggle, these sources of support were regional; no big power politics were involved between the downfall of Haile Selassie and the Soviet agreement of May 1977 to supersede the Americans as arms suppliers. For the previous three years and in spite of the Soviet presence in Somalia since 1967, the US had been intent on reducing its commitment in the area. Somalia could not possibly have posed a serious military threat to the Ethiopian system had it not been for the substantial arms aid it received from the USSR. Having made it possible for Somalia to become an 'aggressor state', the Russians then championed the opposite side, in the process destroying Russian-made equipment and fighting the very soldiers they had trained for nearly ten years.

10

The Western powers had in fact had things pretty much their own way for much of this century, and their decision to pull out made it easier for the Russians to enter the area. But the USSR refused to accept responsibility for reintroducing the danger of big power confrontation in the region, alleging that the Western disengagement was bogus, that the NATO powers were in fact actively engaged in strengthening a new Red Sea alliance through proxies—Saudi Arabia, Egypt, Sudan and Iran. Although these countries were attempting to establish a regional security system in the Red Sea-Gulf area, they were acting out of self-interest and not at the behest of the NATO powers. That such a regional security system (if ever achieved) could at least temporarily serve Western strategic interests gave the Soviets an interest in frustrating the objective. This was quite apart from their other major interest of acquiring 'blue sea' naval facilities.

Israel also looked with concern on the moves to convert the Red Sea into an 'Arab lake', which explains how it found itself on the same side in the Horn conflict as the Russians, Cubans, Libyans, South Yemenis—and to cap the absurdity—the PLO. Such contradictory alliances could not endure, and the Israelis were finally expelled by the Dergue in February 1978 because of Foreign Minister Moshe Dayan's awkward admission of his country's assistance to Ethiopia.

Throughout the developing crisis, the Americans did not want to become active rivals to the USSR. As President Carter explained on 12 January 1978: 'We have taken a position concerning Africa that we would use our influence to bring about peace without our injecting ourselves into disputes that could best be resolved by Africans themselves.' Yet the Americans felt they could not remain entirely passive while the Soviet bloc was strenuously engaged in changing the regional balance of power to suit its own interests. The problem which faced the Carter administration was how to respond without becoming militarily involved. Washington's policy was to try to persuade the Russians and Cubans to withdraw their forces by removing the ostensible reason for their presence—Somali aggression. On 11 February 1978, the US Secretary of State, Cyrus Vance, called on Moscow 'to bring about a withdrawal of Soviet and Cuban forces from Ethiopia'. Backed by the other Western powers, the US set about persuading Siyad Barre to withdraw his regular forces from the Ogaden against a pledge by the Ethiopians that they would not invade Somalia. This commitment was made on 22 February 1978, and on 10 March the Somalis began their withdrawal. But there was no sign whatever of the Russian or Cuban military elements being reduced. On the contrary, the Russians at once turned their attention to Eritrea. A small pull-out of perhaps 3,000 Cuban troops took place in July 1978 after Castro decided not to become involved in Eritrea; but many of these forces went to South Yemen where later in the month there was a pro-Moscow/Havana coup.

Besides avoiding open rivalry with the USSR, a second major aspect of American policy was its commitment to the idea that African problems should be left to the OAU to handle without foreign intervention. But this policy was totally undermined by the OAU's inability to overcome internal differences in approaching such problems as the Somali-Ethiopian conflict.[14]

The blatant Soviet reluctance to reduce its own military commitment or to induce the Cuban forces to withdraw was seen in Washington as a possible threat to detente. On 27 February 1978, the US warned that the continuing Russian military presence in Ethiopia could impede progress in the vital strategic arms limitation talks (SALT). On 2 March, Carter's national security adviser, Zbigniew Brzezinski, spoke of the possibility of Soviet policy in the Horn prejudicing the SALT talks—and especially the chances of Senate ratification of any new agreement that might be reached. The idea of linking concessions made to the USSR in SALT in exchange

11

for Soviet restraint in Africa came to dominate the West's debate about how to respond more adequately to the Soviet 'threat' on the continent. However, the US made it clear that holding up SALT was not an option to be traded against the withdrawal of Soviet and/or Cuban forces in Africa. The reason for this was explained by the US ambassador to the UN, Andy Young: 'We should signal our displeasure in any way that does not hurt us . . . Foreign policy has to be based on a nation's self-interest, and we ought not to react automatically until we determine what our interests are. A SALT treaty is very definitely in our interest.'[15]

While the Western nations anxiously continued the public debate about how to deal with the 'Russian threat in Africa' (not just in the Horn but also in Central Africa, in the dispute between Angola and Zaire,[16] as well as in Southern Africa[17]), the Soviets masterfully continued to hold the initiative. The strains produced on detente by these developments were reflected in Carter's trenchant Annapolis speech on 8 June 1978 in which he finally threw down the gauntlet: '. . . We do recognize that tensions, sharp disputes or threats to peace will complicate the quest for a successful agreement [of SALT]. This is not a matter of our preference, but a simple recognition of facts. The Soviet Union can choose either confrontation or co-operation.'

The West's military establishment (in the form of NATO's Military Committee) displayed considerable concern about the lack of 'political will' shown by their governments, but revealed little inclination to support military intervention in the Red Sea area. In fact, the consensus among NATO military analysts was that the Soviet Union was pursuing two long-term aims in Africa.[18] The first was to establish military bases from which the two most powerful oil-producing States, Saudi Arabia and Iran, together with the oil routes out of the Gulf, could be threatened. The Russians already have the use of the airfield and base facilities at Aden, and are believed to want to base a fleet at Massawa and Assab. According to analysts, the Russians had moved a floating drydock from Berbera to an island near Massawa, with the goal of controlling the southern entrance to the Red Sea leading to the Suez Canal and Israel.

While China strongly inveighed against the Soviet-Cuban intervention in the Horn, it kept to its policy of not becoming militarily involved, choosing rather to encourage Africans to recognize the threat of 'Soviet imperialism' and to urge NATO to confront the Russians more vigorously—an attitude which Moscow described, with some justification, as 'instigating NATO interference' in the Horn.[19] The Chinese naturally welcomed Somalia's break with Moscow, but despite several appeals by President Barre, was reluctant to deliver weapons and spare parts to replace Russian losses. It is still unclear whether any Chinese military shipments were sent to Somalia before that country's withdrawal from the Ogaden. A typical Chinese view of the Soviet-Cuban role in the Horn was expressed by the New China News Agency on 11 March 1978:

'The Soviet Union's interference in the dispute in the Horn of Africa and its incitement of Africans to slaughter Africans is seriously endangering the interests of the African countries and people. In this situation, the Soviet weekly *New Times* has the effrontery to declare that the interests of the Soviet Union and those of the African people "dovetail with each other". . . . The Soviet Union, far away from Africa, persistently extends its claws into the area and intervenes in affairs there in arrogant defiance of the interests of the African people. It aggravates the differences by pursuing a policy of supporting one side while opposing the other and throwing obstacles in the way of peaceful negotiations. The Soviet Union, as a rapacious merchant of death . . . tries in every way to make trouble in Africa and to dump large quantities of war weapons there. Time

12

and again, African public opinion has made it clear that "Africa's developing nations need financial aid rather than arms which are now being used to butcher their brothers". It also expresses the view that the Soviet Union "dispatches excessive amounts of arms to our brothers to destroy each other . . . and it watches the death-duel with intense amusement". Does the Soviet desire to make profits by wars dovetail with the interests of the African people?

'Africa does not want mercenary troops. This was emphatically stated last year at the 14th summit conference of the OAU, where a special document was endorsed which called for a check-up and the suppression of mercenaries. The Soviet Union, however, continues to deliver its hired assassins to Africa. In addition to the large number of Soviet mercenary troops in Angola, there are now over 10,000 Cuban and Soviet military personnel in the Horn of Africa. These highly-trained military men pilot MiG planes to bomb the cities and villages of Somalia, and high-ranking Soviet officers are known to have directly taken part in drawing up plans of war and directed mass massacres. Does this dovetail with the interests of African people? It is blatantly obvious that the Soviet Union's "dovetailing" of interests . . . is a mere pretext for infiltration and expansion into the Horn of Africa and other African areas in a big way, the object being to achieve the Soviet Union's strategic aim of engulfing Africa and outflanking Western Europe. Moscow's "dovetail" theory is dominated by its hegemonic interests. It commends those who act in conformity with its own hegemonic interests, but charges anyone who dares to struggle to safeguard the interests of his own country and Africa with the major crime of insubordination, and is not satisfied until that person is destroyed. This is precisely how the Soviet Union has treated Egypt, Sudan and Somalia. . . .

'The essential fact is that the Soviet Union wants the African countries to "dovetail" with its own hegemonic interests at the expense of the independence of the African countries. The so-called "dovetail" means implicit obedience to the Soviet Union. . . .'

THE SOVIET-CUBAN MILITARY INVOLVEMENT IN THE HORN

In May 1977, a few weeks after the Dergue ended its arms agreement with the US, the USSR and Ethiopia negotiated a secret military agreement in Moscow. No details were published, but informed estimates put the arms aid programme at $400m.[19] However, Soviet military input over the following 12 months is generally believed to have been of the order of $1 bn. Crated MiGs and tanks began arriving in Addis Ababa in September.

The concerted flow of Soviet military supplies got under way between 26–28 November 1977, when US surveillance stations in the Middle East first began monitoring a massive Soviet airlift and an increase in the number of military supply ships passing through the Bosphoros and the Suez Canal. (Between 30 and 50 Russian warships were seen passing through the Canal between June and December 1977.) The initial destination for the Russian military build-up was Aden, where the material was offloaded for onward shipment to Ethiopia by sea (lighter) and air, and the main route for the air supplies was through Iraq. But Iraqi leader, Saddam Hussein, quickly put a stop to the traffic: 'We objected and got a formal undertaking from the Soviets that these planes would go to Southern Yemen instead. We deduced, of course, that some of these shipments were going to Ethiopia by other means of transport, but there was nothing we could do about that. . . . We told the Soviets that if their attitude towards the Eritrean conflict didn't change, we could not allow their transport aircraft to use our facilities.'[20] There is no doubt that, especially after the Iraqi ban, the Russians violated both Iranian and Saudi

13

Arabian air space to maintain their air bridge.

The first reports of a Cuban presence in the Ogaden came in the third week of September when they were seen by Somalis driving some of the 300 newly-arrived Russian tanks and armoured personnel carriers. In November, US intelligence reports put the number of Russian military advisers at 100 and of Cubans at 400, the latter under the command of Gen Arnaldo Ochoa, who had been engaged in Angola in 1976.[21] By January 1978, US intelligence sources estimated the number of Russian military personnel at 1,000 and Cubans at 2,000.[22] However, the Ethiopians insisted that only 450 Russians and Cubans were in the country, none engaged in a military role.[23] By early February, the Somalis claimed that 20,000 Cubans had arrived, but Western intelligence sources put the numbers at 3,000 Cubans and 1,000 Russians.[24] Cubans and Russians became engaged in the Ogaden fighting in the first week of February during the Harar offensive. At the same time, there were reports of Russian troopships landing thousands of Cubans at Assab, the reception area for those coming in by sea.[25] The rapid build-up of Cubans was confirmed by Brzezinski on 24 February when he claimed that between 10,000 and 11,000 Cuban troops had arrived and that many were actively engaged in the Ogaden.[26] He added that c. 400 Russian tanks and 50 MiG fighters were deployed in the area.

Cosmos 964, a military reconnaissance satellite launched by the Russians on 26 November 1977, was generally assumed to have been used to control their overall military supply operation.[27] At the height of the build-up in December–January 1978, it was estimated that 225 Russian transport planes, Antonov 22s and Tupolov 76s—c. 12–15% of their military transport fleet—were involved. In early January, transport carriers were reported to be taking off from airfields north of the Black Sea at 20-minute intervals.[28] Simultaneously, dozens of Russian and East European cargo vessels, escorted by Soviet naval units, were bringing materiel to Massawa and Assab. Their cargo included T-54/55 tanks and MiG-21 fighters, together with missiles and 120mm artillery.[29] Amphibious ships arrived in Massawa and Assab from Aden—vessels which had only previously been supplied to Egypt, India and the Warsaw Pact countries.[30] Two Alligator-class Soviet naval warships operated off Massawa in February and were reportedly used to launch missile attacks against the besieging EPLF forces.[31]

This demonstration of the Soviet's airlift capacity worried NATO strategists. 'We used to console ourselves with the thought that the Soviets were not very good at this kind of thing,' one NATO official commented.[32] 'Now they have shown first in the Middle East, then in Angola and now in Ethiopia that they can organize things very effectively when they want to. They are getting better all the time.' The West German Defence Minister, George Leber, said that Soviet transport capability had become 'a new strategic element' in the East-West balance.[33]

Somalia claimed in January 1978 that the Soviet-Cuban intervention also involved military personnel from other Warsaw Pact countries including East Germany, Czechoslovakia, Poland and Hungary.[34] Somalia's Minister of Information, Abdisalam Hussein, expanded on this claim while on a visit to Peking in late February.[35] He said that at last one East German general, who had not yet been identified, was assisting in the Ogaden campaign. According to Hussein, the East Germans were in charge of communications, security and intelligence operations, Bulgarians of food supplies, while Hungarians and Czechs were engaged in other military roles. However, Moscow angrily denied Somali allegations that the Warsaw Pact powers were planning to invade Somalia, or that they were engaged in any actual military operations.[36]

This denial was aimed more specifically at a Somali claim that Marshal Dimitri

Ustinov, the USSR Minister of Defence, had arrived in Addis Ababa to plan overall strategy in Ethiopia.[37] What was more accurately established was that at least two senior Russian generals had arrived in Ethiopia and were actively engaged in planning the Ogaden campaign. The senior man was Gen Vasili Ivanovich Petrov. According to US intelligence, he is one of Russia's top-ranking soldiers, publicly listed in July 1976 as first Deputy Commander-in-Chief of all Soviet ground forces.[38] Brzezinski claimed that he was in 'direct command' of military operations in the Harar region.[39] The other top military leader was Gen Grigory Barisov who until shortly before had been in charge of the Soviet military aid programme in Somalia.[40]

The Soviet military role was by no means confined to the campaign in the Ogaden. By early February 1978, the Russians were also active in Eritrea. Apart from their naval role off Massawa, the EPLF reported seeing Russian crews operating BM-21 multiple-rocket launchers—the 'Stalin organs'—in Massawa, while South Yemeni pilots were flying MiG fighters in Eritrea.[41] Three squadrons of MiGs, including 24 MiG-21s and 12 MiG-23s were reported to be flying in Ethiopia in February.[42] Arab intelligence sources said that Russian Mil-4 and Mil-8 helicopters, armed with sophisticated anti-missile tank missiles, were engaged in the fighting in the Ogaden.[43]

At the start of the Ogaden campaign, the Ethiopian army had c. 35 American M-60 medium and 50 M-41 light tanks, 50 French AML-60 armoured cars, 90 M-113 armoured personnel carriers and c. 100 American guns and 300 mortars. In addition, 30 American M-47 tanks had arrived from Yugoslavia. At the height of the Ogaden campaign in February and early March, the Ethiopian army was reportedly strengthened by the delivery of 56 T-34 tanks, 400 T-54/55 and a few T-62 tanks, 200 armoured fighting vehicles, more than 300 guns of various calibres from 100mm to 152mm; numerous mortars; several batteries of BM-21 rocket launchers and 57mm anti-aircraft guns and SAM-3 surface-to-air missiles.[44] Several hundred man-portable SAM-7s and Sagger anti-tank guided weapons, together with large quantities of small arms ammunition, spare parts and signal equipment had also been supplied. The air force was understood to have received 60 MiG-21s, 30 MI-8 and some MI-6 heavy-lift helicopters, together with older MiG-17s from South Yemen.

Russian war materiel was reckoned by US intelligence sources in June 1978 to have reached 61,000 tons, transported by 36 freighters and an air ferry of 59 planes.[45] At the height of their strength, the total number of Cubans believed to have been engaged in the fighting in Ethiopia was variously estimated between 11,000 to 19,000. After the Ogaden victory, their numbers were reduced by 2,000 to 3,000.

By July 1978, as the Ethiopian offensive gained momentum, a daily airlift by Russian Antonov freighters from Addis Ababa, and airdrops of supplies to remote and besieged Ethiopian garrisons, were all that was keeping the Ethiopian effort alive. A simultaneous heightening of the diplomatic effort by the Cubans, South Yemenis and Palestinians to press for a negotiated settlement received a setback when Addis Ababa rejected as a 'propaganda manoeuvre' a joint ELF-EPLF offer for 'unconditional' negotiations based on Eritrea's 'right to self-determination'. The Dergue had clearly opted to fight for a military victory, with or without consideration of the possibility that its new allies could not accept such a course of action. Thus, as in the case of Somalia before the Ogaden campaign, ancient appeals to national pride seemed destined to prolong the bloody confrontation into which outside powers could not help being drawn.

15

NOTES
(All references to essays and chapters are to *Africa Contemporary Record 1977-78* unless otherwise indicated.)

1. For background, see all previous editions of *ACR* 1968–69 to 1976–77.
2. Statement by the Somali ambassador to Washington, Abdullahi Addou, to Reuter, 20 January 1978.
3. *The Observer*, London; 12 February 1978.
4. Tass, 20 March 1978.
5. *The Times*, London; 20 January 1978.
6. See *ACR* 1976–77, p. B332.
7. For details of Havana's official stand on Eritrea, see essay on Cuba's role in Africa.
8. See chapter on Ethiopia.
9. *The Guardian*, Manchester; 27 April 1978.
10. For full text, see *Soviet News*, London; 2 May 1978.
11. *International Herald Tribune (IHT)*, Paris; 23 June 1978.
12. *Ibid.*
13. See *ACR* 1975–76, pp. A3ff.
14. See essay, 'The Disunited OAU'.
15. *US News and World Report*, 5 June 1978.
16. See chapter on Zaire.
17. See essay, 'The Crisis in Southern Africa'.
18. Drew Middleton in *IHT*, 6 July 1978.
19. Sergey Kulik in Tass, 8 March 1978.
20. Interview with Arnaud de Borchgrave in *Newsweek*, 10 July 1978.
21. Graham Hovey in the *New York Times*, 15 December 1977.
22. James Reston in *IHT*, 16 January 1978.
23. David Lamb in *IHT*, 7 February 1978.
24. *Ibid.*
25. *The Guardian*, 3 February 1978.
26. *Daily Telegraph*, London; 25 February 1978.
27. Drew Middleton in *IHT*, 10 January 1978.
28. Clare Hollingworth, *Daily Telegraph*, 21 January 1978.
29. *Ibid.*
30. Desmond Wettem, *Daily Telegraph*, 23 February 1978.
31. Mike Wells in *The Guardian*, 20 January 1978.
32. *The Guardian*, 21 January 1978.
33. *Ibid.*
34. *IHT*, 21–22 January 1978.
35. *Daily Telegraph*, 1 March 1978.
36. Tass, 18 January 1978.
37. *Daily Telegraph*, 17 January 1978.
38. *IHT*, 27 February 1978.
39. *Ibid.*
40. *The Guardian*, 11 February 1978.
41. Dan Connel, The Observer Foreign News Service, 10 February 1978.
42. *Ibid.*
43. *The Guardian*, 15 February 1978.
44. Clare Hollingworth, *Daily Telegraph*, 7 March 1978.
45. *IHT*, 19 June 1978.

Ethiopia

'Revolutionary motherland or death' was the choice offered to Ethiopians in 1977 by their new military leaders. For thousands, the choice was all too real. The ruling Provisional Military Administrative Council (PMAC), the Dergue,[1] made death the penalty for opposition to its rule, although official communiqués called it 'revolutionary justice'. Their Marxist opponents were called the 'white terror' against which the Dergue ruthlessly and proudly turned the 'red terror'. 'Counter-revolutionaries' in high places faced firing squads in 1977; they included a Chairman, a Vice-Chairman and at least six other members of the Dergue itself. 'Anti-people forces' of the underground opposition were hunted down and killed by the Dergue-trained vigilantes of the *kebelle* neighbourhood associations. In the provinces, thousands of 'bandits' were 'liquidated' by the people's militia. There were casualties on the government side as well: scores of people associated with the Dergue (trade union leaders, provincial administrators, civil servants, journalists, *kebelle* officials, students, teachers, police officers and members of the PMAC itself) were killed in a furious struggle for control of the revolution. There were also the uncounted casualties of real shooting wars—against the Eritrean secessionists and nationalist EDU rebels in the north, against Oromo and Afar insurgents in the south and east and, most of all, against local Somali guerrillas and troops of the Somali regular army in the south-east. In the arid scrub of the Ogaden, the remote hills of Bale and ragged bushland of Eritrea, in the muddy ditches and foetid prison-yards of Addis Ababa, and in a cemetery outside the city with 2,000 graves reserved for 'glorious martyrs of the revolution'—in fact, all across this beautiful and tragic land—lay the victims of upheaval, reprisal and invasion. The newly-elected Mayor of Addis Ababa, an avid Dergue supporter, said: 'Many fighters for the revolution are dying, and in the future revolutionary process, a lot [more] will die.'[2]

The contenders for power in Ethiopia in the fourth full year of its revolution were numerous. The ruling Dergue, the power of the land since September 1974, imploded into an inner sanctum and, exercising 'Marxism' with an authoritarian ruthlessness, was forced to eliminate its own members and its former closest advisers in order to retain power. As the contradictions sharpened between popular socialism and military rule, the young Marxists—who with some justification saw themselves as the real revolutionaries—pitted themselves implacably against the might of the regime. Caught in the middle were the embryonic popular institutions optimistically set up since 1975 to harvest the fruits of the revolution: the peasants' and town-dwellers' associations. Organized and politicized by the civilian cadres, armed and conscripted into a national militia by the Dergue, these associations epitomized the prevailing contradictions: in a spirit of self-help and hope, they built schools, ran shops and ploughed fields; in a spirit of bitterness and recrimination, they hunted down former landlords, liquidated insurgents and patrolled the towns armed with submachine guns.

The contradictions were also evident in the Dergue's attempts to rationalize its relations with the outside world. Overturning decades of friendship with the US, Britain and other Western 'imperialist' powers, the Dergue entered into an alliance with the Soviet Union which had been massively arming Ethiopia's hostile neighbour, Somalia, since 1974. With the Russians came the rest of the Soviet bloc

17

as well as Cuba, Libya, North Korea and South Yemen. By early 1978, the Russians had poured in an estimated $1 bn worth of supplies—far in excess of the total value of arms received by Ethiopia in the previous 25 years. The Cubans brought in about 11,000 fighting troops and military advisers. This new relationship with the USSR quickly became a principal source of disagreement between the Dergue and its civilian Marxist advisers. Ethiopians began calling each other 'Comrade' (*gwadd* in Amharic) and displayed many of the trappings of revolutionary Marxism: red hammer-and-sickle banners, huge hoardings with Marxist slogans and clenched fist salutes at mass rallies. Forty-foot high portraits of Marx, Lenin and Engels—floodlit at night—looked down over Addis Ababa's Revolution Square, once the arena for Emperor Haile Selassie's festive appearances. The mastermind of the revolution, 'Comrade Colonel' Mengistu Haile Mariam (referred to below as Mengistu), presided over it all as the Chairman of the Dergue and of the Council of Ministers, Head of State and Commander-in-Chief of the Armed Forces.

THE COURSE OF THE REVOLUTION, FEBRUARY-JUNE 1977

The year began and ended with the violent liquidation of Mengistu's two main rivals. While still First Vice-Chairman of the PMAC, Mengistu eliminated the Chairman, Brig-Gen Teferi Banti, in a bloody shoot-out at the Dergue's Grand Palace Headquarters on 3 February 1977. Teferi Banti was the third Head of State to be eliminated: Haile Selassie was deposed in September 1974 and Lt-Gen Aman Andom was shot in November 1974. Six other Dergue members died with Teferi Banti, who had been Head of State for 26 months.[3] Nine months later, on 12 November, it was the turn of Mengistu's Vice-Chairman, Lt-Col Atnafu Abate, who had been the first elected Chairman of the embryonic Dergue in June 1974, when the 'Co-ordinating Committee of the Armed Forces' was carrying out the 'creeping coup' against Haile Selassie.

Both executions were followed by reprisal killings, as opponents of the regime, particularly the underground Ethiopian People's Revolutionary Party (EPRP), increased its campaign of street assassinations of known Dergue supporters;[4] the Dergue responded by ordering the summary shooting of youthful Marxist militants. This violent pattern began immediately after Mengistu declared himself Chairman of the PMAC on 11 February 1977. On the same day, in a broadcast entitled 'Being Young is no Excuse for being Reactionary' the regime warned: 'The patience of the broad masses of Ethiopia is exhausted. They are not willing to sit idly by while their sons are being murdered by fascist youths who are armed by aristocrats and imperialists at a time when they are engaged in an intricate and difficult struggle to straighten the course of the revolution.' In fact, the young targets of these attacks were every bit as hostile to the 'aristocrats and imperialists' as their traducers.

One night in February, nine people, most of them students, were gunned down in a hostel near the university campus. On 25 February, gunmen stormed into the offices of the All-Ethiopia Trade Union, shot dead its chairman, Tewodros Bekele, and seriously wounded his deputy. In the capital and other towns, the terror squads struck daily and the army and police responded in kind. As many as 1,500 EPRP suspects were taken into custody after Mengistu's coup; hundreds more simply vanished. Bodies were increasingly seen in ditches or shallow graves outside the towns, left there for the hyenas.

Nor did the Dergue's enemies further afield let up the pressure. The Eritrean secessionists were besieging a number of army garrisons as they spread their control over widening areas of the province. Nationalist guerrillas of the Ethiopian Democratic Union (EDU) controlled the border grain town of Humera and were broadcasting programmes—widely listened to clandestinely in Addis Ababa and throughout northern Ethiopia—over the transmitters of the Sudan's Omdurman Radio. In the south-east, there were reports on 21 February that 1,500 uniformed Somali troops had launched a 'search and destroy' mission against Ethiopian border positions in the contested Ogaden desert. So it was that Mengistu warned the Adowa Day rally of 'a concerted counter-revolutionary plot to destroy our revolution and test our unity'. From the crowd, the cry went up: 'Let us counter white terror with red terror. Let the enemies of the revolution be crushed.'

The Dergue's response to the state of siege was to step up the arming of civilians—members of urban dwellers' associations (*kebelles*), workers' defence squads and peasants' associations—and to speed the readiness of the 'peasant militia', the force of 300,000 or more civilians who were being trained for eventual deployment in the wars against insurgents in the north and south. Newly-imported small arms were hastily distributed to Dergue loyalists, who were encouraged to 'expose' EPRP or EDU sympathizers in their places of work. In distributing arms to 600 workers and *kebelle* leaders at the Grand Palace on 5 March, the Dergue Vice-Chairman, Lt-Col Atnafu Abate, said: 'Through unfailing vigilance day and night, you guardians of the revolution must cleanse the city of these undesirable elements.' The same day, workers defence squads at the two sugar factories, Shoa and Wonji, were also armed. On 12 March, with the atmosphere of tension and recrimination worsening, the Dergue took over the powerful medium-wave and short-wave transmitters in Addis Ababa of Radio Voice of the Gospel, which went back on the air that evening as 'Radio Voice of Revolutionary Ethiopia' (for details, see below).

The 'offensive' stance of the revolution was confirmed on 23 March with the launching of a house-to-house search in Addis Ababa for 'counter-revolutionaries'. The day before, grenades had been thrown into the city's central bus depot, and the Dergue had charged that the terror campaign was the work of the American CIA. As the city-wide search began, the overnight curfew was extended from 10 p.m. to 5 a.m., and bars were ordered closed from 7 a.m. to 7 p.m. On the first day of the search, five 'anarchists' were killed while resisting arrest. On the third day, a top leader of the EPRP, Dr Tesfaye Debassaye, fell or was pushed from the window of his flat while reportedly resisting arrest. Addis Ababa Radio described his death as 'a great victory for Ethiopian revolutionaries'.

By April, the violence in Addis Ababa had got so out of hand that the Dergue itself was forced to take drastic steps to discourage vigilantes of the *kebelles* from taking the campaign against 'reactionaries' too far. The newspapers and radio reports now carried daily tallies of hundreds of 'anti-revolutionary and anti-unity infiltrators' who were being 'liquidated' in all regions of the country. The nightly television news featured grisly films of mutilated bodies. Families of those executed were being charged a fee of c. £40—'bullet money', it was called—to retrieve the bodies of their loved ones. In the wastes of the Danakil desert, Lieut Negussie Negassa, the Dergue member in charge of liaison with the 'Provisional Office of Mass Organizational Affairs'—the Dergue's civilian politburo—was shot dead after addressing Afar tribesmen at Gawani. At a rally in his memory, Col Atnafu Abate declared that 'a thousand reactionaries will die for every revolutionary murdered'. By mid-April, the Ethiopian News Agency reported that 272 EPRP members had been 'exposed' and 89 killed since the end of February. On 18 April, an army major and corporal were sentenced to death by a court martial for extorting money from a person they had falsely accused of illegal activities.

At this point, on 12 April, Mengistu announced that the 'honour and integrity of

Ethiopia had been violated' by an attack from across the Sudanese border in the north-west (see below Foreign Affairs: Relations with the Sudan). At a rally in Revolution Square on 13 April, he dramatized his exhortation to the people to 'get armed' by picking up six bottles of red-coloured liquid and hurling them to the ground one by one to demonstrate how Ethiopia's internal and external enemies would be crushed. As each bottle exploded on the ground before him, he called out the names of the enemies: the ELF, EPRP, EDU, 'reactionaries', 'imperialists' and 'the Americans'.

THE REVOLUTIONARY AND DEVELOPMENT COMMITTEES

At the rally, Mengistu hinted at an impending mass mobilization of civilians. The peasant militias in the various provinces were by this time in some degree of battle-readiness, though some were still training with wooden sticks rather than rifles. To co-ordinate the coming 'war campaign' (*zemecha*), as it was being called, the government on 21 April established Revolutionary and Development Committees (CRDC) at the national, regional, provincial and district levels, with authority to raise financial and material donations for the war effort, and to 'apply all measures necessary to crush internal and external enemies', including the detention of suspected saboteurs for up to six months without trial. The membership of the CRDC indicated the importance the Dergue attached to it. The members were: Major Endale Tesemma (Chairman), a powerful member of the Dergue with a hard-line reputation; Col Legesse Wolde Mariam (Vice-Chairman), Minister of the Interior; Zegeyye Asfaw, Minister of Agriculture and Settlement; Taye Worqu, Commissioner of Planning; Haile Fida, the Dergue's leading ideologue and chairman of the Politburo; Daniel Tadesse, Minister of Urban Development and Housing; Tadele Mengesha, Minister of Labour and Social Affairs; Baalu Girma, acting Minister of Information; Temesgen Madebo, acting Chairman of the All-Ethiopia Trade Union; Tesfaye Shenkute, Secretary-General. Yet for all the importance initially attached to it, little was heard of the CRDC in succeeding months, as the Dergue, and notably Mengistu himself, continued to assume direct control over all the machinery of army, militia and government. Three CRDC members disappeared: Haile Fida was purged and either killed or arrested in a fierce power struggle with Mengistu (see below); Daniel Tadesse disappeared with him and was believed dead; Temesgen Madebo was assassinated by gunmen in October.

THE TOLL OF REVOLUTIONARY VIOLENCE

Insurgents continued to be reported killed by the hundreds, particularly in the south-east; the assassination of pro-government figures, including Politburo representatives and trade union leaders, also continued. So did the executions. On 27 April, 11 'anti-revolutionaries', including Tadelech Isayyas—daughter of Gen Isayyas Gebre-Selassie, a prominent figure in the *ancien regime* who was himself executed in November 1974—were killed by firing squad in Addis Ababa.

The most crucial development of this period—the Dergue's expulsion on 23–24 April of American military advisers and other officials and the closure of six foreign consulates at Asmara—is discussed separately below. If the expulsions and the subsequent suspension of American military aid to Ethiopia served to clarify the direction of the revolution, the events in Addis Ababa of the weekend of 29 April-1 May only fortified Ethiopia's growing reputation for cruelty and revolutionary instability.

The city was in the throes of preparations for the May Day rally, now an annual fixture. Left-wing EPRP militants opposed to the Dergue also considered it their

20

day, and were determined—despite the continuing wave of killings and arrests—to make a public gesture. It was not until a few days later that the outside world discovered, through the dispatches of an enterprising American reporter, William Campbell, the full horror of that weekend. At 6.30 p.m. on Friday, 29 April, students began distributing leaflets in four areas of the capital. They were quickly set upon by government troops and *kebelle* vigilantes; some were killed on the spot, others were hauled away, tortured and killed. About 40 bodies were thrown into a lake near the Spanish embassy. At the Menelik Hospital, site of the city's morgue, 170 bodies were counted, some mutilated. The bodies were stacked in the corridors for lack of space in the morgue. Relatives had to sort through the piles searching for their loved ones. The killings continued the next day, as troops and civilians roamed the city, bursting into houses and shooting or arresting suspects. Some of the youths were detained at an army headquarters; when relatives brought food for them, as is the Ethiopian custom, they were told: 'Food is no longer necessary.' Forty students were buried in a mass grave on the road to Asmara; 20–30 bodies were stacked near the French embassy. Officials sought to discourage mourning or funeral ceremonies for the dead; one funeral procession of c. 4,000 people was buzzed by air force jet fighters. Mourning mothers protested by wearing their *shamma* shawls inside out. Campbell quoted diplomatic sources as estimating the number of students killed at 300–500. On 13 May, Sweden's 'Save the Children Fund' protested to the Dergue about the killings, alleging that the victims, mostly children aged 11–13, had been dumped alongside the roads leading out of Addis Ababa, the bodies left to the hyenas. Some of the children were said to have been forced to dig their own graves before being mown down by soldiers. One victim was reported reliably to have been a six-year old boy who had shouted 'fascist Dergue' at a soldier.

In a statement on 6 May, the Dergue described the reports of the killings as 'completely baseless', and attributed them to 'a hostile propaganda campaign of international imperialism, led by American imperialism, against the ongoing revolution in Ethiopia'. However, there was a faint acknowledgement of the truth of the reports in the Dergue's accusation that the Western news media were 'distorting and exaggerating minor and isolated incidents'. Verification of the massacre reports was made even more difficult when the last three resident Western correspondents were expelled on 25 April, accused of distorting events in Ethiopia.

Mengistu's May Day speech had a surprisingly defensive tone. He conceded that the Addis Ababa search operation had not been a complete success, and admitted that conditions on the battlefronts in some places 'are getting worse'. He also spoke of 'the present invasion by Saudi Arabia, the Sudan and Egypt'. Two days later, he left for a state visit to Moscow, his first extended trip abroad since the revolution. The authorities resumed the search operation in earnest on 7 May. They claimed that the earlier operation had netted 6,000 weapons of various types, 215,000 rounds of ammunition, 399 binoculars, duplicating machines, typewriters and uniforms. In addition to the daily toll from 'mopping-up operations' conducted by rural militiamen, killings in the towns continued as well; two *kebelle* leaders, a school headmaster, his father and his son were assassinated in Addis Ababa and Gondar; the Roman Catholic Archbishop of Dessie (Wollo) and the Gondar police chief were also killed. Reports continued to appear in the official Press of the wholesale liquidation of 'bandits' and 'infiltrators' in virtually every province. The Voice of Kenya Radio claimed on 9 June that hundreds of Ethiopians were flocking across the border from Sidamo and the Ogaden.

THE DERGUE CALLS OUT THE PEASANTS

The Dergue, meanwhile, prepared to unveil the 'people's militia', a force of 300,000 peasants which had been under training for nine months and which was now to be pressed into active duty against Eritrean and EDU forces in the north, and Somali insurgents and other rebels in the south. In many ways, the militia was now the complete preoccupation of Mengistu's regime, somehow symbolizing that its was a truly 'popular' revolution, while at the same time representing the only means by which the Dergue could remain in power and keep the revolution on its present course. The regular army, particularly in the north, was either on the run or badly dispirited by setbacks, heavy casualties and the capture by Eritrean forces of up to 2,400 of their number. In the south-east, nervous troops guarded the Somali frontier with inadequate tank strength and air cover. Despite the debacle of the previous year, when an earlier—and admittedly untrained and poorly-equipped—peasant army had been ground up at Zalambesa, the Dergue was making preparations for a repeat performance. Some 1,500 regular troops had been turned into road crews to clear the mountain passes for the trucks which would ferry the peasant militia north.

On 17 June, Mengistu visited the *Tateq* ('Be Prepared') camp outside Addis Ababa, where a 'vanguard force' of militia and armed forces had been training for three months. Shouting 'revolutionary motherland or death', Mengistu said Ethiopia was preparing for war. Revolution Square in Addis Ababa was the setting for another mass rally on 25 June—this time a march-past of the militia units. The capital was put under even stricter curfew. An estimated 80,000 militiamen—eight divisions—in camouflage battle dress and small boys carrying dummy wooden rifles filed past the reviewing stand. 'Our struggle is waged to consolidate our gains, the gains which we acquired as a result of the revolution. Our struggle is waged to protect the dignity, unity and existence of revolutionary Ethiopia. This struggle is being waged to start a new life.' In evoking an Ethiopia encircled by enemies, threatened with disintegration and demanding struggle and sacrifice of its patriots, Mengistu's speech—eloquent, impassioned, skilfully demagogic—was no exaggeration.

THE INTERNATIONAL DIMENSION OF THE REVOLUTION

The violence from March to May came at a difficult time in Ethiopia's relations with the outside world. The Dergue had finally cut Ethiopia's 25-year old arms supply relationship with the US, and had begun discussions instead with the USSR. (These developments are dealt with under Foreign Affairs, below.) The threat of Ethiopia's encirclement evoked by Mengistu was not farfetched. Ethiopian Airlines was banned from Sudanese airspace on 17 June. A few weeks earlier, on 31 May, the Addis Ababa-Djibouti railway—Ethiopia's main trading link with the rest of the world—was sabotaged when five bridges were blown up between Miesso and Dire Dawa. The Ministry of Information said both these acts were 'pre-planned and co-ordinated efforts by the reactionary leaders of Sudan and Somalia to subvert the unity and disrupt the revolution of Ethiopia. Their aim is to isolate Ethiopia and her popular revolution by landlocking her.' The sabotage of the 784-km railway line was blamed on 'infiltrators trained and armed by Somalia'. But on 10 June, in a communique issued in Beirut, the Oromo Liberation Front claimed responsibility. That the rail line was out of action for nine months had crippling effects on the economies of both Ethiopia and Djibouti (see Economy, below).

MOBILIZATION AND WAR

On 24 June, the day before the people's militia was paraded before the nation, Ethiopia alleged that 'uniformed Somali soldiers' were operating on its soil. Major Dawit Wolde Giorgis, Permanent Secretary in the Ministry of Foreign Affairs, said he did not know if the intruders were regular or irregular forces, but added: 'We want to drive out all elements which are working against the Government in Ethiopia, either from the Somali side or from the Sudanese side. We can only fight up to our borders. We will fight to clear these reactionary and expansionist forces from our country.' The week before, residents of the eastern city of Harar reported watching from their balconies as Ethiopian troops and unidentified insurgents fought a skirmish outside the walls of the ancient city.

By 29 June, the first militia units were being airlifted aboard Boeing 720Bs of Ethiopian Airlines to both the north and south-east of the country. On 23 July, Ethiopia formally reported an invasion from Somalia in the Ogaden. On 27 August, the nation was mobilized with the formation of a National Revolutionary Operations Command (NROC) to co-ordinate the marshalling of 'the regular forces, police force and people's militia in the defence of the country's unity, freedom and revolution'. Ethiopia was at war.

THE DERGUE'S OPPONENTS

THE ERITREAN LIBERATION MOVEMENTS

Under the impact of the gravest threat in the 16-year history of the Eritrean liberation struggle, two of the major rival fronts seemed finally to have agreed to unite in March 1978. Although previous announcements of agreement between the leaders of the Eritrean Liberation Front (ELF) and the Eritrean People's Liberation Front (EPLF) have proved premature, the March 1978 agreement was thoroughly prepared and carefully discussed at grassroots level. After the defeat of the Somalis at the hands of the Ethiopian army, the Russians and Cubans in the Ogaden, Eritrean unity became more imperative than ever. Moreover, the ELF had lost much of its strength in 1977. However, one weakness in the new agreement was that it excluded the third and smallest group, the ELF-PLF (also known as the Third Force), led by Osman Saleh Sabbe, head of the Eritrean Foreign Mission in the Arab world.

The ELF and EPLF agreed in Khartoum in June 1977 to work towards establishing 'a national democratic front' eventually to achieve the reunification of all Eritrean guerrilla and political forces. This agreement in principle was followed by a meeting, also in Khartoum, between the ELF and Sabbe's ELF-PLF who similarly agreed to form a 'democratic national front' as a prelude to achieving 'comprehensive national unity'. However, the EPLF refused even to consider negotiating with Sabbe's Third Force. On 20 October 1977, at a further meeting in Khartoum, the ELF and EPLF agreed to form a joint political command—but not a joint military command. An agreement was signed by Isayas Afewereke, the EPLF assistant secretary-general, and Ahmed Nasser, ELF chairman, providing for practical steps to achieve organizational unity (for details see Documents section). Both parties agreed that the Third Force was to be excluded, and its members encouraged to join either the ELF or EPLF. In the spirit of this agreement, Sabbe's right to facilities at Radio Omdurman was withdrawn, but Mogadishu agreed to allow him to use its radio. Another meeting was held on 27 November—this time in Eritrean 'liberated territory'—to clear up persisting disagreements. The ELF appeared to favour a single national democratic organization with a single liberation army under joint leadership, while the EPLF favoured a popular front with the two groups working independently. The EPLF tactical approach was that while the

23

fighting front against Ethiopia should be unified immediately, more careful preparation at grassroots level was needed to achieve genuine political support. The weaker ELF was suspicious that such an approach would result in an EPLF political takeover.

Although the earlier Muslim/Christian divisions have ceased to be as important as in the earlier phase of the struggle, political differences still persist. The EPLF adopts a Maoist tactical approach to achieve 'national democratic revolution', which requires intensive politicization of 'workers and peasants' to achieve a complete social and political restructuring of society as part of the struggle for national liberation. The ELF adopts a more pragmatic approach of 'non-capitalist development' for Third World countries as defined by Moscow-oriented Marxists. The Third Force, on the other hand, regards these ideological theories as irrelevant to the independence struggle, which Sabbe insists should come first, leaving the political decisions to be taken after independence. He fears that the emphasis on Marxism will discourage Saudi Arabia and other conservative Arab states from continuing their important financial support.

Notwithstanding these political disagreements, the ELF and EPLF military cadres have co-operated in the conduct of the war. Each has respected the area of control of the other—with the EPLF largely occupying the highlands up to the Sudan and Tigre borders, and the ELF stronger in the coastal areas. However, it was the EPLF which made the attack against Massawa, and the two forces are contiguous on the perimeter around Asmara; both have links inside the capital which have allowed them to enter it almost at will, even in daytime. However, the ELF lost a substantial part of its force between July and August 1977 when 1,500 military cadres around Asmara elected to join the EPLF. Later, an estimated 3,000 crossed into the Sudan in opposition to the October agreement between the ELF and the Third Force. There were reports that this latter group was rallying around Heroui Tedla, the former ELF military commander, and Azen Yasin, both of whom had been demoted in 1976 for opposing an earlier move at unification. The defection of the men at Asmara was caused by the lack of ELF military success as opposed to those of the EPLF. By early 1978, a fair estimate of the EPLF strength was c. 30,000, while that of the ELF appears to have shrunk to below 10,000. Sabbe's forces were never large (perhaps less than 1,000), but his strength has always rested on the ability to retain the confidence of both conservative and militant Arab states, who still regard him as 'treasurer' for the Eritreans.

The EPLF administrative and military organization was astonishing. They have built a usable 1,000-km road all the way from Port Sudan (the port of entry for their supplies) to Asmara, with underground repair shops on the way and well-camouflaged fuel depots. They have also established efficient administration in the liberated towns, even keeping the electricity supply going in Keren.

THE TIGRE PEOPLE'S LIBERATION FRONT (TPLF)

The TPLF, a Marxist-led group formed in 1974, played only a minor role in the military struggle in 1977, its military cadres numbering fewer than 2,000. In the latter part of 1977, three of its central committee members—Atakilte Ketsela, Sebhatu Negga and Abai Tsehai—met with EPLF leaders to seek closer relations. It also engaged in talks with the nascent EPDRP (see below). Although the TPLF originally favoured full independence for Tigre, in 1977 it emphasized a 'national struggle with a class character'. Dan Connell, an American journalist who spent some time with the TPLF in 1977, found that its members were concentrating their activities on political education in the countryside. They have formed cultural troupes on the Chinese model, which play traditional tunes with revolutionary lyrics. One of the members of a troupe told Connell: 'Through our revolutionary songs we are trying to instil confidence in the people themselves, telling them that they are the source of political power and that they will one day destroy their oppressors.' One of their main difficulties has been in combatting traditional prejudices about the role of women in Tigre. Connell found the TPLF had full control over Intechew, only 25 miles east of Adowa, a city from which they have drawn much of their élitist support.

THE ETHIOPIAN DEMOCRATIC UNION (EDU)

Although the EDU kept up its military operations in 1977 in Tigre, Begemder and Semien (see below), its political organization ran into serious difficulties due to two different causes. The first was a bitter conflict between Ras Mengesha Seyyoum, the traditional royal leader of Tigre, and the military commander, Gen Nega Tegegne, a Shoan, which produced a rift between Tigres and Shoans. The second was due to the emergence of a radical group within the EDU's ranks which wished to rid it of any connection with members of the former Imperial establishment—like Ras Mengesha and Gen Nega. This group blamed the death of Dr Teferi Tekle-Haimanot on an internal power struggle within the EDU, and demanded the replacement of its 'feudalist-controlled Supreme Council' and 'reactionary field commanders'. A faction actually broke away to form the Ethiopian People's Democratic Revolutionary Party (EPDRP). The EDU's prestigious chairman, Gen Iyassu Mengesha, resigned in the middle of this dispute, but was later persuaded to resume the leadership, thereby limiting the damage caused by the disagreements.

The Dergue has always deliberately encouraged the idea that the former Crown Prince Asfa Wossen and other members of the Imperial family in exile were closely associated with the EDU—thereby characterizing it as a 'feudalist-monarchist group'. However none of the Crown Prince's entourage has ever been associated with the EDU; on the contrary, they are suspicious of its predominantly anti-monarchist tendencies.

THE ETHIOPIAN PEOPLE'S REVOLUTIONARY ARMY (TIGRE)

Although the Marxist-Leninist EPRA continued to maintain its separate existence, mainly localized in a small part of Tigre, it failed to make any substantial inroads during 1977 on its principal rival in the area, the TPLF. Nor did it appear to have any strong links with the EPRP.

THE ETHIOPIAN PEOPLE'S REVOLUTIONARY PARTY (EPRP)

The EPRP continued in 1977 and early 1978 to be the main enemy of the Dergue, whose policies it repeatedly denounced as a betrayal of true Marxist-Leninist principles to which it is itself committed. Nor did the EPRP relent in its bitter hostility towards the other Marxist-Leninist party, *Me'ison*, even after it broke with the Dergue in 1977 and also became a target of red terror. Despite the tight security maintained by the Dergue, the EPRP was still able to produce two publications, *Democracia* and *Labader* (The Workers), and to keep up nightly clandestine operations in the capital, suggesting that it had supporters in the police. To judge by Dergue reports, the EPRP has managed to establish cells in most of the major towns in Shoa and Hararghe (Harar and Dire Dawa), and even in the southern provinces. Its main strength continued to come from students, teachers and trade unionists. Although the EPRP seemed to have lost up to 10,000 of its supporters by February 1978 and although serious inroads were made on its chain of command, the organization nevertheless remained an active threat to the military regime. (See Red Terror vs White Terror, below.)

THE AFAR LIBERATION FRONT (ALF)

The ALF, which has close links with the EDU, continued to be led by the former Sultan of Aussa, Ali Mirreh, and his son, Hanfare Mirreh.[5] The Sultan remains in exile in Saudi Arabia, while his son is in Mogadishu, a tactical arrangement which gives the ALF a foot in the conservative Arab camp as well as in a radical one. But father and son co-ordinate their activities closely; they also maintain close links with a section of the Afari leadership in Djibouti (see chapter on Djibouti). After two years of relative military inactivity, the ALF seemed to have reassembled its fighting command during the latter part of 1977 when its guerrilla activities became more pronounced. However, the ALF felt that it was being crushed between the territorial limits set on the one side by the Eritreans (who lay claim to Assab, usually regarded as an Afari port), and on the other by the Somalis, as the WSLF aspires to control the whole of the Awash valley where the Afari nomads also have traditional rights.

THE WEST SOMALI LIBERATION FRONT (WSLF) AND
ABBO SOMALI LIBERATION FRONT (ASLF)

Assisted by the Somali army, the WSLF was central in the initially-successful struggle in 1977 and early 1978 to liberate the Ogaden province. The structure of the WSLF underwent considerable changes on 15 January 1976 at a conference held at Firq near Harar. One crucial decision was to form two wings of the West Somali liberation movement: Wariya (WSLF) and Abbo (ASLF)—the first to represent the Somali inhabitants of Ogaden, and the second those living in three other Ethiopian provinces—Bale, Arussi and Sidamo. The WSLF has also put forward the claim that most of those previously classified and accepted as Oromos by the Ethiopian authorities in these latter provinces were, in fact, members of a Somali linguistic group who spoke Abbo. The Firq conference also claimed that the *majority* of the inhabitants of Bale, Sidamo and Arussi are Somalis. The WSLF substantially enlarged the Somali territorial demands on Ethiopia, insisting that the traditional Somali lands covered the whole of the territory to the east of the Awash river, extending right up the highlands as far as Nazareth (known formerly by the Somali name of Hadamo), less than 100 km from Addis Ababa itself. This hugely enlarged Somali claim provided an entirely new dimension to the conflict in the Horn.

The leader of the Wariya wing is Abdullah Hassan Mahmoud. He was born in Jijiga in 1942 and taught Arabic in Egypt after qualifying at Cairo University. His deputy is Sherif Hasein Mohammed, who was born in 1940 in Degahabur, where he was a teacher until he became a military leader in 1963. A separate command within the Wariya wing—named after the sixteenth century Islamic warrior, Ahmed Gran (Ahmed the Left-handed, who once threatened to overrun the Ethiopian highlands)—operates from Hargeisa in the former Haud and Reserve areas which were transferred by the British to Ethiopia before their surrender of power over the former Somaliland Protectorate. The charismatic leader of the Abbo wing is Ibrahim Waago Gutu Usu, who for many years led the resistance to Haile Selassie in Bale province. Its secretary-general is Mohammed Ali Rubey. Waago Gutu, now in his early fifties, explained to the author: 'The people in Bale, Arussi and Sidamo are not Oromos but Somalis. The Somali people are divided between two language groups—Wariya and Abbo—which both mean *You*. We all stand together in the West Somali Liberation Front in demanding our independence.' He was emphatic that his struggle had nothing at all to do with the Oromo Liberation Front, and that the decision about whether the Abbo wing would favour Bale, Sidamo and Arussi being joined to Somalia or achieving a separate independence would have to be decided by the people themselves after their liberation. However, the Wariya wing leaders insist that as the representatives of their people, they wish to have the entire region east of the Awash river joined up with Somalia.

THE OROMO LIBERATION FRONT (OLF)
The Oromos (better known in modern times as Gallas) still occupy their traditional lands which stretch in a horseshoe all the way from Ethiopia's southern border to Wollo province in the east. Numerically, they form the largest group of the country's population and comprise a considerable proportion of the regular army. Although still well represented in the PMAC, their role in the officers' ranks of the army has decreased since Haile Selassie's time. The OLF's programme was first published at 'Finfine, Oromia' (Addis Ababa) in October 1974 and was later amended in June 1976. Its fundamental objective is 'the realization of national self-determination for the Oromo people and their liberation from oppression and exploitation in all their forms'. They claim this can be achieved only through a 'new democratic revolution . . . and by the establishment of the People's Democratic Republic of Oromia'. The OLF describes its enemy as 'Great Amhara chauvinism'.

THE THREE WAR FRONTS
By mid-1977, Ethiopia was fighting on three vast and widely-separated fronts, in wars almost entirely unobserved except for a handful of Western journalists who travelled with the guerrillas in Eritrea and a few carefully stage-managed trips for correspondents to both the Ethiopian and Somali sides of the Ogaden front.

1. THE NORTHERN FRONT
ERITREA
The Eritrean story in the first seven months of 1977 was one of almost unbroken success for the three wings of the secessionist movements: the Eritrean Liberation Front-Revolutionary Council (ELF), the Eritrean People's Liberation Front (EPLF) and the Eritrean Liberation Front-Popular Liberation Forces (ELF-PLF). With their victories on the battlefield, the three movements also managed to move further towards unification than at any time since the EPLF was formed in 1971 (see above). The first significant victory of the year, if not the entire 15-year guerrilla campaign, came on 23 March, when EPLF forces captured the town of Naqfa, in the northern tip of the province, after a five-month siege of the garrison there in which 840 Ethiopian troops were said to have died. In the final attack, 420 Ethiopians were claimed to have been killed and 100 captured. In April, the ELF claimed to have seized Tessenei, 25 km from the Sudanese border in southern Eritrea, after driving 3,000 Ethiopian soldiers back to a nearby camp, where they were being supplied by helicopter. The ELF forces were also besieging Barentu, between Tessenei and Asmara, and claimed to have captured its airstrip. The Dergue admitted on 21 April that Eritrean guerrillas had attacked the Soviet-built oil refinery at Assab. In May, Eritrean forces put Barentu, Agordat and Keren—all within 160 km of Asmara—under siege, while 120 Ethiopian troops fled to the Sudan from the garrison at Tessenei. Kuwait and other Gulf states stepped up their financial backing of the guerrillas, and an ELF leader told a Kuwait newspaper that any kind of federation with Ethiopia was out of the question, but that an independent Eritrea would grant Addis Ababa access to the Red Sea ports of Massawa and Assab.

The airlift of the Ethiopian peasant militia to Asmara, Massawa and Keren began in earnest in June. By July, the secessionists claimed to control 80% of the province. Guerrillas from both main movements were in position around Asmara and were making nightly forays into the city, sometimes taking Western journalists along to demonstrate the degree of their control. By 9 July, the guerrillas claimed to hold the key towns of Keren and Decamere, both major Ethiopian positions, north and south of Asmara. A Belgian journalist who witnessed the fall of Keren estimated Ethiopian casualties there at 2,000. At the same time, Agordat, north-west of Asmara, came under ELF attack and was reported captured on 26 July. A government counter-attack on Umm Hagar, a town in the far south-west corner of Eritrea, was repulsed on 18 July. By the beginning of August, the towns of Saganeiti (an Ethiopian telecommunications microwave relay centre) and Digsa, south-east of Asmara, had fallen as the secessionists completed their encirclement of the capital. Conditions in Asmara itself were reported 'intolerable' by a correspondent of the London *Observer* who went into the city with an Eritrean band in late July. 'After two and a half years of siege,' he reported, 'life is rapidly breaking down. Public services are ceasing to function, electricity fluctuates, luxury items are unobtainable, basic foodstuffs are rationed and there is a thriving black market.'

The increase in fighting sent fresh waves of Eritrean refugees fleeing across the border into Sudan. President Numeiry claimed on 9 June 1977 that his country had already received more than 1m Ethiopian refugees since Mengistu came to power in February. An additional 200,000 Ethiopians were in the Sudan before that time.

With their hold on the territory tightening, the Eritrean movements turned in June and July to the urgent necessity for unification, lest the spoils of victory be snatched away in an Angolan-style civil war among the three groups. (For relations among the Eritrean fronts, see The Eritrean Liberation Movements, above.)

Agordat, west of Asmara, was taken in mid-September by a combined force of Ahmad Nasser's ELF-Revolutionary Council and Osman Saleh Sabbe's ELF-PLF following the collapse of the 4,000-strong Ethiopian garrison there. The seven remaining Ethiopian garrisons in Eritrea, all encircled by guerrillas and deprived of vital strategic support and supplies because of the shift of Ethiopian firepower to the Ogaden, held out only because of continuing disunity among the three Eritrean guerrilla organizations. The surviving Ethiopian strongholds were at Asmara and the Red Sea ports of Assab and Massawa; and the towns of Ginda and Dongolo on the Asmara-Massawa road; Barentu, south-west of Asmara, and Adi Keih, south-east of Asmara. The critical road from Assab was cut for the first time in late September 1977.

The ELF claimed on 14 October to have cut the road between Massawa and Asmara in an ambush—described as the biggest and most successful of the 16-year war—in which 600 Ethiopian troops were reported killed or captured and c. 100 vehicles, including newly-delivered Soviet armoured cars, destroyed.

The Ethiopian forces tried twice after October to reopen the road winding down the escarpment from Asmara to Massawa, which was controlled by the EPLF. In the first attempt, the Ethiopian peasant militia, backed by Russian tanks (driven by South Yemenis) and artillery, were no more successful than the peasant army which was annihilated at Zalanbesa in 1976. According to the EPLF, the militiamen closed their eyes when they fired and threw their new Kalashnikovs away when the ammunition ran out. A few weeks later, the Ethiopians tried again, sending a column of 300 vehicles up the road from Massawa. But in their own terrain, the outnumbered Eritreans broke the attack and the Ethiopians started to retreat. 'It was a ruthless hunt,' Simon Dring of the BBC reported, 'the EPLF advancing hill by hill, outmanoeuvring and outflanking the Ethiopians each time the officers tried desperately to regroup their men. Within 24 hours, the battle was won. The guerrillas had captured the main pumping station of Massawa and, almost unintentionally, found themselves on the outskirts of the city itself, 18 miles from where the battle had begun.'

Taking over abandoned Ethiopian quarters at Dogoli, the EPLF simply brought forward their plans for the final capture of Massawa and patiently resupplied themselves, using Ethiopian trucks to make the tortuous run into the highlands to collect reinforcements, arms and ammunition. The final attack began on 19 December, as the guerrillas fought their way past the two main defensive camps outside the city and captured the airport with hardly a shot fired. More than 20,000 civilians were evacuated from parts of the city controlled by the EPLF; convoys of trucks removed valuable items, all carefully labelled to be eventually returned. The Ethiopians allegedly moved their rocket launchers onto a Russian Alligator-class support vessel photographed by reporters lying off Massawa. Ethiopian radio messages intercepted by the EPLF said bluntly: 'Do not expect reinforcements'.

On 23 December, the guerrillas made their move. From their emplacements behind a sand embankment, they suddenly emerged in a human wave that swept across the salt pans between them and the Ethiopian naval base. For four hours the battle raged; but the guerrillas were unsuccessful and eventually fell back to their positions, where they were still waiting for their opportunity in March 1978. According to Simon Dring, who observed the whole operation, casualties in the battle for Massawa were estimated at 4,000 with 600 on the guerrilla side. Overall, about 8,000 Ethiopian prisoners were held by the guerrilla movements, and a steady stream of Ethiopian defectors told of continuing executions of dissident officers and men within the Ethiopian ranks.

The situation in Eritrea early in 1978 was desperate. A first-hand report of the seemingly hopeless position was given by Mengesha Gessesa, formerly the third-ranking member of the martial law regime in Eritrea, to an American journalist, Dan Connell, after he had escaped in mid-January 1978. At that stage—before the Russians began pouring weapons into Asmara at a rate of 15–20 planeloads a day as well as into Massawa—Mengesha Gessesa said: 'It is becoming clear that Eritrea will be a free country in a matter of months'. He had been sent to Asmara in June 1975 as the assistant chief administrator responsible for economic, political and social affairs under Gen Getachew. 'I came with the idea that if we gave the Eritrean people justice the problem could be solved, but with the military situation as it was, there was nothing I could do.' When Getachew reported in similar vein to the Dergue, he was executed (see above). The same fate befell the Vice-Chairman of the Dergue, Atnafu Abate, after he had come to the same conclusion in November 1977 (see below).

Following Atnafu's execution, the Dergue launched a wave of killings in Asmara in December. According to Mengesha Gessesa, 100 Eritreans were executed on 14 December alone. He complained to the colonel in charge of security in Massawa, but on the following day another 160 were killed. A week later, the colonel himself was killed by his own soldiers near the Massawa hospital when they refused to carry out any more of his orders. Mengesha reported: 'After the attack on Massawa, our morale really deteriorated. We expected an attack against us at any time. Civilians are no longer being arrested in Asmara. They are just killed in the streets or in their homes at night by the *Afagne* (literally the 'strangling squad'). Mengesha said that after one of the *Afagne* was killed, the administration found Birr 150,000 hidden in his home. 'You can trust no one but yourself,' Mengesha added. 'It has gone too far now for anything but a military solution.' He decided to contact the EPLF for three reasons: to oppose the Dergue's policies in Eritrea and Ethiopia, particularly its campaign against the educated youth; to encourage the other Ethiopian provinces to follow Eritrea's example in freeing themselves, not only from the Dergue but from the strong and bureaucratic central government which has existed for a century; and in order to save his own neck in order to help promote what he had come to believe in.

THE EDU FRONT

In contrast to the relentless drive of the Eritreans, the EDU guerrillas seemed to have fallen largely on the defensive by mid-1977, apparently unable to sustain the momentum started with their capture in January of the border grain town of Humera. They did score some further territorial gains, taking control in April of Metemma, another border town 160 km south of Humera, and Dabbat, 35 km north of the provincial capital of Gondar. They appeared capable of striking into Gondar itself, which, as the ancient capital of Ethiopia, was their prime target. And, in July, they extended their campaign into Tigre province—where the Marxist-led Tigre People's Liberation Front (TPLF) appeared to have declined in significance, by capturing Enda Selassie, near Axum. But there were major EDU losses as well. Throughout April and May, the Dergue reported killing hundreds of 'EDU bandits' in Gondar, Gojjam and Wollo. Some of the claims, including the killing of an important EDU leader, Dr Teferi Tekle-Haimanot, were clearly true. Another EDU leader, Lt Bayu Gidey, captured by the Dergue and interviewed on television in Addis Ababa, said on 11 June that the EDU was 'on its deathbed'. He had been captured as 3,000 Dergue troops briefly retook Humera. There were also reports of a rout at Dabbat, and EDU leaders in the field conceded that it might have been a mistake to try to 'capture' the towns, instead of just 'controlling' them.

Still, the EDU's battle was as much political and psychological as military. Judging only from the fury of the sustained Dergue propaganda attacks on the EDU, they had made themselves a force to contend with. In February 1977, EDU had started regular broadcasts, in Amharic and Tigrinya, over Radio Omdurman in Sudan. The programmes were widely listened to in Ethiopia. EDU claimed to be winning the allegiance of the growing legion of defectors from the Ethiopian diplomatic corps and civil service, as well as deserters from the Ethiopian army itself; these often came over with their arms and equipment. There was no question that the EDU field command, under Lt-Gen Nega Tegegne, was growing in sophistication and tactical ability. New avenues of financial support also opened up to EDU in 1977, with the main backer thought to be Saudi Arabia; but EDU's arms purchases had for the most part to be conducted on the open market. Sudan provided unflinching support by giving sanctuary to the EDU political command, which moved to Khartoum from its previous remote base in London in the spring of 1977. The military command was by that time well-established in the field. What EDU seemed to lack was a clear ideology and the ability to co-ordinate disparate and far-flung forces, all opposed to the Dergue and prepared to take up arms against it, in various corners of the country.

Ideologically, the EDU was stung by the Dergue's repeated characterization of it as a 'monarchist' group seeking to restore the old feudal order, a portrayal un-wittingly helped by careless Western news reports. EDU's assertion that it was a 'broad movement of no particular ideological affinity welcoming all shades of political opinion and world outlook' seemed noble enough, but it lacked the ideological fervour of the Marxist opposition movements.

The Dergue announced a 'full general amnesty' for EDU followers on 1 July, saying they were free to 'return to their homes and engage in normal life'. Throughout the rest of the year and into 1978, the Dergue reported the continuing surrender and capture of EDU leaders and their followers. One group of 80, under Grazmatch Ayele Chekul, was reported 'liquidated' near Metemma in February 1978.

THE AFAR FRONT

Between Addis Ababa and its Red Sea outlets of Assab and Djibouti, and between the war zones of Eritrea and the Ogaden, lies the desert homeland of the nomadic Afar people, centred on the Sultanate of Aussa, with its seat at the dusty desert town of Assaita in the Danakil region of Wollo. These Hamitic cousins of the Somalis have not accommodated themselves to the Dergue's rule. The disaffection they share with other Ethiopian nationalities awaiting the 'liberation' promised by the Dergue is heightened by their links with fellow nomadic tribesmen who live in an uneasy marriage with the Somali Issa people in Djibouti (see section on the Afar Liberation Front above, and chapter on Djibouti).

The ALF's significance lies in the Afar country's position astride Ethiopia's main routes to the sea—the high-speed road to Assab and the road and rail links to Djibouti. The Front was severely mauled by the Ethiopian army in 1975 and did little more than periodically harass Ethiopian traffic on these routes. But it appeared to have re-established its fighting command in the latter part of 1977. In a communiqué broadcast from Somalia on 21 September, the ALF claimed to have blown up a bridge on the Assab road, inflicting heavy casualties on Ethiopian guards. Although fuel supplies from Ethiopia's only refinery at Assab were rerouted via dry river beds nearby while a temporary bridge was constructed, the Afars said they cut the road again in December with an attack on government posts at Harawe and Burie.

Earlier, in October, the Western Somali Liberation Front's daily communique claimed that Afar 'freedom fighters' had killed 460 Ethiopian troops, captured arms and ammunition, and destroyed supplies of food in an attack on a Government emplacement at Assaita.

The Addis Ababa regime announced on 3 October that Afar, Oromo and Issa nationals 'who had fled to the bush' because of the Somali invasion were being resettled with State assistance in their former homes at Melka-Jedu. Five followers of Ali Mirreh were reported to have returned to Aussa from Somalia and Djibouti, and appealed for amnesty in February 1978.

2. THE EASTERN FRONT

THE OGADEN

The first indication that the Ethiopian and Somali tanks, which had glowered at each other for years across the Ogaden desert frontier, had gone into action came in February 1977 when bush pilots flying for a Western drought relief organization claimed to have been hit while passing over the scene of a tank skirmish. The pilots claimed that Somalia had sent troops and tanks on a 'search and destroy' mission against Ethiopian desert outposts. Somalia denied this, and Ethiopia said it knew only of 'some Somali-trained insurgents', but of no actual Somali troops in the Ogaden region. But, by May, it was clear that the insurgents of the Western Somali Liberation Front (WSLF), taking advantage of the Dergue's preoccupation with Eritrea and with urban and rural discontent, had begun a military drive to reclaim the Somali-speaking areas of eastern Ethiopia. They were surprisingly numerous (c. 3,000–6,000), well-organized and well-armed. The first engagements took place along the westernmost edge of the desert and scrubland region claimed by Somalia, when the towns of Imi and El Kere were 'liberated'. In his first interview with a Western correspondent, on 25 May, the WSLF commander, Abdullah Hassan Mahmoud, said his forces were fighting in four Ethiopian provinces—Hararghe, Bale, Sidamo and Arussi—against an Ethiopian force of 20,000, mostly militiamen and frontier police. He said the Ethiopian Third Division was for the most part bottled up in small towns scattered across the region. In another interview in June, Hassan claimed that the WSLF controlled 60% of the 'Somali territory under Ethiopian occupation'. Throughout June, the Dergue daily reported the 'liquidation' of 'Somali-trained infiltrators', and the WSLF made announcements from Mogadishu of their successes in capturing a succession of waterholes. The signal for an all-out campaign by Somali forces, and a critical setback for Ethiopia, was the destruction of five bridges on the Addis Ababa-Djibouti railway, which cut Ethiopia's lifeline to the sea. The bridges hit were to the west of the railhead town of Dire Dawa, which meant that trains could go no further east than Awash. Ethiopia blamed the sabotage on Somalia. Ethiopian import-export trade, as well as the supplies of Soviet arms to the Dergue which had been carried over the railway, were shifted to Assab, itself divided from Addis Ababa by stretches of rebel-held territory across which traffic could move only under armed escort. On 24 June, Ethiopia alleged that Somalia had sent uniformed troops into the Ogaden to fight alongside the WSLF guerrillas. On 29 June, Ethiopia claimed to have killed 150 Somali-trained infiltrators who had camped 45 km from Dire Dawa. Far more serious was Kenya's claim the same day that 3,000 regular Somali troops had attacked one of its border police posts, at Ramu, and that 13 men had been killed in the fighting there. Somalia vehemently denied the charge. The truth, it seems, is that Somali liberation fighters had crossed Kenya's territory to make a new thrust into the border province of Bale. Nevertheless, the incident set off the alarm bells in Nairobi and led to Kenya officially taking the side of Ethiopia against Somalia.

By mid-July, Ethiopia admitted that a state of war existed in the Ogaden. For weeks, charges and counter-charges emanated from the national radios of Ethiopia and Somalia—to the point where no analyst could keep track of the rival claims of troops killed or captured, tanks destroyed, aircraft shot down or towns seized. Yet it was clear—confirmed by observation from US 'spy-in-the-sky' satellites—that this was no simple desert skirmish on the order of previous Ethio-Somali confrontations in the early 1960s. By early August a serious war was raging in the Ogaden. Somalia continued to deny direct involvement, while conceding that 'off duty' regular soldiers were being allowed to 'volunteer' for duty with the WSLF. It became clear that Somali forces had succeeded in capturing a series of towns, villages and waterholes in Hararghe, Bale and, to a much lesser extent, Sidamo and Arussi provinces. The names of the places were read over radio Mogadishu: Gode, Kebri Dehar, Warder, Tog Wajale, Dudub, Aware, Bokh, Imi, Dolo, Danan, Fiq, Fer Fer, Qalafo, Mustahil and Bur Hukur. By the end of July, 100 towns were claimed, some within striking distance of Dire Dawa, many over 250 km inside Ethiopia. Ethiopia said that a 'full-scale' Somali invasion began on 23 July. Two days later, there were reports of heavy fighting around Jijiga, for decades the easternmost stronghold of the Ethiopian army. The claims on both sides of tanks and aircraft destroyed quickly exceeded any semblance of credibility. By 9 August, the Ethiopian ambassador in Nairobi was admitting that Somali forces had gained control of 'most parts' of the Ogaden. Within 10 days, both sides were claiming to have killed, wounded or captured hundreds of each other's forces; the Ethiopians were displaying corpses dressed in the uniform of the regular Somali army as well as Somali MiG jet fighters said to have been shot down; advance units of Somali guerrillas, operating well beyond what were then their lines of communication and supply in the easternmost tip of the Ogaden, had staged attacks on Dire Dawa, Ethiopia's third largest city, an important rail, industrial and commercial centre and a strategic forward air base. Addis Ababa became an international arms bazaar, as small arms were ferried in from Romania, East Germany and Czechoslovakia; Vietnamese delegations arranged the sale of US war surplus equipment; and Israeli pilots allegedly flew in spare parts and ammunition for Ethiopia's American-made equipment.

Mengistu ordered a national mobilization on 20 August against the 'open invasion' by Somalia. Four days later, he called for a 'total people's war against aggressors and interventionists.' Ethiopia, he said, was engaged in a 'life-and-death struggle' in the Ogaden: 'War fronts are being opened against us from every corner.'

An attempt was made on 8 August by a special OAU mediation commission, convened in Libreville, Gabon, to work out a peaceful settlement. But it failed when Somalia walked out after the commission refused to admit a delegation from the WSLF. Addis Ababa radio reported: 'Facts are facts. A full-scale war is going on between revolutionary Ethiopia and Somalia. We cannot sit idle while our sacred right to live as a free and proud people is trampled upon by the conceited and chauvinistic designs of the fascist authorities in Mogadishu. We are assured of victory. We shall punish the aggressors.'

On 5 September, Addis Ababa reported that a 'fierce and bloody battle' was being fought with 'Somali regulars' around Jijiga, the base for Ethiopian tanks east of Harar. Fighting was also reported at Dire Dawa, the Djibouti railhead and important airbase north-west of Harar. The report claimed that five more Somali MiGs had been shot down in the fighting around Jijiga, bringing the total to date to 28; it also said that 62 of the Somalis' 93 tanks had been put out of action, 22 armoured cars destroyed and 778 Somali soldiers 'wiped out'. Five days later, on 10 September, Somalia reported that Ethiopian aircraft had bombed Hargeisa, its main city in the north and the staging base for Ogaden attacks. A Mogadishu statement confirmed for the first time that Somalia was giving 'all-out moral, material and other support' to the WSLF; but it firmly and repeatedly denied that any Somali regulars were involved in the Ogaden—a pretence kept up until late February 1978. Correspondents taken into the Ogaden from the Somali side on 12 September said Ethiopia clearly no longer controlled the entire southern part of the disputed area. On the next day, after a mutiny in the demoralized Ethiopian ranks, Jijiga fell to the Somalis who thus acquired substantial quantities of abandoned Ethiopian equipment, including tanks and ammunition.

The Dergue, now exercising virtual martial law through the National Revolutionary Operations Command, called up all retired servicemen under the age of 60 on 16 September. Drivers, medical staff and mechanics were also conscripted for immediate combat duty. Motor vehicles were commandeered to take supplies to the front, and Addis Ababa was jammed with thousands of buses, trucks, vans and taxis queueing to transport conscripts. The mobilization instructions also spoke of food rationing: 'If there are people who eat three meals a day, let them eat twice; if there are those who eat two meals a day, let them eat once. We are fighting not only the invading forces, but also time.'

At his first news conference for the world Press, held in Addis Ababa on 18

33

September, Mengistu predicted a long war to 'throw out the invaders' and also conceded that Ethiopia was trying to secure fresh American arms supplies. Mohammed Aden, a Somali envoy, said in Rome on 20 September that 'Western Somali' forces were prepared to negotiate a ceasefire—but only if Ethiopia recognized their right to self-determination. He added that Somalia would consider joining a federation with Ethiopia if the rights of Somali-speaking people under Ethiopian rule were recognized.

Ethiopia began receiving the crated airframes of knocked-down Soviet MiG-21 jet fighters at the end of September; these were assembled at Addis Ababa airport with the help of Soviet and Cuban technicians. Some Soviet armoured vehicles, ferried across the Red Sea from Aden, also began arriving at Assab, from where they were driven direct to the Ogaden front.

By October, after successfully breaching the Gara Marda Pass—gateway to the Ahmar mountain range—and knocking out an Ethiopian radar station on a peak above Jijiga, the Somalis were pushing through the mountain passes behind Jijiga towards Harar, 80 km to the west. Fierce fighting occurred in the first two weeks of October as the Somalis approached Babile, 32 km east of Harar. The Somali push through the mountains met little resistance, as after abandoning Jijiga, the Ethiopians fell back towards Harar and Dire Dawa. The WSLF claimed to have killed 300 Ethiopians in the capture of Babile.

Meanwhile, diplomatic activity gathered momentum. Ethiopia's Foreign Minister, Felleke Gedle Giorgis, travelled to Havana for five days of talks with the Cubans, stopping in New York to meet the US Secretary of State. The East German leader, Erich Honecker, urged a peaceful solution, saying the Ogaden war 'endangered the achievements of both countries' revolutions'. The Soviet Ambassador in Addis Ababa, Anatoly Ratanov, said in October that the USSR had stopped supplying arms to Somalia and was now providing Ethiopia with 'defensive weapons to protect her revolution'. Two weeks later, on 13 November, Somalia cancelled its 1974 Treaty of Friendship with the USSR, withdrew all Soviet military and air facilities and expelled the 5–6,000 Soviet diplomats, technicians and advisers. Diplomatic relations with Moscow were retained, but not with Havana. All Cuban advisers, numbering c. 400, were ordered to leave.

By the end of November, some Somali units (helped by torrential rains) had penetrated the defences of Harar. Although the WSLF claimed 'absolute control of Harar and the surrounding area', it was clear that the Ethiopian Third Division was holding out against the attack.

Earlier, in November, the Soviet Union launched one of the largest military support operations in recent history. It transported, by air and sea, an estimated $1 bn worth of equipment: MiG fighter aircraft, heavy and light tanks, multi-barrelled rocket launchers, artillery, small arms, ammunition, vehicles, medical supplies, food and petroleum. Flight after flight of Antonov and Tupolev transport planes (carrying equipment) and Ilyushin airliners (carrying personnel) landed at Addis Ababa airport. Some flew from South Russia via Iraq and Aden; others from eastern Russia to Libya. They filed misleading flight plans and violated the airspace of Turkey, Sudan, Pakistan and other countries en route. At the same time, c. 30–50 Russian ships travelled through the Black Sea and the Suez Canal into the Red Sea to Assab. Monitored by a Russian satellite, launched specially for the purpose, the airlift and sealift were a test of the USSR's global tactical capacity; they were also a powerful demonstration of Moscow's active interest in the Red Sea region and therefore a source of concern to those Western, Arab and African countries who view with suspicion any expansion of Soviet influence.

The strategic command of the Ogaden campaign was taken over by two generals—Vassily Petrov, a Deputy-Commander of the Soviet ground forces, and Arnaldo Ochoa, who was in Angola in 1976. Over the next two months, an estimated 11,000 Cubans and 1,000 Russian military personnel arrived to put the Ethiopian army through a crash programme in the use of Soviet aircraft and equipment, while the Cuban combat troops were integrated into the Ethiopian front-line units. On 13 February 1978, Somalia openly committed its regular forces to the war, and a few days later the strengthened Ethiopian army went into the counter-offensive in the Ogaden.

Pushing forward in four fronts from Dire Dawa and Harar, they rapidly drove the Somalis back towards Jijiga. One counter-thrust was along the rail line to Djibouti. Mengistu had pledged at a Press conference on 14 February that his forces would not cross the Somali border. 'The defensive war we are waging goes as far as our frontier.'

The big breakthrough came on 5 March, when Ethiopia recaptured Jijiga. The victory was achieved with the help of Soviet Mi-6 helicopters which airlifted Ethiopian tanks, two at a time, from Dire Dawa around the back of the Ahmar mountains to Jijiga. Four days later, on 9 March, the Ethiopian victory was assured when Mogadishu broadcast a statement by the Acting Information Minister, Abdisalam Sheikh Hussein: '[Since] the big powers have suggested that the problem of the Horn of Africa be solved peacefully and that all foreign troops withdraw, and that Somalia withdraw her units, at the same time promising that the rights of Western Somalia will be safeguarded, the Central Committee of the Somali Revolutionary Socialist Party has decidéd that Somali units be withdrawn.' The Somali withdrawal was announced simultaneously by President Carter in Washington, who also urged the progressive withdrawal of Soviet and Cuban forces from Ethiopia. However, the Dergue declined to accept a ceasefire until Somalia publicly renounced for all time any claims on the Ogaden.

The WSLF also refused to accept the defeat as final. Its leader, Abdullah Hassan Mahmoud, said at a Press conference in Mogadishu on 11 March 1978 that Somalia's decision to withdraw its regular forces 'will not bring peace; it will bring more bloodshed and war. The masses will continue to wage the war until complete success, no matter how long or how many sacrifices it takes.' He blamed the defeat equally on the two super-powers. 'They have both adopted identical policies and attitudes towards this problem. The US has approved the Soviet plan, so it doesn't matter if one was absent from the battlefield.'

3. THE SOUTHERN FRONT

This front covers the three provinces west of the Ogaden and south of Addis Ababa: Bale, a mountainous province which has been rebellious since the early 1960s; Sidamo, a fertile province on the southern border with Kenya; and Arssi (until 1977 known as Arussi), a scenic lakeland region just south of Addis Ababa. The Oromos have always been considered predominant in these provinces. A Hamitic people like the Somalis, as opposed to the Semitic Amharas and Tigres, they speak their own language (Oromigna) and have developed a national consciousness (and a national liberation movement) in recent years. Nomads, who speak the Abbo dialect of Somalia, have from time immemorial formed important communities among the Oromos and in some parts a majority. But Abbo claims to being a majority in Bale, Sidamo and Arrsi are strongly contested by the Oromos. However, with the rise of militant Somali nationalism, the Abbos decided to link their fortunes with the WSLF.

The traditional leader of the Oromo Liberation Front is 'General' Ibrahim Waago Gutu Usu, who began his insurrectionary movement in Bale against Haile Selassie in the early 1960s. In an ambiguous move in 1977, he announced himself as leader of the Abbo Somali Liberation Front, linked to the Western Somali Liberation Front. (See the Oromo Liberation Front, above.)

Since 1974, the Ethiopian army has virtually had no control over Bale, outside of its main towns, Goba and Ginir, where there were reported clashes throughout 1977, but especially from September onwards. There were similar reports of continued activities against insurgents at Negelle (a major garrison town) and Borena in Sidamo. Though less serious, the situation in Arssi also deteriorated during 1977. This southern front remains one of the major military and political problems for the regime.

THE DERGUE AND ITS RIVALS
While waging his three-front war, Mengistu was engaged in an equally momentous battle for control of the revolution, and perhaps for preservation of his own position as well. In consolidating his personal grip in the first half of 1977, Mengistu had all but scrapped the last vestiges of civilian government. The National Democratic Revolution Programme of 21 April 1976[6] had promised a 'single party of the proletariat', but this remained unfulfilled. The Dergue's civilian Politburo—the Provisional Office for Mass Organizational Affairs (POMOA)—was split between 'militants' who saw pragmatic reasons for functioning in the shadow of the Dergue, and 'moderates' who demanded immediate civilian rule. Mengistu himself had increasingly assumed the trappings of autocratic personal power, even in a faintly imperial style: he lived in one of Haile Selassie's palaces, sat on his throne and rode in his limousines; in receiving the Vice-President of Tanzania in February 1978, he put on a white suit, rolled out the old royal red carpets and turned on the palace fountains.

THE DECLINE OF ME'ISON
Although longstanding socialists, by no means all of Mengistu's civilian advisers and 'allies' favoured the growing role of the Soviet Union, which was regarded as the intrusion of 'social imperialism'. Most critical was the All-Ethiopia Socialist Movement (known by its Amharic initials as Me'ison), the only political movement even unofficially sanctioned by the Dergue. Me'ison had dominated POMOA from the start through Haile Fida, a Sorbonne-trained Marxist who had returned from exile in 1975 to advise the Dergue on ideology and who became chairman of the Politburo. Its small élite membership represented the last civilian link with the military; this link was snapped in August 1977 after a period of internecine fighting.

The orthodox socialist Haile Fida and his followers (many of them compatriots from his home province of Wollega) were not the only Marxists to sprout up suddenly on the previously barren Ethiopian political landscape. Their bitterest rivals were the Ethiopian People's Revolutionary Party (EPRP). It was between these two groups that the blood feud, already described, claimed so many victims in the street killings in Addis Ababa and other towns. Me'ison had secured from the Dergue the responsibility for the organization and politicization of the peasants' and urban dwellers' associations (kebelles) upon which the Dergue staked the success of the revolution. It set up and ran the Ideological School in Addis Ababa and, when the People's Militia was formed, took over their political education as well. It was a group with particularly strong Oromo representation. As it gained influence with the Dergue, its revolutionary zeal—particularly in pressing the campaign to exterminate the EPRP—took on the appearance of tribal and factional vendettas. The Dergue leadership grew increasingly wary of the power of *Me'ison*, particularly over the mass organizations and the burgeoning militia, and Mengistu quietly encouraged the formation of an alternative 'party', *Seded*.

Russian advisers are believed to have proposed to Mengistu that he convert his military regime into a revolutionary mass movement. When a *Me'ison* activist, Girma Kebede, ran amok, the Dergue felt constrained to impose 'revolutionary justice' on him and his five accomplices. Girma Kebede was the chairman of a *kebelle* in the vicinity of the state-owned Berhanena Selam printing press. He was accused with five accomplices of having 'mercilessly and inhumanely executed the children of the broad masses'. They were charged with the 'dastardly murder of 24 persons and gruesome maiming of six others' so as to 'create misunderstanding between the oppressed people and the government'. Among these, the *Ethiopian Herald* reported, were nine employees of the printing press, including a woman eight months pregnant, who were falsely accued by Girma and his accomplices of being anarchists, taken from their place of work, hideously tortured and eventually killed. After having been found guilty of the murders by a special court martial, Girma Kebede and his five accomplices—all teachers or civil servants—were publicly executed at the foot of Mount Entoto on the morning of 2 April. Of all the Dergue's executions to date, this was the first to be carried out publicly, being witnessed by members of Girma's *kebelle*, employees of the printing press, relatives and friends of the murder victims and a large crowd of onlookers. The press reports noted the next day that Girma Kebede had been the son of a nobleman 'whose interests have been adversely affected by the revolution', and had been brought up 'in a highly pampered manner' by Lt-Gen Debebe Haile Mariam, a senior official of Haile Selassie's regime who was executed in November 1974. The bloody and tragic story thus neatly encapsulated the contrasting tempests at work in the revolution.

By August, POMOA itself was in disarray, just when Mengistu was coming under increasing pressure to form the single 'proletarian party' he had promised more than a year earlier. There were now five distinct factions: besides *Me'ison* and *Seded*, there were the Marxist-Leninist Organization (*Malered*) the 'Oppressed Masses' organization (*Echat*) and the Labour (*Waz*) League. On 14 July, the Dergue had 'reorganized' POMOA and the Ideological School. A month later, Mengistu disclosed cryptically that 'a few in whom we have placed our trust have deserted the revolutionary ranks'. It soon became clear that he meant none other than Haile Fida himself, by then perhaps the second most influential man in Ethiopia. Haile had disappeared, together with his most loyal followers, including *Me'ison*'s nominal chairman, Kebede Mengesha; Minister of Housing, Daniel Tadesse; Minister of Education, Teferra Wolde Tsadiq; and two leading women activists. Haile Fida's top deputy, Negede Gobezie, who was vice-chairman of POMOA, failed to return from an overseas trip. Altogether, some 70 *Me'ison* members were reported to have disappeared; they were rumoured to have made their way towards Wollega, although there were reports that some of them, possibly including Haile Fida, had been caught and possibly killed.

By the time of the third anniversary of the revolution on 12 September, the government was laying at *Me'ison*'s door responsibility for much of the internecine bloodshed of the previous nine months, including the slaughter of 300–500 students and young children over the weekend before May Day. The main reason given for *Me'ison*'s fall from grace was its insistence that the People's Militia be used to 'consolidate' the revolution by exterminating all remaining 'bourgeois' and 'reactionary' elements, including former landlords, EPRP members and even members of the government, civil service and elements in the army who did not subscribe to *Me'ison*'s philosophy. More to the point was an attempt by Haile Fida and his comrades to 'grab power', as the acting Ethiopian chargé d'affaires in London, Mismaku Asrat, disclosed on 12 September. Referring to the May Day killings, Mismaku said, after a thoughtful pause: 'I cannot categorically say that most of those killed were innocent (of anti-government activities), but I can say that most were killed as part of *Me'ison*'s political process.' Moreover, the ambassador stated bluntly, now that *Me'ison* had been curbed, there would be 'no more killings without due process of law' in Ethiopia.

That remained to be seen, for none could forget the many killings carried out under the Dergue for which only Mengistu and his Dergue colleagues could be blamed. Every bit as surprising as *Me'ison*'s decline was the inference that the regime had taken on a more 'liberal' complexion. Official spokesmen pointed out that 'progressive' elements were emerging from the Eritrean movement; this was a 'hopeful' sign, and these elements were invited to participate in the quickening political process. There were even hints of a willingness on the Dergue's part to come to an accommodation with the EPRP, or at least with its 'progressive' elements. There was known to be a quiescent 'moderate' faction within the armed forces who were embarrassed by the Dergue's excesses, and the reality of three wars going badly simultaneously, while perhaps strengthening Mengistu's personal allure as a military leader, could well have strengthened their hand.

In fact, there were recurring rumours of plots against Mengistu, particularly as the Soviet links became tighter. Some of these centred on Maj-Gen Gizaw Belaineh, the Armed Forces Chief of Staff, who was alleged to be 'pro-American'. He was replaced in a Cabinet reshuffle on 9 September, becoming military adviser to the PMAC Chairman—a seeming one-way ticket to limbo. In the same reshuffle, the last *Me'ison* activist in the Cabinet, Culture Minister Aklilu Habte, was sacked.

THE LIQUIDATION OF ATNAFU ABATE

The PMAC's Vice-Chairman, Lt-Col Atnafu Abate, carried special responsibility for raising and arming the people's militia. He had come up from the ranks as the NCOs representative in the original Dergue in 1973, and kept the NCOs as his personal power base. He also had strong links with his home province of Gojjam. Atnafu disappeared from public view after his return from a trip to Eritrea in October. In a long statement on 13 November, the Dergue announced that a 'revolutionary step'—a favoured euphemism for execution—had been taken against Atnafu the previous day. Recalling previous 'plots' to reverse the revolution—involving Maj Sisay Habte in 1976 and Capt Alemayehu Haile in early 1977—the statement said that Atnafu had been 'thrown out of the revolution' accused of five specific 'crimes': 1) at a time of revolutionary struggle, he 'argued that the interests of Ethiopia should be put before ideology'; 2) he did not subscribe to socialism or believe it could be applied in Ethiopia; 3) he ridiculed the idea of a proletarian party; 4) he took the part of the reactionary aristocracy, rich landlords and imperialists; and 5) he favoured a mixed economy and friendship with both East and West. In a departure from previous purges, a 'tribal element' was also mentioned (Atnafu was the son of a clergyman from the Amhara heartland of Gojjam; Mengistu of a Wollamo woman from Sidamo who had served in an Amhara aristocratic household).

There is direct evidence that Atnafu's real 'crime' may have been his decision to urge the Dergue to accept Eritrea's independence. According to Mengesha Gessesa, who went into exile after Atnafu's éxecution (see Eritrea, above), Atnafu had

38

concluded during his visit to Eritrea in November that there was no alternative to independence. Without doubt, the elimination of Atnafu was a defiant demonstration to the people of the Dergue's power.

RED TERROR VS WHITE TERROR, SEPTEMBER 1977-FEBRUARY 1978

It was Atnafu Abate who had said after the assassination of a Dergue member in April 1977 that 'a thousand reactionaries will die for every revolutionary murdered'. In fact, between November 1976 and April 1977, over 1,250 EPRP supporters had been killed; the toll of students in street fighting in the capital in April alone was estimated between 700 and 1,200. Atnafu's own death unleashed the bloodiest series of random killings and assassinations in the brief history of the revolution. The Dergue unleashed the 'red terror' of its own security forces as well as the 'revolutionary defence squads' of the *kebelles* and peasants' associations against the 'white terror' of the EPRP. Col Debela Dinssa, a member of the Dergue's standing committee, was put in charge of the 'red terror'.

The killings had been mounting since October when the Dergue's officer in charge of military and political affairs, Second-Lieut Legesse Asfaw, had warned that the 'counter-revolutionary activities' of the regime's opponents were more dangerous than the 'situations prevailing on the war fronts in the east, north, south and west of the country'. During October, 385 EPRP suspects were secretly executed in prisons. By mid-November, the underground assassination squads' victims had included another Dergue member, Lieut Solomon Gessesse, and the Chief Administrator (Governor) of Shoa, the province around Addis Ababa, Dr Makonnen Jotte. The mayor of Addis Ababa admitted that killings in the capital alone had numbered at least 3,000. Two US Congressmen who visited Addis Ababa in mid-December were shocked to see bodies of 'red terror' victims in the streets, often young children tagged with placards reading 'I was a counter-revolutionary'.

In late November, a leader of the EPRP's women's group, Tegest Gebre Selassie, and three of her comrades were killed when tanks were sent to blow up a house in which they had taken refuge.

There was another massacre in mid-December when a number of the EPRP's Youth League were killed, including Nebeleul Gebre Michael, a member of its Central Committee. According to one report, a senior EPRP leader had revealed himself to the authorities sometime in November and identified others.[7] Under torture, some had revealed further names. This led to the EPRP command chain being broken, but by no means totally so.

This wave of killings reached a crescendo between mid-December 1977 and February 1978. During one stage, again according to Addis Ababa's mayor, 'five or six of our comrades were being killed every day'. In order to teach its opponents a lesson, the Dergue decided in December to leave the bodies of those killed in reprisals attacks unburied. One diplomat said in February 1978 that 'every morning between five and 20 bodies are found around the city'.[8] His own estimate was that 10,000 young Ethiopians had been arrested or killed since the beginning of the red terror campaign.

There was also growing opposition to the Dergue among Ethiopians outside the country. Much speculation centred on Commodore Tassew Desta, former commander of the Ethiopian Navy and at one stage the Dergue's Ambassador to North Yemen, who had defected to the Sudan. He was said to be organizing a counter-coup, with American, Sudanese and West German help, and was thought to have some following in the Ethiopian armed forces among the anti-Mengistu and anti-Soviet factions.

Five opposition groups—the Ethiopian People's Revolutionary Party, the Ethiopian Democratic Union, the Western Somali Liberation Front, the Orormo Liberation Front and the Afar Liberation Front, met in Khartoum on 22 June to co-ordinate their policies, but nothing further came of the attempt to form a national coalition.

The Ethiopian Teachers' Association, a frequent Dergue target and a leading force in the overthrow of Haile Selassie, issued a statement in February 1978 accusing the Dergue of 'mass killing and torture' and demanding a popularly elected people's government.

DEFECTIONS FROM THE DERGUE

Ministers and ambassadors who were able to make arrangements for their families, or who were prepared to sacrifice them, deserted the Dergue in growing numbers. The Foreign Minister, Kifle Wodajo—who had lasted since the end of 1974—failed to return from an OAU ministerial meeting in March 1977 and took up asylum and a university post in Liberia. Getachew Mekasha, Minister of Information under Haile Selassie and later Ambassador to India and to Egypt, turned up in California on 10 March, denouncing the brutality of the Dergue. 'At the slightest excuse, soldiers will arrest and kill anybody considered an opponent,' he said. 'The only law and order is that imposed by the men with guns. Those of us who had welcomed the revolution are now embarrassed.' Other ambassadors who declined to return to Addis Ababa when recalled were: Kebede Gebre-Wold (Athens); Million Neqniq, once a Minister under the Dergue (Tokyo); Bekele Endeshaw (Bonn); Col Belachew Jemaneh, a former Interior Minister (Belgrade); Ayele Moltotal (Mexico); Ayalew Assaye (Rome); Brig Yohannes Wolde Mariam (military attaché in Washington). One envoy who dithered too long before returning home, and who was dismissed summarily by the junta, was the Ambassador to Britain, Zaudie Mekuria. In July, Abdullah Abdurahman Nour, ambassador to Saudi Arabia and the man charged by the Dergue with the task of negotiating with moderate Arab regimes over Eritrea, resigned and took up political asylum in Britain. The chargé d'affaires in Washington, Mekbib Gebeyehu, was said to have left his post in August. He was succeeded by the first ambassador to be posted to Washington since 1975, Ayalew Mandefro, the former Defence Minister. He too defected from his Washington post in January 1978.

There were frequent reports of members of the armed forces deserting their posts in northern and southern Ethiopia and turning up in Sudan, Somalia, Kenya and Djibouti for asylum. In May, the Secretary-General of the Ethiopian Teachers' Union, Kassahun Bisrat, defected to the Sudan and claimed that 30,000 people, including thousands of students and teachers, had been killed or sent to concentration camps. He put the death toll of the pre-May Day massacres in Addis Ababa at 2,000, and said 500 teachers had been murdered by the regime.

POLITICAL PRISONERS

The London-based group, Amnesty International, released a long-awaited report on 29 March, alleging a 'consistent and continuing pattern of gross violations of human rights under the rule of the Dergue'. The report estimated that there could be as many as 8,000 political prisoners in Ethiopia, in eight categories: members of the former royal family, including women and young children; members of former governments, plus prominent civil servants and businessmen; senior armed forces officers and other soldiers, including members of the Dergue itself, suspected of 'subversion'; Eritreans suspected of sympathizing with the Eritrean liberation movement; leaders of various associations—students, teachers, trade unionists, women—which resisted reorganization and purging by the Dergue; church leaders, including the deposed patriarch, Abune Theophilos; alleged members of EPRP, some as young as nine or ten years of age (the largest category of detainees so far); and those arrested by *kebelles* in towns or rural areas. The report particularly deplored the Dergue's frequent practice of 'extra-judicial execution' of widespread torture.

A US State Department report on human rights conditions in 105 countries, released on 9 February 1978, said of Ethiopia: 'Respect for human rights, not well observed by the autocratic regime of Emperor Haile Selassie, has deteriorated since the assumption of power by the Provisional Military Government in September 1974. The use of arbitrary arrest and the lengthy imprisonment of opponents of the Government has been common. . . . Denial of fair public trial is a common occurrence. We have received a few allegations of torture which appear to be valid.'[9]

The Dergue used random arrests and then mass amnesties of suspected political opponents as a propaganda device to suggest both that they were on top of the situation and that the 'confessions of errors', justifying clemency, proved that they were rallying public support. Reported amnesties of political detainees totalled c. 2,200 from April 1977-February 1978. Two large batches of suspected 'counter-revolutionaries' were released: 708 on 10 June and 894 on 9 September. They were freed 'in the belief that they would correct their attitude towards the revolution'. At the Dire Dawa textile factory, 271 workers were detained in February 1978; 67 were released, while the rest received 'political education'.

Ten great-grandchildren of the former Emperor Haile Selassie, aged from four to 22, escaped from Ethiopia in August with the help of Swedish missionaries. Six of them, three boys and three girls aged 13-21, were the children of Princess Ijigayehu Asfa Wossen, the Emperor's eldest granddaughter, who died after an abdominal operation in a prison hospital in Addis Ababa on 31 January 1977, aged 42. The remainder of the 14 Royal prisoners, women and children, remained in custody where they have been since September 1974.

DEFENCE AND SECURITY

The strength of Ethiopia's armed forces grew to an unprecedented level between May and December 1977. Soviet military supplies were valued at $850m to $1 bn, for which Ethiopia would have to pay either out of its coffee-rich foreign exchange reserves, through barter deals (again mostly in coffee) with the Russians, or through the generosity of Libyan aid. Although the actual size of the Soviet airlift is not known, the following inventory of new equipment has been compiled from various reports: 60 MiG-21s, 12 MiG-23s and possibly some MiG-17s; 300 T-54/55 medium tanks, 30 T-34 light tanks; 300 armoured cars; 40 BTR-152 armoured personnel carriers; six 57mm towed anti-aircraft guns, and a number of 155mm and 185mm guns.

At the beginning of 1977, Ethiopia also had the following US equipment: 24 M-60 medium and 54 M-41 light tanks; c. 90 M-113 personnel carriers; 56 AML-245/60 armoured cars; 12 M-109 155mm self-propelled, 36 75mm pack, 52 105mm and 12 155mm howitzers; 146 M-2 107mm and M-30 4.2-in mortars (with 24 M-60 and some M-113 on order). The Air Force in 1976 consisted of 36 combat aircraft, including a light bomber squadron with four Canberra B2s; one fighter ground-attack squadron with 11 F-86Fs; two fighter ground-attack squadrons with 16 F-5A/Es; one reconnaissance squadron with five T-28As; one transport squadron with 12 C-47s, two C-54s, 12 C-119Gs and three Doves; three training squadrons with 19

Safirs, 13 T-28A/Ds and 11 T-33As; one helicopter squadron with 10 AB-204s and six UH-1Hs.

There were also massive changes in the strength of the armed forces (except, perhaps, the Navy) as the regime stepped up regular recruitment of soldiers and conscripted a vast 'people's militia' (c. 500,000). The total strength of the regular forces stood at perhaps 51,000.

The Dergue reorganized the Army into seven divisions from the previous four: the First had comprised the former Imperial Bodyguard; the Second, Third and Fourth Divisions had been based in Eritrea, Harar and Addis Ababa respectively. The new Fifth Division was the crack *Nebelbal* or 'Flame' division of paratroopers and counter-insurgency specialists, trained by the Israelis. Only the Third Division, which later led the defence of the Ogaden, was mechanized. A police commando unit formed the Eighth Division.

The armed forces command was reshuffled on 23 July 1977 to comprise six 'People's Divisions' under a new 'Revolutionary Campaign Co-ordination Centre', established in Addis Ababa. It was headed by Mengistu. Two other Co-ordination Centres were established at Asmara and Harar. The new army commanders were Col Aberra Haile Mariam, Commander of the Eastern People; Col Hailu Gebre Michael, Commander of the Northern People; and Cols Demissie Gultu, Regassa Jimma, Asrat Birru and Merid Negussie, Commanders of the Second, Fourth, Sixth and Seventh Divisions. The Commander of the Ground Forces, Brig-Gen Bahru Tuffa, appointed in 1976, died of natural causes on 11 May 1977.

Just over a month later this new institution was superseded by yet another. On 27 August, the Dergue announced the formation of a National Revolutionary Operations Command (NROC) to 'co-ordinate the performance of government and public organizations' in mobilizing 'the regular forces, police force and people's militia in the defence of the country's unity, freedom and revolution'. Heading the NROC was a 28-member Council of six Dergue members, five Cabinet Ministers, five senior military commanders, five members of the Provisional Office for Mass Organizational Affairs (POMOA) and representatives of trade unions and mass organizations. Mengistu was to be chairman of the NROC, which was to meet at least every fortnight. The Council was in direct charge of the armed forces and had the power to commandeer facilities and manpower for the war effort. On the regional level, it superseded the Revolution and Development Committees formed earlier in the year and took over their role in safeguarding the revolution against 'reactionaries'. Those who refused to co-operate with the NROC mobilization were threatened with life imprisonment or death.

GOVERNMENT CHANGES

The Dergue, thought to have been whittled down to c. 45 members from the original 120, took on more definition in 1977 as more of its members were publicly identified and as those in the inner circle—the 16-man Standing Committee—were given specific 'portfolios'. This made* members* of the Dergue—those closest to Mengistu—responsible for many of the same areas as Ministers of the mostly-civilian Cabinet, which also underwent many changes of personnel in 1977.

The structure of the Dergue, first established on 31 December 1976, was modified after Mengistu's 'palace coup' in February 1977 to comprise the Standing Committee of 16, a Central Committee of 32, and a General Congress of all PMAC members (number unspecified). The General Congress, under a new Secretary-General, Capt Fikre-Selassie Wogderes, did not hold its first meeting until 16 May 1977. After the elimination of Atnafu Abate in November, Second-Lieut Legesse

Asfaw (newly promoted from sergeant-major), was put in charge of political and military affairs and appeared very much as the new 'number two' to Mengistu. For members of the Dergue known by the beginning of 1978 (listed with their areas of special responsibility), see below.

The Council of Ministers, formed on 11 March 1977, was reshuffled on 9 September to include a new batch of 'technocrats'. Two Ministers—Teferra Wolde Tsadiq (Education) and Daniel Tadesse (Urban Development and Housing)—had disappeared in August with the purge of *Me'ison* members. The positions of Permanent Secretaries in the Ministries seemed to gain in importance. Their occupants are listed below where available. Hailu Yimenu, the Cabinet's 'Senior Minister'—apparently a sort of Premiership—had not been heard of since his appointment in March and his role remained unclear. So did that of Lij Michael Imru, a former Prime Minister, once the most influential civilian in the regime and now a political adviser to Mengistu. Well to the Left at the start of the revolution, Lij Michael probably now stands well to the Right in the PMAC spectrum. Mengistu told a Press conference after the OAU Summit in Gabon in July that his regime was 'neither civilian nor military' and would hand over power to others 'when there is a workers' party which can lead and become the vanguard party for the development of the masses'.

THE PROVISIONAL MILITARY ADMINISTRATIVE COUNCIL (PMAC)

Chairman	Lt-Col Mengistu Haile Mariam
Assistant to the Chairman	Second-Lieut Mengistu Gemechu
Secretary-General	Capt Fikre-Selassie Wogderes
Political and Military Affairs	Second-Lieut Legesse Asfaw
Central Committee Affairs	Maj Endale Tesemma
Foreign Affairs	Maj Berhanu Bayeh
Administration	Maj Fisseha Desta
Defence	Lt-Col Tesfaye Gebre Kidan
Militia	Maj Addis Tedla
Security	Maj Kassahun Tafesse
Economic Affairs	Second-Lieut Gessesse Wolde Kidan
Information and Public Relations	Second-Lieut Tamrat Ferede
Justice	Capt Wubishet Dessie
Militia Political Affairs	Lieut Gezahegn Worqe
Addis Ababa Revolutionary	
Operations	Col Debela Dinssa
Shoa Administrative Region	Capt Kassaye Argaw
Hararghe Administrative Region	Lt-Col Zelleke Beyene
Sidamo Administrative Region	Sgt Petros Gebre
Gondar Administrative Region	Capt Melaku Teferra
Gojjam Administrative Region	Second-Lieut Eshetu Alemu
Kaffa Administrative Region	Lieut Tesemma Belai
Other members	Maj Nadew Zakaria
	Capt Gizaw Wolde Michael
	Second-Lieut Negussie Wolde
	Lt-Col Getachew Shibeshi
	Second-Lieut Demeke Banchew
	Sgt-Maj Getahun Aboye
	Senior Technician Demsew Kassaye
	Col Tekka Tulu

THE GOVERNMENT (as at 9 September 1977)

Head of State and Chairman of the Council of Ministers	Mengistu Haile Mariam
Senior Minister	Hailu Yimenu
Political Advisers to the Chairman	Getachew Kibret
	Lij Michael Imru
Military Adviser to the Chairman	Maj-Gen Gizaw Belaineh

Ministries

Foreign Affairs
  Minister — Col Felleke Gedle Giorgis
  Permanent Secretary — Major Dawit Wolde Giorgis
Defence
  Minister — Brig-Gen Taye Tilahun
  Permanent Secretary — Capt Haile Wolde Michael
Finance
  Minister — Teferra Wolde Semayit
  Permanent Secretary — Asfaw Damte
Commerce and Tourism
  Minister — Ashagre Yigletu
  Permanent Secretary — Abebe Worqu
Industry
  Minister — Tesfaye Dinka
Urban Development and Housing
  Minister — vacant
Education
  Minister — vacant
  Permanent Secretary — Hussein Ismail
Agriculture, Land and Settlement
  Minister — Zegeyye Asfaw
  Permanent Secretary — Dr Girma Tolessa
Public Health
  Minister — Dr Teferra Wonde
  Permanent Secretary — Wogayehu Sahle
Interior
  Minister — Col Legesse Wolde Mariam
  Permanent Secretary — Lt-Col Mersha Ketsela
Labour and Social Affairs
  Minister — Tadele Mengesha
  Permanent Secretary — Maj Mehari Maasho
Information and National Guidance
  Minister — vacant
  Permanent Secretary — Baalu Girma
Justice and Judgement
  Minister — Amanuel Amde Michael
  Permanent Secretary — Kebede Gebre Mariam
Communications and Transport
  Minister — Yusuf Ahmed
  Permanent Secretary — Dinssa Gutema
Mines, Energy and Water Development
  Minister — Ezzedin Ali
  Permanent Secretary — Assefa Tilahun

Culture, Sports and Youth Affairs	
Minister	Dr Haile Wolde Michael
Permanent Secretary	Desta Tadesse
Commissioners	
Relief and Rehabilitation	Shimelis Adougna
Science and Technology	Haile-Leul Tebeke
Higher Education	Yayeh Yirad Kitaw
Planning	Taye Worqu

SOCIAL AFFAIRS

PEASANTS' ASSOCIATIONS AND KEBELLES

On paper at least, the Ethiopian people appear to be the beneficiaries of a true communist revolution—perhaps the most sweeping Africa has ever known. In the rural areas, c. 25,000 peasants' associations have been organized with c. 6m members. Theoretically, they allow peasants to farm the land collectively and to administer their own affairs at grass-roots level; they are invested with broad powers of self-government, including juridical powers. Because many of these associations have simply superseded earlier co-operative groupings, while others have become vehicles for the expression of existing tribal and clan tensions, it is still hard to determine their effectiveness in transforming the once feudal life-style of rural inhabitants. But there was some evidence, particularly in the south, that standards of living, nutrition and health have improved substantially.

The urban equivalent of the peasants' association is the *kebelle* (Amharic for neighbourhood) or urban dwellers' association. There are c. 290 of these in Addis Ababa alone, the smallest covering 3,000 residents, the largest 12,000. *Kebelles* have also been established in Dire Dawa, Harar, Dessie, Gondar, Jimma and other large towns. These, too, were extensions of pre-revolutionary institutions (the *edirs* or neighbourhood self-help and savings associations), but quickly assumed (or were given) a decisive political role in the revolution. They became the focal point of a power struggle between the Dergue and its civilian rivals, and more than any other institution were both the victim and instrument of revolutionary violence.

In their ideal form, the *kebelles* were an impressive accomplishment in social organization. They were run by democratically-elected committees, administered their own courts, managed their own shops and built and ran their own schools. Their membership embraced the gamut of social classes. In Addis Ababa, districts of 25 *kebelles* each sent representatives to a higher urban council which served as a regional planning agency and acted on appeals of lower *kebelle* tribunal decisions. The higher urban councils in turn elected delegates to a city-wide council which virtually replaced the former Addis Ababa Municipality. It was through this procedure that a new 'mayor' of Addis Ababa, Dr Alemu Abebe, a veterinarian and committed Marxist, was chosen in 1977.

Both the peasants' and urban dwellers' associations became sources of manpower for the 'people's militia'—c. 500,000-strong by the end of 1977—recruited to 'protect the revolution' from both its internal and external enemies. The risks involved in arming the civilian population were significant, especially where the urban associations were involved, and were the subject of heated debate within the Government. As Dr Alemu Abebe put it: 'With guns there can be few restraints. But it was ultimately decided that people felt a need to protect themselves that the army could not provide, and that we must respond to that need even if there is a risk that the guns might some day be turned against us.'[10]

At the outset, the arming of the *kebelles* was a means by which the Dergue sought to reassert its control over institutions which had evolved a political life of their own under the guidance of the Dergue's civilian rivals in *Me'ison*. The 'revolutionary defence squads' formed within each *kebelle* (c. 15 men per *kebelle*, trained by the Dergue—with East German assistance—in secret police techniques) became the spearhead of the Dergue's 'red terror' campaign against 'counter-revolutionaries'; they had the authority to shoot first and ask questions later. As the struggle over the *kebelles* intensified, the Dergue felt constrained to create an 'Addis Ababa Overall Revolutionary Operations Co-ordinating Committee' under one of the more ruthless PMAC members, Major Debela Dinssa, to take control of the situation.

PMAC members were also sent to the countryside to oversee the creation of cadres in the peasants' associations. On 17 September, the Dergue decreed the establishment of an All-Ethiopia Farmers' Association to 'create conditions facilitating the complete destruction of feudal rule' and to 'strengthen the transitional period during which the feudal system of production is to be transformed'. Its members were to be elected from regional associations consisting of two representatives of each peasants' association in a given region. The fact that the decree acknowledged that the 'feudal system of production' had yet to be transformed, and that Mengistu indicated at a Press conference in February 1978 that the farmers' association had still not been formed, demonstrated how far the revolution had to go in transforming Ethiopian society. The All-Ethiopia Peasants' Union, with c. 9m members, was finally inaugurated on 5 May 1978.

TRADE UNIONS

The All-Ethiopia Trade Union (AETU), formally inaugurated on 8 January 1977, was one of the key instruments through which the Dergue sought to eliminate the influence of its Marxist rivals in *Me'ison* and EPRP. It was from activists in the now-banned Confederation of Ethiopian Labour Unions (CELU) that much of the impetus for revolution had come before the Dergue appeared in 1974. Even after the Dergue assumed power, CELU continued vigorously to oppose military rule. Its entire leadership was imprisoned, and after severe strife in 1975–76, it was disbanded as 'reactionary'. The Dergue then set about creating more amenable workers' organizations, such as the 18,000-strong Union of Transport and Communications Workers. At its inauguration, the AETU embraced eight unions with a total membership of 200,000.

The EPRP never forgave the Dergue for banning CELU, and the AETU became a prime target for its assassination squads. Its first chairman, Tewodros Bekele, a former seamen's union leader, was shot dead in his office on 25 February 1977, just six weeks after taking office; his deputy, Getachew Legesse, was seriously wounded. His successor, Temesgen Madebo, who had been a member of the Dergue's national Revolutionary and Development Committee, was assassinated on 30 September. The AETU's treasurer, Kebede Gebre Michael, was killed on 3 December.

HOUSING AND EMPLOYMENT

The Ministry of Urban Development and Housing announced in June 1977 that Birr 10m (over £2.5m) in housing loans had been granted to Addis Ababa residents in the previous year, enabling 1,200 familes to acquire their own homes. Homebuilders had each been given 500 sq metres of government land free of charge. The Ministry handed over 20 newly-built houses in Addis Ababa to 20 families who had helped build them under a self-help scheme. The houses were to be let to the families for Birr 16.50 (£4) a month. An official study released in November 1977 showed that 62.3% of the capital's population live in rented houses.

Unemployment continued to be a problem in urban areas though, judging from presence of fewer idlers in city streets, perhaps not in the epidemic proportions of pre-revolutionary days. The *Ethiopian Herald* reported on 19 December that thousands of unemployed had been 'rounded up' by security forces in Addis Ababa and sent to the countryside to help with the harvest (the rural workforce having been depleted because of militia call-ups).

An official study released in November 1977 put the 'crude' rate of economic participation in Addis Ababa—i.e. the ratio of economically active people to the total population of the city—at 42.4% for males and 23.2% for females. The 'refined' rate—i.e. the ratio of the economically active to the working-age population—is 60.4% for men and 31.6% for women.

EDUCATION

The most tragic aspect of the revolutionary violence of 1977 was that its main civilian victims were the youth of Ethiopia. Hundreds of children aged 12–16 were killed in the campaign against 'counter-revolutionaries' in April and May; many of the victims of the 'red terror' campaign later in the year were similarly youthful. To this extent, the nation's schools were severely disrupted although, from the Dergue's point of view, the campaigns did seem to have the desired effect of dampening the student activism which had crippled the educational system in 1976.[11]

Reports from academic sources indicated a complete absence of political activity at Addis Ababa University and in the high schools. One professor vividly described the scene in his university classroom: at the beginning of the year he had told his students that 'none of us want to be here, but we shall have to make the best of it'; he said he looked out on a sea of 'dead' faces as the students listened blankly to his lectures, fumbling in their pockets for a scrap of paper if they wished to make a note of something.

The University awarded its first degrees and diplomas since the revolution on 11 September, when Mengistu conferred degrees on 952 graduates and awarded certificates to 524 extension students. In an address, he admonished them to 'work hard to give depth to the revolution'.

The Dergue created a Higher Educational Commission on 13 January 1977 which later decreed that foremost among the aims of higher education should be 'teaching, expanding and propagating socialism'. In 1976, primary and secondary schools had been placed under the 'control of the masses' through a system of committees drawn from peasants' and urban dwellers' associations.

Addis Ababa University started construction of a new Faculty of Sciences in February 1977, costing Birr 8.4m and including chemistry, physics and geology laboratories.

RELIGIOUS AFFAIRS

Abune Tekle-Haimanot, Patriarch of the Ethiopian Orthodox Church installed after 'democratic elections' in 1976,[12] seemed less prominent in political circles than his controversial predecessor, Abune Theophilos. However, he frequently graced the dais (together with the Imam of Addis Ababa's Central Mosque) at rallies in Revolution Square. Visitors to Ethiopia during the periods of strife in the capital reported a tangible upsurge in religious expression—in what is already one of the most fervent Christian communities in the world. Churches were reported to be crowded at all hours every day of the week.

The Dergue was careful to eschew even implied criticism of the Church or interference in its affairs. The only mention of religion in official statements dealt with religious liberty and equality, particularly concerning the Muslim population (perhaps 40% of the total). Nevertheless, the former Imam of the mosque at Dire Dawa, Sheikh Omar Ahmed Seif, and a Muslim leader from Harar fled to Somalia where they allegedly spoke of persecution.

A new Roman Catholic Archbishop of Addis Ababa, Abba (Father) Paulos Zedua, was installed on 5 June 1977, replacing Abba Asrate Mariam Yemiru, the first Ethiopian to hold the post, who retired after 19 years' service. The Roman Catholic Archbishop of Dessie, Abba Wolde-Mariam Tesfa-Giorgis, was assassinated at his home on 6 May.

Israel said on 13 July that it was ready to receive Ethiopian Jews who found themselves in physical danger. About 28,000 Jews—the 'Falasha' who consider themselves one of the lost tribes of Israel—live near Gondar, but only 150 have gone to live in Israel in recent years.

PRESS AND INFORMATION
The Government gained a powerful new voice for its propaganda with the nationalization on 12 March 1977 of Radio Voice of the Gospel (RVOG), a station with one 1-kilowatt medium-wave and two 100-kilowatt shortwave transmitters. Operated since 1963 by the Lutheran World Federation, the station's religious, news and music programmes in 14 languages had been heard by millions throughout Africa, the Middle East and Asia. Accused by the PMAC of spreading 'bourgeois ideology', RVOG was henceforth to be used 'for the intensification and advancement of the revolution of the broad masses'. The station went back on the air that evening as Radio Voice of Revolutionary Ethiopia, with programmes in Amharic, Arabic, English and French, and has since been the main platform for the Dergue's policy statements to the outside world. Retaining many of the 180 skilled Ethiopian staff who had worked at RVOG, the new station took over all English programming formerly carried by the official Radio Ethiopia on 18 July. However, the foreign staff of c. 20, who included Europeans and Africans, left Ethiopia soon after nationalization. The Lutherans maintained that RVOG had been a voice for 'justice, peace and human rights'.

The PMAC announced on 23 January 1978 that 'the former Radio Voice of the Gospel has merged with Radio Ethiopia . . . so that it will agitate the broad masses to enable the revolution to achieve its objectives'. At the same time, the radio's Oromigna (Galligna) programmes were extended to four hours a day, and broadcasts in Tigrigna and Tigre, the two northern languages, were extended to an hour each. Amharic programmes are broadcast from 8 a.m. to 11 p.m. daily.

The State-owned newspapers, the daily *Addis Zemen* and *Ethiopian Herald* and the weekly *Yezareitu Ethiopia*, remained under the Dergue's strict control and devoted most of their space to official propaganda and discussions of the finer points of Marxism-Leninism. A new quarterly magazine, *Yekatit* (*February*), began publication on 2 March 1978.

The last Western correspondents resident in Addis Ababa, those of the *Washington Post*, Reuters and the French News Agency, were given 48 hours to leave the country on 25 April 1977. Other Western journalists were only allowed into the country intermittently. By contrast, the number of Soviet Bloc journalists increased, and the Cuban news agency Prensa Latina opened a bureau in Addis Ababa on 23 January 1978.

REFUGEES AND RESETTLEMENT
The fighting in the north, east and south of the country sent refugees fleeing into neighbouring states in record numbers. There were c. 150,000 Eritrean and Ethiopian refugees in Sudan; c. 10,000 in Djibouti (see chapter on Djibouti); and an undetermined number in Somalia, Kenya, North Yemen and Saudi Arabia.[13] The refugees included Eritreans fleeing from zones of fighting or from Ethiopian reprisals; Somalis, Afars and Oromos caught up in the fighting in their areas or accused by the regime of subversion; victims of drought and famine, and political opponents of the regime (particularly students). There was also a steady flight of educated Ethiopians, including Government officials, who could afford and get permission to travel abroad, or who were prepared to escape. Most of these made their way to Western Europe and North America.

International organizations, including the UN High Commissioner for Refugees, the International Committee of the Red Cross, and the Swedish Save the Children Fund provided aid to Ethiopian refugees. UNHCR aid to refugees in Sudan was co-ordinated by the Ethiopian Refugees Self-Help Organization (ERSHO), which was associated with the EDU. The UNHCR estimated in February 1978 that c. 300,000 Ethiopians, mostly nomads, have fled to Somalia since the Dergue came to power.

Under the agreement with Sudan on improving bilateral relations (see Foreign Affairs), the Government offered an amnesty to Ethiopian soldiers who had fled to Sudan. About 400 officers and men who took up the offer were returned to Ethiopia in January 1978.

Mengistu announced on 20 June that 'all genuine refugees who had left Ethiopia before and after the revolution could return safely', and that a special commission had been set up to help them.

The resettlement of drought victims was a priority of the Government's Relief and Rehabilitation Commission (see The Drought in 1977, below). Special projects were initiated in Eritrea and Hararghe.

POPULATION
The population was last estimated in 1976 at 28.68m, of whom 10.9% (3m people) live in towns. The population growth rate was 2.6% in 1970–75. The urban population increases by c. 6.6% pa, (cf a total population growth rate of 2.5% annually). A study of the c. 1m residents of Addis Ababa, carried out by the Central Statistical Office, revealed that 42% are under the age of 15 and only 10% over 45. The growth rate of the capital's population was put at 7% pa, of which 4.5% is due to annual migration and 2.5% to natural growth. The study said that 48.5% of the city's population were born in Addis Ababa, 30.2% came from other parts of surrounding Shoa province, and 5.7% from Wollo. The literacy rate in the city for those over the age of 10 was given as 69.5% for males and 38.5% for females.[14]

FOREIGN AFFAIRS
A remarkable aspect of the Ethiopian revolution during its first three years had been the way the careful balance of foreign relations maintained by Haile Selassie was preserved by the new regime—until finally in 1977 the Dergue began to unravel this widespread network of relationships with East and West, Africa and the Middle East and to throw out new lines of friendship (and dependency) to the Communist bloc. Centuries-old friendships with Western nations, even with those heavily engaged in development and aid projects in Ethiopia, were erased almost at a stroke; relations with the US, Britain and Sweden swiftly degenerated into open hostility. The new ties were firmly with the Soviet bloc—with Russia, with East Germany,

Czechoslovakia, Poland, Hungary, Bulgaria, as well as with Cuba and Yugoslavia. While in some ways patterning its agrarian revolution and militia tactics on the Maoist model, the Dergue did not rush into the arms of Peking. The Chinese, while continuing their previous level of development aid, showed no wish to compete with the Russians in building up Ethiopia's military strength. Relations with African states remained cool. Although no black African government openly supported the secessionist ambitions of the Eritreans and Somalis, only one, Kenya, put itself actively on the side of the Dergue for reasons of its own national interest. The Dergue's real failure was over its attempts to emulate the old Emperor in preventing open Arab hostility to Ethiopia. Only two Arab states—Libya and the People's Democratic Republic of Yemen (PDRY, Aden)—took Ethiopia's side for their own particularist reasons. Despite its new allies, the Dergue continued to maintain a clandestine relationship with Israel. Although the Israeli military role shrank to a token involvement for a time, neither they nor the Ethiopians wished to see it ended altogether, despite the Dergue's public protestations to the contrary. The Israelis saw Ethiopia as the instrument of their strategy to keep Arab influence from extending the whole length of the Red Sea.

RELATIONS WITH THE USSR
When the USSR President, Nikolai Podgorny, toured Africa in early 1977, Ethiopia was not one of the countries he visited, although Somalia was. Less than a year later, the USSR was the Dergue's staunchest ally and the Somalis' bitterest enemy; the Russians were more deeply committed in Ethiopia than in any other African country. The first signal that the Dergue was finally about to commit itself to Moscow came, ironically, from Atnafu Abate, nine months before he was liquidated (see above), in an announcement on 11 February 1977 that Ethiopia would in future turn to the 'socialist countries' for its arms supplies. A PMAC delegation had gone to Moscow in December 1976 to secure agreement in principle on future Soviet arms supplies. Presumably, a Soviet condition was that military links with the US must first be cut. Washington made that step easier for the Dergue by winding down its own commitment to Ethiopia on human rights grounds (see Relations with the US, below); many pro-Western Ethiopians continue to argue that the US 'forced' Ethiopia into Russia's arms.

There had been earlier signals from Moscow of its willingness to assist Ethiopia's revolution, even at the expense of upsetting long-time friends in Eritrea and Somalia. Moscow Radio commented on 24 April 1976 that 'the strength of the Ethiopian revolution lies in its very inevitability in the world revolutionary process . . . [its] progress puzzles the uninitiated, maddens its enemies and is a source of satisfaction for the true friends of the new Ethiopia.' In June 1976, the USSR endorsed the PMAC's nine-point peace plan for the 'administrative region' of Eritrea[15] and underscored this in a Moscow Radio broadcast on 7 March 1977 which said that 'those countries in which national democratic systems have been established cannot be considered non-progressive just because they suffer from some complex problem or other, which is just a vestige of the past and is awaiting a solution.'

A PMAC delegation first visited Moscow in July 1976, when a joint communique stated: 'The sides noted with satisfaction that, at the present time, new favourable conditions are coming into being for broadening relations between the Soviet Union and Ethiopia and for the development of all-round co-operation. . . . During the talks the coincidence or proximity of the positions of the Soviet Union and Ethiopia on many international problems was noted.' The leader of the delegation, Capt

Moges Wolde Michael (who was killed in the purge of February 1977), spoke of the support received 'from the great country of the Soviets, the first in the world to build the most humane socialist society'.

Mengistu himself went to Moscow for five days, beginning on 4 May 1977—his first official trip abroad. A joint communique signed on 6 May included a declaration (but not a treaty) of friendship as well as agreements on economic, scientific and cultural co-operation and a consular convention. The communique stressed the Soviets' 'solidarity with the efforts of the Ethiopian people to defend their revolutionary gains'. It also condemned the 'intrigues of imperialists' in the Horn of Africa, and the 'efforts of certain states to impose their control on the Red Sea at the expense of the legitimate rights of other states and peoples of this region'. There was no mention—apart from an emphasis on 'strengthening security'—of Soviet military aid, but it was no coincidence that Mengistu's visit came just ten days after the remaining US military and information facilities in Ethiopia had been closed down. From subsequent developments, it seems clear that in Moscow, Mengistu put the seal on the December agreement which opened the way and defined the terms of payment for $1 bn worth of arms shipments. On his return home on 10 May (he had stopped in Bulgaria and possibly also in Libya on the way), Mengistu said 'all the socialist countries were ready to give the necessary support for the bitter revolutionary struggle of the broad masses of Ethiopia'.

The first trickle of Soviet arms' deliveries to Ethiopia were monitored shortly before Mengistu's Moscow visit. At the beginning of May, observers in Djibouti reported seeing consignments of Soviet tanks—outdated T-34s and more modern T-54s—being loaded onto the railway to Ethiopia after having been shipped across the Gulf of Aden aboard amphibious craft from South Yemen. Le Monde reported that the tanks and some armoured cars were then offloaded at Dire Dawa and driven north-west towards Gojjam and Gondar. By July, the reported rate of Soviet arms shipments to Addis Ababa was five planeloads a week. Arab intelligence reports cited a Soviet commitment to supply Ethiopia with $385m worth of military equipment, including 48 MiGs and up to 200 T-54 and T-55 tanks. By September, the large-scale Soviet airlift and sealift was under way. (See War in the Ogaden above.)

RELATIONS WITH OTHER COMMUNIST COUNTRIES
A marked upsurge in Ethiopia's contacts with Eastern European countries was evident in 1977, with East Germany, Czechoslovakia, Hungary and Bulgaria quickly stepping into the trade and aid-giving roles once occupied by Western nations (see Economy, below). Yugoslavia, which had close economic and aid relations with Haile Selassie's regime, also increased its activities. Mengistu visited Bulgaria in May, and PMAC delegations visited most other Warsaw Pact states, which in return sent repeated diplomatic, economic and cultural missions to Addis Ababa. The ties with East Germany were especially close; the GDR State Planning Commission provided experts to plan and direct the Ethiopian economy. Even more important were the direct ties between the Dergue and East Germany's ruling Politburo. The prime mover of this relationship was the leading GDR Politburo member, Werner Lamberz, who was a frequent visitor to Addis Ababa during 1977. (Lamberz died in a helicopter crash in Libya in March 1978, apparently while on a visit to discuss mediation in the Horn of Africa.) The Ethiopian Minister of Commerce and Tourism noted on 10 March 1978 that trade between his country and GDR amounted to Birr 200m in 1977.

The Dergue also exchanged visits during 1977 with representatives of the

Communist parties of North Korea, Vietnam and Mongolia.

RELATIONS WITH CUBA

Ethiopia was linked with Angola by Cuba's leaders as a genuine revolutionary force deserving of support against its enemies. The Cuban commitment was entered into personally by Fidel Castro after his visit to Addis Ababa on 14 March 1977. This followed a visit to Mogadishu and two days of secret talks with the Somali and Ethiopian leaders in Aden. (Cuba's role in Ethiopia is examined in detail in the essay, 'Crisis in the Horn of Africa'.)

By the beginning of 1978, Cubans were a common sight on the streets of Addis Ababa; c. 11,000 Cuban military personnel, including combat forces, were estimated to be in the country. In his Adowa Day address on 2 March, Mengistu confirmed that 'the Cubans, renowned for shedding their blood anywhere and at any time for a just struggle and cause, are bracing themselves with the Ethiopian people's army'. Mengistu was reported to have made a secret visit to Havana (and to Moscow) at the end of October 1977, after which the pace of Soviet and Cuban military assistance picked up. His Foreign Minister, Felleke Gedle Giorgis, visited Cuba from 15-19 October.

RELATIONS WITH THE US

A quarter of a century of close relations with the US, cultivated by Haile Selassie and maintained in the first three years of the Dergue's rule, all but came to an end after Washington's announcement on 25 February 1977 that it was reducing foreign aid—including military grants worth $6m—to Ethiopia because of its consistent violations of human rights.[16] The Dergue responded on 23 April by ordering the closure of four US agencies and expelling c. 100 American officials and their dependents. The facilities affected were the Military Assistance Advisory Group (MAAG), the Naval Medical Research Unit (NAMRU), the US Information Service (USIS), and the Kagnew communications station at Asmara. The most significant closure was MAAG. For 25 years it had administered the US military assistance programme, worth c. $11m in 1976; at its height, there were 300 American military advisers attached to the programme, but this had already begun to decline under Haile Selassie in 1973-4 so that at the time of their expulsion, there were only 46 Americans in MAAG. The Dergue statement said: 'The existence of an American Military Assistance Advisory Group is useless at a time when the American government takes every opportunity to create hatred against revolutionary Ethiopia by depicting her as a country where human rights are violated.' Kagnew—at one time a key communications link between Western fleets in the Indian Ocean and the Mediterranean as well as an important US 'listening post' for the Middle East—was already regarded as obsolete, and the US had decided even before the Ethiopian revolution to phase it out. The run-down was to have been completed in 1977, and there were only a handful of US civilian technicians minding the base. The Dergue statement said the US had used Kagnew 'to secure its economic, political, social and military interests in the world, particularly in the Middle East, Asia and Africa'. The Naval Medical Research Unit was described by the Dergue as 'no longer of any importance to revolutionary Ethiopia', while the USIS was accused of 'transmitting the cheap culture of imperialism'. This move was followed on 24 April by an order closing all six diplomatic missions in Asmara: the consulates of the US, Italy and Sudan and the honorary consulates of Britain, France and Belgium.

The US formally retaliated against the expulsions on 28 April by suspending the Foreign Military Sales Credit programme, under which Ethiopia had purchased

$25m worth of arms in 1975 and was authorized to receive $10m in 1976 and 1977, including F-5E Tiger jet fighters and M-60 tanks. Ethiopia replied on 30 April that the decision did not come as a surprise and would not 'make revolutionary Ethiopia kneel before imperialists'. Mengistu declared in a May Day speech that the action against the Americans had ended an era of 'slavery' imposed on Ethiopia by Washington. Keeping up its pressure, the US delegate on the World Bank Board of Directors abstained on 12 May when the Board approved two IDA loans worth $57m for Ethiopia. The abstention was designed as an expression of American concern for human rights.

There was a further move on 30 May when the US was ordered to cut its Addis Ababa Embassy staff by half and reduce the Embassy's Marine Corps guard by two-thirds. This left c. 50 American officials in Ethiopia, most of them attached to USAID, which was not affected by the closures and continued to administer programmes worth several million dollars. The US, Britain and Egypt were also ordered to withdraw their military attachés.

The US House of Representatives passed and sent on to the Senate a foreign military aid bill omitting all previous provisions for Ethiopia on 21 July. Five days later, the State Department announced that the US had decided 'in principle' to authorize the sale of military equipment to Somalia. This offer, in which Britain had concurred, was clumsily withdrawn a short while later when the extent of Somali involvement in the Ogaden fighting became clear (see chapter on Somalia). The Ethiopian Foreign Minister, Col Felleke, summoned the US and UK *chargés d'affaires* on 2 August to demand an explanation. Both assured him that their countries respected the 'unity and territorial integrity' of Ethiopia, and that Somalia would be obliged not to use the proposed arms against her.

There has been no US ambassador in Addis Ababa since May 1976, and the Ethiopian ambassadorship in Washington was similarly vacant until September 1977 when Ayalew Mandefro, previously Ambassador in Mogadishu and then the Dergue's Defence Minister, was appointed. He presented his credentials on 22 November but, after being ordered back to Addis Ababa for consultations, resigned on 29 January 1978 and asked permission to remain in the US (but did not request political asylum). A US university graduate, Ayalew had defended his country's ending of military ties with the US, saying that Washington had dragged its feet on Ethiopian arms requests since 1973, despite the massive Soviet build-up in Somalia.

Several attempts were made in the course of 1977 by both Ethiopia and the US to improve relations. On the Ethiopian side, the main concern was to secure c. $40m worth of military equipment, already paid for, which was in the pipeline when military ties were broken in April. In the face of the Somali onslaught in the Ogaden, the Ethiopians were also able to refer to several treaties signed over the years, including one in 1960 which committed the US to help preserve Ethiopia's territorial integrity. Finally, many senior Ethiopian officials were anxious to strike a balance in foreign policy befitting the country's non-aligned status. Col Felleke said in an interview with the *Washington Post*: 'We want to become a kind of Yugoslavia in this region and have the same kind of relations the US has with that country'. He said Ethiopia had decided to turn to the Soviet Union for military assistance after being 'betrayed at a critical time' by a 'virtual blockade' on US arms.

Two US envoys, Paul Henze of the National Security Council and Richard Post of the State Department's Africa section, visited Addis Ababa in September to discuss the arms request. It was later decided to maintain an arms embargo on both Ethiopia and Somalia as long as the Ogaden fighting continued.

Two US Congressmen, Don Bonker and Paul Tsongas, both liberal Democrats, visited Addis Ababa on 13 December and met Mengistu. He told them that Ethiopia's anti-imperialism did not mean that it was anti-American, anti-Europe or against the peoples of any country, but that Ethiopia 'opposed the exploitation and oppression which flowed from imperialism'. Replying to the Congressmen's concern about human rights, Mengistu said Ethiopians had 'gained democratic and human rights by being organized in farmers', workers' and urban dwellers' associations'. The Congressmen were impressed with Mengistu's intelligence and obvious patriotism, but were shaken by the sight of 'red terror' victims in the streets of Addis Ababa. On arrival in Nairobi, they spoke of a 'reign of terror' in Ethiopia.

In February 1978, David Aaron, President Carter's deputy assistant for national security, accompanied by Mr Henze and by William Harrop, Deputy Assistant Secretary of State for Africa, held talks with Mengistu in Addis Ababa. The atmosphere for the meeting, which had been planned for some time, was clouded by Ethiopia's 14 January threat to break off diplomatic relations with the US. This was in response to statements by Carter at a Press conference on 12 January in which he criticized the Soviet Union's 'unwarranted involvement in Africa', and blamed Moscow for contributing to the war in the Ogaden—first by arming both sides, and then by massively arming Ethiopia. In Addis Ababa, this was interpreted as an endorsement of the Somali position; the US was accused of 'prodding the Somali expansionists to launch their aggression'.

In the Aaron-Mengistu talks, the US stressed the American commitment to Ethiopia's sovereignty and territorial integrity, while at the same time expressing concern over the Russians' role. The main purpose, however, was to obtain assurances that Ethiopia would not invade Somalia's territory if Mogadishu agreed to withdraw all its regular troops from the Ogaden. Both sides expressed satisfaction with the talks, and a week later the US authorized the delivery of the 'non-lethal' part of the $40m consignment the Ethiopians wanted unfrozen, i.e. $1.1m worth of trucks and vehicle spares. The shipment was due to leave Baltimore on 23 February 1978.

RELATIONS WITH WESTERN EUROPE

Britain, France, West Germany and Italy tended to share the brunt of Ethiopian criticism against the US, particularly over the Ogaden conflict, where Ethiopia accused all the Nato countries of backing Mogadishu and of indirectly arming the Somalis through Western allies such as Saudi Arabia and Iran.

West Germany, which continued to maintain substantial economic aid programmes in Ethiopia—and even to supply and train the Ethiopian police—came in for particular disapproval. The West German military attaché was described as 'unnecessary' and expelled on 17 January 1978. On the same day, Ethiopian militiamen occupied the West German school in Addis Ababa in an argument over its immunity from teaching Marxism-Leninism. But the real rift came on 22 January after West Germany announced a DM 25m credit to Somalia. While designed strictly for economic and social development, the credit had 'no strings attached' and was widely interpreted as an expression of gratitude for Somalia's assistance in the West German commando raid on a hijacked Lufthansa airliner at Mogadishu in October 1977 (see chapter on Somalia). The Ethiopian Ambassador in Bonn, Dr Haile Gabriel Dagne, said the credit was 'probably just the tip of the iceberg'. Convinced that Somalia would be free to use the money to purchase arms, Ethiopia retaliated by expelling the West German Ambassador in Addis Ababa whose presence had been found 'detrimental to the traditional relations between the two countries'. Denying any intention of assisting Somalia militarily, Chancellor Helmut Schmidt said: 'It will continue to be our policy not to supply weapons to areas of tension in the Third World'.

Protest notes alleging Western diplomatic and military assistance for Somalia were delivered on 1 February 1978 to the US, UK, French, West German, Saudi Arabian and Iranian embassies in Addis Ababa. Mengistu said on 14 February that if the Western powers 'continued their policy of devising secret means of causing the bloodshed of the peoples of Africa and widening the scope of destruction and annihilation . . . maintaining diplomatic relations with them would become totally meaningless.

Britain was accused in an *Ethiopian Herald* editorial on 4 June 1977 of helping 'members of the self-exiled feudal monarchy', providing facilities for the EDU, and platforms for the EPRP and Eritrean groups. The British Press was further accused of misinterpreting the Ethiopian revolution by attempting to give a false picture of alleged genocide. 'In short, London has become a principal centre for sustained propaganda campaigns aimed at weakening the revolution and unity of the Ethiopian people.'

RELATIONS WITH SOMALIA
The war over the Ogaden is discussed separately. Ethiopia broke off diplomatic relations with Somalia on 6 September 1977, saying that they served no useful purpose 'in view of the continuing war of invasion which the Mogadishu regime is waging aginst Ethiopia'. Somalia in turn broke off relations the next day. Throughout the war, Ethiopia continued to maintain its position, stated at the UN on 3 October, that 'there can be no ceasefire or negotiations until the forces of aggression are completely withdrawn from Ethiopian territory'. Even in the initial days after the announced withdrawal of Somali regular forces from the Ogaden, Ethiopia refused to accept calls for a ceasefire, insisting that there could be no peace until Somalia publicly renounced all claims to any part of Ethiopia.

RELATIONS WITH SUDAN
The sharp deterioration in relations, which threatened to break out in open war early in 1976,[17] was reversed by the end of 1977 when the Sudan—strengthened by its alliances with Egypt and Saudi Arabia and exhausted by the burden of c. 200,000 Ethiopian and Eritrean refugees—showed a positive interest in reconciliation with its eastern neighbour. At the root of the conflict between the two once-friendly regimes were mutual allegations that each was harbouring elements hostile to the other. Sudan accused Ethiopia of sheltering and training members of the Sudanese National Front (led by former Premier Said Saddiq al-Mahdi) who had sought to overthrow President Numeiry; Ethiopia cited Sudan's assistance to the Eritrean guerrilla movements and to the Ethiopian Democratic Union, both of which enjoyed privileges on Sudanese territory. Numeiry's internal position changed after his reconciliation with al-Mahdi in the autumn of 1977. Nevertheless, the Sudanese leader continued to speak out strongly against Soviet military involvement in the Horn.

The Sudan alleged on 10 April 1977 that Ethiopian troops had attacked the Sudanese border town of Qallabat. At the same time, Ethiopia reported to the OAU that Sudanese forces had committed 'direct aggression' in the north-west, and that 'serious clashes' were occurring with 'invading Sudanese troops and mercenaries' well inside Ethiopia. In a broadcast on 12 April, Mengistu charged that the 'honour and integrity of Ethiopia had been violated' in an attack, backed by artillery and tanks, from across the Sudanese border. Blaming the attack directly on President Numeiry, who was 'supported by international imperialism and reactionary Arab regimes', Mengistu claimed that fighting was occurring in Tessenei, Umm Hagar, Naqfa, Afabet, Abderafi, Humera and Metemma—the very towns captured in preceding weeks by rebels (the first five by Eritrean guerrillas and the other two, in Begemder province, by the EDU). A rally of several hundred thousand Ethiopians in Revolution Square on 13 April was exhorted by Mengistu to 'get armed' and prepare to fight their enemies. An effigy of Numeiry was hanged, and demonstrators later marched on the Sudanese and Egyptian embassies. However, Sudan rejected the Ethiopian allegations as 'baseless' and repeated its charge that Ethiopian troops and aircraft had repeatedly attacked border areas in pursuit of Eritrean guerrillas.

Remarkably, despite the heat of the propaganda battle between the two countries, the tenseness of the border areas and occasional clashes along the frontier, Ethiopia and Sudan steered clear of all-out war, confining themselves to other forms of pressure. In June 1977, Numeiry launched a campaign to remove the OAU headquarters from Addis Ababa, in protest at the 'horrible crimes' committed by the Dergue. On 17 June, the Sudan banned Ethiopian Airlines planes from its airspace and closed the airline's Khartoum office, Sudan Airways flights from Khartoum to Addis Ababa having been suspended five months earlier. Ethiopia described the ban as 'part of the systematic campaign of reactionary regimes whose mission is to bring about the abortion of the Ethiopian revolution'.

Just four months later, on 15 October, Ethiopia expressed its readiness to support 'sincere efforts' to normalize relations with the Sudan through a mediation committee set up during the OAU Summit at Libreville. A conciliatory statement said that Ethiopia was not a threat to any of its neighbours and its revolution was 'purely an internal affair'. Numeiry announced his willingness in early December to join in reconciliation talks, saying that he was 'greatly concerned about increased Soviet influence which is developing a strong base in the brother country of Ethiopia'.

Under the auspices of the OAU's mediation committee, agreement was reached by Ethiopia and the Sudan at Freetown (Sierra Leone) on 19 December 1977 on immediately ending all hostile acts and propaganda against each other, re-opening air links and seeking a solution to all other outstanding problems, including that of refugees. After the talks, Numeiry repeated his readiness to mediate between the Dergue and the Eritreans. Civil aviation links were restored a month later.

RELATIONS WITH THE ARAB STATES AND IRAN
The 'conservative' Red Sea powers—Saudi Arabia, Egypt and (despite its improved relations with Ethiopia) Sudan—were deeply suspicious of Soviet designs in the region and were prepared to challenge them in ways that the US could not. Egypt supported the Eritreans and ferried arms to Somalia during the Ogaden fighting. Saudi Arabia harboured a wing of the Afar Liberation Movement and reportedly gave financial support to the Eritreans, Somalis and the EDU. Both Cairo and Riyadh were described by Ethiopia as 'agents of international imperialism'; much of the Dergue's propaganda was directed against 'the forces of Arab reaction'. Ethiopia contended on 13 September 1977 that forces from Egypt, Sudan, Saudi Arabia, Syria and Iraq were all fighting on Somalia's side in the Ogaden.

While Somalia and the Eritrean liberation movements received broad support in the Arab world, there were some divergences. Libya and South Yemen supported Ethiopia (see below). Iraq, long-time principal arms provider for the Eritreans, allowed Baghdad airport to be used as a refuelling stop for planes in the Soviet airlift to Ethiopia. In spite of Israeli assistance for Ethiopia (see below), a Palestinian delegation visited Addis Ababa in March 1978 and decided to open a PLO office there.

The Afro-Arab summit conference in March 1977 rejected two Ethiopian proposals: the inadmissability of any form of assistance to secessionist and 'counter-revolutionary' movements, and an oil embargo on SA, Rhodesia and Israel. Ethiopia in turn reacted strongly to the decisions of the Arab Information Ministers' meeting in Tunis in August 1977, which were seen as pledging Arab propaganda support for Somalia and the Eritrean secessionists. However, a meeting of Arab League Foreign Ministers in Cairo in September failed to support Somalia (a League member) against Ethiopia, and called on them to settle their dispute peacefully.

Iran was the most active Muslim country backing Somalia in 1977, primarily out of concern over the Russian role in the Red Sea area. The Shah announced in January 1978 that Iran would not remain idle if Ethiopia attacked Somalia, a statement which brought a sharp warning from the OAU about Iranian 'meddling' in African affairs.

A diplomatic row occurred in Moscow in January 1978 when the Ethiopian Embassy issued a statement accusing the Arabs of 'slave trading' in Africa in the past and, at present, of systematically employing 'direct and indirect military aggression, pressure, bribery and other subtle means to achieve the control of and expansion into Africa'. Arab diplomatic missions in Moscow replied angrily, accusing Ethiopia of 'lies and fabrications'.

RELATIONS WITH SOUTH YEMEN (PDRY) AND LIBYA
The rulers of Tripoli and Aden, until 1976 among the chief supporters of the Eritrean struggle,[18] remained out of step with the rest of the Arab world in 1977 by maintaining close links with the Dergue, but once again there were subtle diplomatic shifts. Libya continued to pledge its support 'to ensure the fullest possible success' of the Ethiopian revolution. On 26 June 1977, it concluded a trade protocol and six agreements on co-operation in agriculture, mining, industry, social services and transport, including the establishment of a joint Ethio-Libyan shipping company. More important, Libya was reported to have guaranteed Ethiopia's oil supplies, to be assisting in paying for its arms purchases from the Soviet Union, and to be helping to transport Soviet equipment to Ethiopia. Mengistu was reported to have stopped over in Tripoli on his way back from the Soviet Union in May for six hours of talks with Col Gaddafy, during which, in addition to the proposed arms aid, they were said to have discussed possible Libyan mediation over Eritrea. In March 1978, just before the Somali withdrawal from the Ogaden, President Siyad Barre of Somalia also visited Tripoli. He was believed to have discussed with Gaddafy the possibilities of both a Libyan mediatory role in the Ogaden conflict and a renewed Soviet role in Somalia. After the visit, Libya called for the 'cutting off of non-African connections' with the Ogaden conflict and for an African solution.

South Yemen also served as a conduit—the principal one—for Soviet arms shipments to Ethiopia, which were landed by air at Aden and transported across the Red Sea to Assab. Ethiopian army and navy officers who defected to the Eritrean movements also reported that South Yemeni jet and helicopter pilots, artillery and tank crews were playing a combat role in Eritrea. A State Department spokesman in Washington said in January 1978 that there were c. 300 South Yemenis in combat zones in Eritrea and the Ogaden. A number of trade and co-operation agreements were signed between Ethiopia and South Yemen in 1977. In July, the PDRY denied reports from Beirut that it was to mediate in the disputes in the Horn.

RELATIONS WITH ISRAEL

The Israeli Foreign Minister, Moshe Dayan, confirmed on 6 February 1978 that Israel was providng 'certain arms' to Ethiopia as a means of safeguarding the sea lanes to Israel's southern port of Eilat. The confirmation, in an interview in Zurich, embarrassed the Ethiopians, aroused the already anti-Ethiopian Arabs, and even infuriated members of the Israeli government. Dayan said: 'For years, we've co-operated with Ethiopia, never with Somalia. So when they were interested [in Israeli arms] and were being attacked, they asked us for help and we granted it to them.' He said the aid did not include warplanes or soldiers; Israeli Defence Ministry sources stated that it consisted of ammunition, tents, sleeping bags and first aid supplies. Other sources said the ammunition included napalm and deadly cluster bombs, some of which had already been seized by Somali forces in the Ogaden. Reports from Washington indicated that Israel was supplying spare parts for both Russian and American tanks and aircraft. There were persistent reports, even from sources in Jerusalem, that Israel was also providing teams of instructors in military aviation and logistics to Ethiopia. One indication that this might be so was that Ethiopia, angered at Dayan's disclosure, ordered all Israelis—an indeterminate number doing unspecified jobs—out of Ethiopia. The Ethiopian Embassy in London issued a statement citing Dayan's remarks as 'a deliberate and sinister act designed to isolate Ethiopia from the revolutionary and progressive Arab states'—presumably meaning that the disclosure would make it difficult for Libya and South Yemen to continue their vital assistance to Ethiopia (see above).

There had previously been considerable speculation about Israeli military and security personnel helping the Dergue, although Ethiopia had technically broken off all relations with Israel in October 1973. An Israeli contingent of about a dozen instructors, who had trained the Dergue's Fifth or *Nebelbal* (Flame) Division, was known to have left Ethiopia in 1976. In early 1977, Ethiopia stoutly denied any Israeli connection but on 24 July, US officials in Washington said c. 20–30 Israelis were now back in Ethiopia, training forces in anti-guerrilla and counter-insurgency techniques, while also working for Israeli intelligence.

Ethiopia dismissed as 'malicious' a *Newsweek* report in November 1977 that Israelis were training Ethiopian tank crews in Israel, and that Israeli mechanics were servicing Ethiopian jets. A Kuwaiti newspaper reported in January 1978 that the US had asked Israel to withdraw its military advisers from Ethiopia. At home, Dayan was taken to task in the Knesset for his disclosure, which one MP said had done 'hair-raising' damage to Israel in the military, economic and diplomatic fields.

RELATIONS WITH CHINA

The Chinese played a growing economic role in Ethiopia, but kept a low profile diplomatically. A Chinese statement in August 1977 accused the Soviet Union of trying to build spheres of influence in north-east Africa and the Red Sea, and of trying to cover up Russian 'expansion' by blaming the Horn of Africa conflict on the US. Arab newspapers reported that China had made contacts with Iran, Somalia and South Yemen about its concern that the Red Sea might come under the 'hegemony' of either the US or USSR.

RELATIONS WITH KENYA

Because of its strong resistance to Somalia's claim to the Northern Frontier District (NFD) as part of the 'Somali nation', Kenya in September 1977 became the first black African state to ally itself openly with the Dergue—despite the Kenyans' strong opposition to the Ethiopian regime's violent Marxism-Leninism and to its close alliance with Moscow. It was probably only because of the shared Somali threat that the longstanding ties developed between Ethiopia and Kenya under Haile Selassie survived the Ethiopian coup intact. The two countries exchanged visits, forged ahead with joint projects (including the Addis Ababa-Nairobi highway, completed in 1977), and generally enjoyed exemplary relations. In November 1977, Kenya made the port of Mombasa available to Ethiopian import traffic (see below). Kenya also donated food supplies, including 10,000 tonnes of maize, to Ethiopia in November 1977. It impounded two Egyptian aircraft carrying arms for Somalia which were caught overflying Kenyan airspace early in 1978.

At the eighth conference of Ethiopian and Kenyan border administrators, commissioners and experts (held in Nazareth, south of Addis Ababa, from 5–8 September 1977), captured Somali tanks, armoured vehicles and artillery were on display.

RELATIONS WITH DJIBOUTI
As its independence on 27 June 1977, Ethiopia recognized the new Republic of Djibouti, denied ever having laid claim to the former French territory, and pledged itself to safeguard Djibouti's security and unity. Ethiopia continued to accuse Somalia of intending to annex Djibouti as part of its 'expansionist' aims. The Afar people of Djibouti, whose ethnic roots are in the Sultanate of Aussa in eastern Ethiopia, developed divisions for and against the Government in Addis Ababa in 1977 (see chapter on Djibouti).

RELATIONS WITH OTHER AFRICAN STATES
Ethiopia enjoyed the tacit approval of virtually all black African states for its determination to preserve its territorial integrity (a sacred African principle enshrined in the OAU Charter). This was true even of African states which strongly disapproved of the Dergue and especially of the deep Russian involvement in Ethiopia. Likewise, over Eritrea, Ethiopia enjoyed the tacit support of the numerous black African states which have themselves faced secessionist threats.

With the Ethiopia-Somalia dispute on the agenda virtually since its inauguration in 1963, the OAU made yet another attempt in August 1977, under rather more urgent conditions, to settle the conflict. The OAU 'good offices' committee—comprising Nigeria, Liberia, Senegal, Sudan, Cameroon, Tanzania, Mauritania and Lesotho—made an attempt to reduce tensions at a meeting in Libreville, but nothing came of it.

Ethiopia established diplomatic relations with Angola on 13 July 1977.

The Dergue announced on 20 October 1977 that it would boycott the Africa Games eliminating matches in Cairo in November, in protest against Somalia's participation.

ECONOMIC AFFAIRS (Birr 3.77 = £1 sterling; Bir 2.4609 = SDR 1)
The economic promise of the 1974 revolution has remained largely unfulfilled due to dislocation and war. In its preoccupation with the political aspects of revolution, the regime has allowed the economy to drift without a new Development Plan or even a published budget. Its emphasis on developing agriculture (which provides a living for 90% of Ethiopians, mostly at subsistence level) has been offset by labour problems in the industrial sector. Laudable efforts to cope with the continuation of drought and famine conditions—which did so much to spark off the revolution in

1973—have been hampered by the war and the accompanying refugee problem, especially in the most drought-stricken region, the Ogaden. There was no shortage of offers of external economic assistance in 1977—especially from Eastern Europe. Yet $10m in foreign aid was believed swept away by the Ogaden conflict, and at the time of the country's greatest need, the regime's capacity to absorb aid declined markedly, leaving c. $658m in longstanding aid commitments unspent. One indicator of the parlous state of the economy was an estimate by the World Bank in March 1978 that the per capita GNP growth rate, which averaged 2% over the period 1960–75, was a mere 0.4% in 1970–75. The World Bank estimated Ethiopia's 1975 GNP at $2,730m, or roughly $100 per capita.

Almost in spite of these shortcomings, Ethiopia's economic position at the end of 1977 was relatively healthy, thanks to record coffee prices. Although reduced in volume, coffee exports were worth Birr 324.6m ($155.6m) in 1976—a 112% increase over 1975's earnings of Birr 152.7m ($73.2m). Coffee's share in total exports in 1976 was 55.6%. The record earnings, due to an eightfold increase in world coffee prices since 1975, helped to offset declines in other exports (except hides and skins) and huge jumps in the import of textiles, machinery and transport equipment, thereby contributing to an overall balance of payments surplus.

But the coffee trend was not altogether encouraging. Figures for the first quarter of 1977 (the most recent available) showed earnings at Birr 198.1m ($95m), an increase of 41% over the same period of 1976; but the volume of coffee exports was down by 41% from 31,200 tonnes to 18,400. (In fact, for the first time since the revolution, the volume of coffee exports had only begun to pick up in 1976.) With world coffee prices expected to stabilize soon, the Commercial Bank of Ethiopia warned that the country's payments surplus could quickly turn to deficit, particularly if spending on mechanical imports continued at its current rate.

The 1976 trading account was in deficit by Birr 149m ($71.4m), an improvement of only 1% on 1975's deficit. Exports totalled Birr 580.5m ($278.3m), an increase of 16.6% from 1975, while imports cost Birr 729.5m ($349.8m), up 12.6% from 1975. Non-coffee exports fell from Birr 345.1m ($165.5m) in 1975 to Birr 246m ($118m) in 1976.

BALANCE OF PAYMENTS

The 1976 surplus was Birr 32.4m ($15.5m), an increase of Birr 24.9m ($11.9m) from 1975. However, it was believed that Ethiopia's petroleum import bill of c. Birr 10.6m ($5m), unrecorded in the trading figures, plus estimated 'errors and omissions' worth c. Birr 55.8m ($26m), would wipe out the recorded surplus. [19]

The rise in the official payments surplus was attributed to increased earnings from services (up 50% from 1975) and to a large influx in both private and public foreign capital, including Birr 32.7m ($15m) from the EEC's Stabex commodity support programme. However, the National Bank warned that the increased cost of imports—particularly machinery, vehicles and oil—could produce a payments deficit in 1977. In its 1976 annual report, the bank took the bold step of warning the regime of the dangers of deficit financing, which it said could imperil the country's strong foreign reserve position unless accompanied by increased export revenue. 'If credit is made to expand faster in the private sector (for example, the commercial banks), additional borrowing by the Government would fan the inflationary fires,' the report said. [20] It also drew attention to declining imports of industrial plant, despite an abundance of obsolete equipment, and deplored the increase (30.6% in 1975–76) in textile imports, which 'consume a substantial amount of foreign exchange earnings' when such textiles could be produced locally.

Foreign reserves continued to rise, standing at Birr 649.3m ($311.3m) at the end of 1976 (cf Birr 591.3m in 1975) and at Birr 679m ($328.6m) at the end of the first quarter of 1977. The Government's borrowings from the Central Bank increased in 1975–76 from Birr 259.3m ($124.3m) to Birr 445.1m ($213.4m), while credits to the private and nationalized sectors increased only marginally in the same period, from Birr 494m ($236.9m) to Birr 497m ($238.3m).

FOREIGN EXCHANGE

Following the tightening up of exchange control regulations on 5 January 1977 (which prohibited Ethiopians from maintaining bank accounts abroad),[21] the Government imposed new customs duties on imported luxury goods on 17 May, ranging from 185% on motor vehicles and 80% on alcoholic beverages to 200% on jewellery. Luxury taxes were also increased on alcohol and perfume. Nevertheless, the country's overall tax rate structure was still considered by economists to be remarkably low.

The introduction of the new *birr* banknotes, which became legal tender on 12 January 1977 (replacing the old Haile Selassie Ethiopian dollar notes)[22] was followed on 23 January 1978 by the introduction of new coins, in denominations of 50, 10, 5 and 1 cents. The birr retained the former dollar's face value.

THE STATE OF THE ECONOMY

Activity in the agricultural, industrial and commercial sectors was characterized in 1977 by irregular production and returns due to continuing political and social chaos. The organization of 6m rural dwellers—21% of the population—into 25,000 peasants' associations had many positive effects. A 'self-help' consciousness was encouraged; areas under cultivation increased; and the production of crops for the rural subsistence diet went up, so that many Ethiopians ate more and better food than before. The associations became the proprietors of the rural land 'returned' to the peasants from their former 'feudal landlords'; instead of tributes in cash and kind going to the landlords, taxes were paid to the State. However, the transportation system remained in a state of disarray due to the widespread rural insurgencies; it was even difficult to maintain existing roads. Products did not find their way to market and townspeople experienced severe shortages. As prices for basic commodities rose—even when put under Government control—crops were withheld. A quintal of the staple *teff*, used for making the spongy unleavened bread *injera* which, with a fiery stew called *wat* is the national dish—cost Birr 30 ($15) in 1973. In February 1977, its price was fixed at Birr 41 ($20), but by August, it was up to Birr 67 ($32) at official prices and Birr 90 ($43) at black market rates. These prices represented more than a month's salary for most Ethiopians.

The regime maintained that agricultural production had increased steadily since the nationalization of rural land in 1975. The Minister of Agriculture and Settlement said on 3 March 1977 that production was running at 120,000 tonnes a year, and that State-run farms now employed 100,000 people. Yet there were reports that the State takeover of the large former commercial farms had been far from successful: at one project which was producing 4,000 tonnes of grain when taken over, output was reported to have fallen to 1,600 tonnes in the first year of State operation and to 500 tonnes in 1976.

The Commercial Bank extended over Birr 400m ($193.3m) in agricultural and industrial credits in the first half of 1976. The agricultural credits, worth Birr 131.4m ($63m), had gone to State investment and marketing agencies, local agricultural development units at Tendaho, Abadir, Wollaita and Awassa, and to the Livestock and Meat Board. Birr 15m ($7.2m) had been advanced to agricultural co-operatives. The Agricultural and Industrial Development Bank lent Birr 327.9m ($157.2m) to the rural sector in 1975–77, including Birr 38m ($18.2m) to peasants' associations.

In an official and unprecedented PMAC statement on 18 October 1977, the regime came close to acknowledging economic realities. It reported that Birr 80m ($38.3m) worth of crops had been left to rot in the fields because of 'sabotage' by the 'anarchists' of the EPRP and EDU. It said 'subversives' had crippled industrial machinery, left the harvest to be destroyed by frost and rain, disrupted transport thus preventing farmers from taking their produce to market and so causing food shortages. Subversives were also responsible for the closure of schools which had put 20,000 teachers out of work.

The insurrections and security problems all took their economic toll. About 40% of Ethiopian industry was traditionally based in Eritrea, and this production—from beer to processed foods and matches—was for the most part no longer available to the national economy. The important agricultural regions of Tigre, Gondar and Gojjam in the north-west and Sidamo, Kaffa, Gamo-Goffa and Illubabor in the south-west were all affected by rebellion. Several rural development projects being carried out with foreign technical assistance had to be abandoned. Another factor in the rural decline was the conscription, sometimes under duress and at harvest time, of c. 500,000 able-bodied men and boys into the peasant militia. These conditions also had drastic consequences for both internal distribution of goods and the delivery of export commodities to the world market (see Transportation and Communications, below). At the height of the Ogaden fighting, the Minister of Commerce and Industry said in Kenya that Ethiopia was facing acute shortages. Kenya agreed to make Mombasa available for the trans-shipment of Ethiopian goods, which could then be either flown to Addis Ababa or taken in along the 1,600-km Nairobi-Addis Ababa highway, the final asphalted section of which was opened to traffic in June 1977.

INDUSTRY

There was some progress in diversifying, expanding and improving the productivity of the industrial sector, which accounts for less than 10% of GDP. Particular successes were reported in textiles, shoes and cement (which were being developed with Chinese aid), and in sugar refining and salt mining, two commodities being developed for export by British companies. The three domestic sugar producers—Metahara, Wonji and Shoa—were expected to boost production by 12% in 1977–78. Production in 1976–77 was 1.24m quintals (cf 1.08m in 1975–76 and 1.28m in 1974–75).

The Ministry of Industry reported on 2 February 1978 that 131 nationalized firms had been grouped into 14 State corporations and nine share companies. The Ministry said that 'in view of the prevailing reality in the country, these corporations and companies are facing a variety of problems, including delays in getting raw materials and spare parts'. The textile, leather and silk industries, it said, had been particularly affected by the situation in Eritrea.

COMMERCE AND TOURISM

There was general stagnation in the commercial and tourist sectors of the economy in 1977. Many companies were forced to close down, including local export-import firms as well as foreign-owned groups such as the United Touring Company. Singer, one of the first foreign companies set up in Ethiopia 50 years ago, was nationalized in January 1978.

The tourist trade fell to negligible levels in 1977. The capital's luxury hotels remained all but empty, and passenger traffic on Ethiopian Airlines dropped dramatically (although no official figures were published).

THE DROUGHT IN 1977

Drought and famine continued to affect large areas, particularly in the Ogaden and Danakil regions. The Relief and Rehabilitation Commission, under its able and energetic commissioner, Shimelis Adougna, continued to canvass the world for assistance, though the distribution of relief supplies was hampered by security problems. The Commission was preoccupied in 1977 with resettling nomads in the Afar region and in the vicinity of the Wabi Shebelle river in the Ogaden, and with distributing seeds and seedlings to farmers. Poor harvests were again reported in Wollo, scene of the disastrous 1973–74 famine.

The longer-term problems of soil erosion and deforestation were being tackled through a Forestry Institute set up with Swedish help. A US aid team continued to monitor climatic conditions, crop patterns and the food intake of farming families as a kind of 'early warning' protection against future famine. The US agreed on 21 December 1977 to provide $2m to purchase 150 trucks specifically to distribute famine relief supplies.

TRANSPORTATION AND COMMUNICATIONS

The Eritrean guerrillas deprived Ethiopia of the use of one Red Sea port, Massawa, and were able to harass the other, Assab, where Ethiopia's only oil refinery was attacked on 21 April 1977 with the loss of 4m litres of petrol. The road across the Danakil from Addis Ababa to Assab was subject to constant harassment by Afar guerrillas and was cut completely in September and November when several bridges were blown, necessitating the rerouting of traffic across dry river beds. Conditions at Assab were the despair of international shippers, particularly towards the end of 1977 as several of the port's six berths were permanently given over to 'priority cargo'—namely, incoming Soviet arms shipments. Hefty congestion surcharges were imposed by the shipping conferences on Assab-bound cargo, and some lines stopped calling there altogether. Some ships were forced to wait three weeks or more to unload vitally needed drought relief supplies. The UN Disaster Relief Agency reported in December 1977 that a third of the grain imported by Ethiopia in 1977—42,000 out of 114,250 tons—had been bottled up at Assab since May. Access to the main outlet for Ethiopian trade, the port of Djibouti, was curtailed on 30 May when three railway bridges were destroyed (by either Afar or Somali guerrillas), putting the 784-km line out of action for the rest of the year (see chapter on Djibouti). About 10,000 tonnes of Ethiopian cargo remained stored at Djibouti all year. A road link to Djibouti, running roughly parallel to the railway, was inaugurated on 23 March 1977 by a convoy of 177 Ethiopian trucks loaded with drought relief grain. The 250-km road, built with French aid at a cost of $17m, connected with the Addis Ababa-Assab highway.

The Ethiopian Road Authority began a five-year (1977–81) programme to build 6,248 km of roads at a cost of Birr 1,070m ($513m), with credits from the World Bank and other international organizations. Total aid required was Birr 291m ($140m), of which Birr 171m ($82m) had been secured by December 1977. The programme includes the completion of 2,710 km of rural and 3,455 km of urban roads, as well as the construction of 5,400 km of new rural and 848 km of new urban roads.

Ethiopian Airlines started or planned new services during 1977 to Seychelles, Tokyo and Kilimanjaro airport in Tanzania.

TRADE AND AID AGREEMENTS
Ethiopia established its most active external economic relations with the Soviet Union and East Germany in 1977, although the US, Britain, Japan, West Germany and Italy continued to be major trading partners. Agreements on economic, scientific and cultural co-operation were signed with the USSR during Mengistu's visit to Moscow in May (see above), followed by trading agreements in July. Economic relations with GDR developed even more dramatically; a joint committee was established in which East German experts virtually took over the planning of the Ethiopian economy. Trading agreements were also signed with China, Poland, South Yemen and Libya (which set up a joint shipping line with Ethiopia). Economic co-operation agreements were signed during 1977 with Yugoslavia, Czechoslovakia, Romania, Bulgaria, North Korea, Cuba and China. Aviation agreements were signed with the USSR (Aeroflot began weekly flights to Addis Ababa), China, Poland, North Yemen, South Yemen, Angola and the West African airline, Air Afrique.

The IDA agreed on 12 May 1977 to lend $57m for road-building and agricultural projects. The EEC granted $14.2m to expand rural water services, and $16.8m for an irrigation project at Amibara, in the Awash Valley. This will cover 10,300 hectares, provide for the settlement of 800 Afar families and development of four State-run cotton plantations.

One of the biggest aid agreements, announced in February 1978, came from Czechoslovakia, which will provide Birr 93m ($44.6m), 5% as an outright grant and the rest as a 15-year loan, for industrial development. The West German government lent Birr 21.1m ($10m), bringing its total contribution to the construction of the Addis Ababa-Nairobi highway to Birr 68m ($32m). Bonn also provided a $7.4m loan for rural electrification, and continued a programme which pre-dates the revolution of training and equipping the Ethiopian police. Loans also came from the European Development Fund ($14m for coffee cultivation), the African Development Fund ($19m for sewerage facilities), and the OPEC Special Fund ($4.8m). Sweden provided $30m in general economic assistance, and the Netherlands donated $16m worth of chemicals and spraying equipment to combat coffee diseases. The FAO donated $2.6m worth of drought relief food.

Britain reduced its aid programme from an average £2.4m a year since 1974 to £1.47m in 1977. Only three British aid projects, involving fewer than 20 personnel, remained; these dealt with village water resources, road surveying and mapping.

NATIONAL ACCOUNTS (million Birr, year ending 7 July)

	1973	1974	1975	1976
Exports	654	828	683	760
Government Consumption	538	586	730	832
Gross Fixed Capital Formation	569	549	580	594
Increase in Stocks	—	—	—	—
Private Consumption	3,797	4,244	4,407	4,711
Less: Imports	−552	−655	−875	−855
Gross Domestic Product	**5,005**	**5,551**	**5,525**	**6,043**
Less: Net Factor Payments Abroad	−47	−36	−30	−3
Gross National Expenditure = GNP	**4,958**	**5,515**	**5,495**	**6,040**
GDP 1970 prices	5,014	5,144		

Source: IMF, *International Financial Statistics.*

NET BALANCE OF PAYMENTS 1973–76 (million Birr)

	1973	1974	1975	1976*
A Trade balance	**55.5**	**−46.8**	**−202.0**	**−215.3**
Exports (fob)	503.7	556.5	497.8	580.6
Coffee	189.8	151.9	152.7	324.6
Non-coffee	313.4	404.2	345.1	256.0
Non-monetary gold	0.5	0.5	—	0.5
Imports (cif)	−448.2	−603.3	−699.8**	−795.9†
of which freight and insurance	71.9	96.4	113.3	129.7
B Services (net)	**49.9**	**70.9**	**25.6**	**50.7**
Travel	5.8	6.2	—	−2.5
Other transport††	47.7	33.2	43.2	31.6
Investment income	−41.7	−23.1	−24.1	−8.3
Government transaction, nie	40.5	51.0	40.8	33.5
Other services	−2.1	3.6	−34.3	−3.6
C Goods and services (A + B)	**105.4**	**24.1**	**−176.4**	**−164.6**
D Transfer payments (net)	**53.8**	**108.0**	**82.7**	**125.0**
Private	23.8	37.7	30.0	44.0
Public	30.0	70.3	52.7	81.0
E Current account balance (C + D)	**159.2**	**132.1**	**−93.7**	**−39.6**
F Long-term capital (net)	**112.5**	**106.3**	**149.1**	**123.8**
Private	64.2	60.3	35.3	3.5
Public	48.3	46.0	113.8	120.3
G Basic balance (E + F)	**271.7**	**238.4**	**55.4**	**84.2**
H Short-term private capital	**−23.1**	**−18.4**	**−19.4**	**−41.4**
I Net errors and omissions	**−30.3**	**−30.6**	**−28.5**	**−10.4**
J Net monetary changes (surplus−)	**−218.3**	**−189.4**	**−7.5**	**−32.4**

*Preliminary.
**Includes customs figures plus 8 per cent of total imports (cif) estimated for grants and other unrecorded merchandise.
†Includes customs figures and adjustments for crude petroleum imports. In addition, import figures for the second half include 15 per cent of imports (cif) estimated for grants and other unrecorded imports.
††Freight on exports earned by the Ethiopian Shipping Lines included.
Source: National Bank of Ethiopia, Addis Ababa.

INTERNATIONAL LIQUIDITY (million US dollars, at end of Period)

	1975	1976	1977 (Jan–Sept)
International Reserves	287·9	305·9	273·3
Gold	11.2	11.2	11.2
Reserve Position in IMF	8.0	7.9	8.5
Foreign Exchange	268.7	286.8	253.6
IMF Position			
Fund Sales of Currency to Date	—	—	0.6
Quota	31.6	31.4	31.4
Commercial Banks:			
Assets	40.0	38.6	56.5
Liabilities	9.8	10.3	10.2

Source: IMF, *International Financial Statistics.*

MONETARY FACTORS (million Birr)

	1976 March	1976 December	1977 March
Foreign reserves	641.8	649.3	679.0
Domestic credit	860.5	942.1	1,036.2
Credits to Central Government	340.8	445.1	402.1
Credits to non-Government Sector	519.7	497.0	634.0
Money supply	1,331.7	1,259.6	1,403.6

MONEY AND QUASI-MONEY (million Birr)

	1976 March	1976 December	1977 March
Money in circulation	765.7	574.7	675.9
Current accounts	259.9	235.0	256.0
Total (money)	**1,025.6**	**809.7**	**932.2**
Savings deposits	200.4	308.9	316.0
Deposit accounts	105.6	141.0	155.0
Total (quasi-money)	**306.1**	**449.9**	**471.4**

Source: Marchés Tropicaux, 14 October 1977.

DIRECTION OF TRADE (million US dollars)

	1970	1974	1975	1976
Main Suppliers				
United States	14.61	15.52	56.51	84.59
Japan	25.44	35.41	38.76	62.72
West Germany	23.55	33.02	30.27	43.86
Iran	10.42	23.83	30.41	36.49
Italy	29.04	42.19	33.27	32.47
United Kingdom	12.80	21.26	23.64	24.63
Saudi Arabia	0.32	11.64	10.51	12.61
Netherlands	4.36	6.01	9.57	11.04
Total (including others)	**171.64**	**286.48**	**327.38**	**409.66**
Main Purchasers				
United States	59.61	64.77	41.14	90.09
Saudi Arabia	6.67	19.42	26.95	32.34
Djibouti	6.60	25.43	27.71	27.71
United Kingdom	2.33	10.28	6.24	23.47
Italy	7.60	18.74	10.25	20.49
Japan	6.64	24.40	20.59	20.10
Egypt	0.18	4.81	19.92	19.92
West Germany	8.90	20.34	26.79	16.06
France	2.65	18.82	5.57	13.16
Total (including others)	**122.73**	**295.07**	**236.15**	**322.63**

Source: IMF, Direction of Trade 1970-76.

ETHIOPIA'S FOREIGN TRADE 1974-76 (million Birr)

	1974	1975	Change 1974-75	1976	Change 1975-76
Exports	**556.2**	**497.8**	**−58.4**	**580.5**	**+82.7**
Coffee	151·9	152.7	+0.8	324.6	+171.9
Hides and skins	47.1	34.5	−12.6	55.4	+20.9
Meat and meat products	14.6	7.1	−7.5	6.8	−0.3
Oil seeds	95.9	84.0	−11.9	31.2	−52.8
Pulses	101.9	64·8	−37.1	55.9	−8.9
Re-exports	8.9	29.4	+20.5	7.7	−21.7
Others	135.6	125.3	−10.6	98.9	−26.4
Imports	**590.2**	**647.9**	**+57.7**	**729.5**	**+81.6**
Petroleum products	101.7	141.7	+40.0	111.0	−30.7
Chemicals	89.9	125.4	+35.5	110.0	−15.4
Textiles and clothing	48.2	46.7	−1.5	77.2	+30.6
Machinery and transport equipment	147.3	152.2	+4.9	218.9	+66.8
Others	203.1	181.9	−21.2	212.4	+30.3
Trade balance	**−34.0**	**−150.1**	**−116.1**	**−149.0**	**+1.1**

Source: Commercial Bank of Ethiopia, Annual Review, 1977.

VOLUME OF EXPORTS 1977 ('000 tonnes)

	1st quarter 1976	1st quarter 1977
Coffee	31.2	18.4
Skins (million units)	3.5	2.6
Hides	0.5	0.9
Pulses	27.7	35.1
Oilseeds	8.3	16.8
Livestock ('000 head)	87.0	5.0
Fruit and vegetables	4.3	6.5
Other food products	3.5	1.6
Sugar	5.5	1.5

Source: Marchés Tropicaux, 21 October 1977.

COFFEE EXPORTS, 1971/72–1976/77

	Volume ('000 tonnes)	Value (million Burr)
1971–72	77.7	164.6
1972–73	81.4	200
1973–74	61.7	166
1974–75	68.9	117.4
1975–76	77.1	297
1976–77*	47.9	652.1

*Provisional estimate.
Source: Marches Tropicaux, 5 August 1977.

NOTES
1. See *Africa Contemporary Record (ACR)* 1974–75, pp. B160ff; 1975–76, pp. B186ff; 1976–77, pp. B187ff.
2. Interview with Jonathan Dimbleby, 'This Week', Thames Television, London, 23 February 1978.
3. See *ACR* 1976–77, p. B179 and p. B194.
4. See *ACR* 1976–77, p. B186-7.
5. For a fuller discussion of the Afars, see Colin Legum and Bill Lee, *Conflict in the Horn of Africa* (London, 1977), pp. 27–29.
6. See *ACR* 1976–77, p. B182.
7. Roger Mann in *The Observer* Foreign News Service, 9 February 1978.
8. *Ibid.*
9. *The New York Times*, 10 February 1978.
10. *Ibid*, 3 September 1977.
11. See *ACR* 1976–77, p. B205.
12. *Ibid.*
13. See *ACR* 1976–77, p. B204.
14. *Ethiopian Herald*, 11 November 1977.
15. See *ACR* 1976–77, pp. B197-8.
16. See *ACR* 1976–77, p. B210.
17. See *ACR* 1976–77, pp. B207-9.
18. See *ACR* 1976–77, p. B212.
19. *Marchés Tropicaux et Meditérranéens*, Paris, 1 July 1977.
20. *Middle East Economic Digest*, London, 25 November 1977.
21. See *ACR* 1976–77, p. B214.
22. See *ACR* 1976–77, p. B212.

Somali Democratic Republic

There was no disguising the extent of the military, political, diplomatic and economic setbacks which Somalia suffered in 1977–78. The bold and carefully timed attempt to retrieve from a disintegrating Ethiopia one of the 'five constituent parts of the Somali nation'[1] ended in a humiliating withdrawal from the Ogaden battlefield. That acknowledgement of defeat was brought about only by the intervention of what, until 1977, had been two of Somalia's closest allies, the Soviet Union and Cuba.[2] President Siyad Barre's failure to acquire a source of significant arms supplies after breaking with the Russians in November 1977 left him politically exposed at home and militarily outflanked on the battlefield; while his failure to get significant African support for the Somali cause left him at a serious diplomatic disadvantage. His tough, well-trained army—reputedly one of the best on the continent—was crippled in the Ogaden in early 1978. Half a million war refugees crowded into Somalia's towns and villages, critically overstretching their meagre resources. Perhaps most damaging of all, the grand objective which most Somalis regard as their national destiny—the unification of the entire Somali 'family'—now seemed even more remote. Not only had the Somalis lost their attempt to 'liberate' eastern Ethiopia (after having taken over most of the areas they laid claim to there by the summer of 1977), but Djibouti had hoisted its own flag of independence earlier in the year, and Kenya was mobilizing its powerful Western friends to defend the integrity of its largely Somali-inhabited Northern Frontier District (NFD).

Yet even in defeat, Siyad Barre still had some options. In spite of angrily evicting the Russians in November 1977, he had not broken with them altogether.[3] From over the border in Ethiopia, their new centre of influence, the Russians dictated the terms of a settlement they were willing to underwrite: a guarantee of peace without Ethiopian reprisals; assurance of aid to rebuild Somalia's army and economy; and a formula for incorporating the Somali-speaking peoples in a single political entity. An alternative was to build on the Arab-Iran-Western friendship which had developed especially after the break with Moscow. The choice Barre had to make, therefore, was whether to accept the terms of his old enemy, the Soviets and Cuba, or to rebuild Somalia's future with the help of the anti-Communist group of Red Sea and Gulf States and with the West. But first he had to ensure his personal survival and that of his Marxist-Leninist regime.

In fact, it was not long before simmering dissatisfaction within the armed forces over the outcome of the Ogaden war erupted on 9 April 1978 in a brief, disorganized and ultimately unsuccessful coup against President Barre. An attempt on Sunday morning to seize a military communications centre outside Mogadishu was crushed by loyal troops, but not before the rebels had killed 20 people and wounded 34 others (by official count). Tanks and armoured cars appeared in the streets after the attempt, but shops remained open and life continued virtually as normal. The President himself announced the crushing of the coup in a radio broadcast in which he claimed that 'colonialism, which has many faces, both old and new, all along wanted to stir up chaos' through its 'lackeys'. There were reports that the coup attempt followed the execution of c. 80 officers in Hargeisa for their opposition to the handling of the war.

OGADEN: THE WAR FRONT

A narrative account of the war is given in the chapter on Ethiopia in this volume. What follows is a summary of the fighting with emphasis on the Somali viewpoint.

First reports of hostilities along the disputed Ogaden frontier came on 21 February 1977 from independent sources in Nairobi. Somalia denied them, saying that it had 'always advocated the peaceful settlement of problems of any nature'. Between February and June, Somalia was preoccupied with the impending independence of the French Territory of the Afars and Issas (see chapter on Djibouti), and with Ethiopian allegations that Somalia was planning to annex the territory. On 21 March, Siyad Barre challenged Ethiopia to accept the right of self-determination for its peoples, and said Somalia could not accept Ethiopia's 'continued colonization of Somali territory'. On 15 May, he offered to make his army available to assist Djibouti if the territory was invaded by Ethiopia. This statement was seized upon by an Ethiopian spokesman on 17 May as evidence of a 'projection of Mogadishu's intentions to annex Djibouti'. By early June, Ethiopia was blaming 'Somali-trained infiltrators' for the attacks on the Addis Ababa-Djibouti railway; Somalia replied that Ethiopia was trying to draw attention away from its own 'liberation wars'. It added that it would never desist from supporting those liberation struggles in general, and that of the Western Somali Liberation Front (WSLF) in particular.

In mid-June, Mogadishu Radio began to broadcast the communiqués of the WSLF, which at the time was thought to have c. 6,000 armed guerrillas operating in the Ogaden and other parts of Ethiopia's Hararghe province. The first report, on 16 June, claimed 352 Ethiopian soldiers killed and 176 captured in a skirmish at Babile, in the mountains near Harar. This was followed by extravagant claims of hundreds of Ethiopians killed, of aircraft shot down, of tanks and armoured cars destroyed and of large quantities of arms and ammunition captured in clashes around Harar and Dire Dawa. On 19 June, the WSLF claimed it had captured the Ogaden towns of Sagag and Fiq. It was about this time that Ethiopia began to accuse Somalia of having sent its regular forces into the Ogaden.

Kenya entered the fray on 29 June with a report that 3,000 Somali troops had attacked a police post near Rhamu in the NFD, which turned out to be closer to the Kenyan-Ethiopian border than to the Kenyan-Somali frontier. Mogadishu repudiated these reports as part of an Ethiopian plot to damage its relations with Kenya. Nairobi Radio said on 12 July that Kenya would not allow itself to be used as a thoroughfare by Somali troops on their way to attack Ethiopia, and urged Somalia to 'stop enhancing its expansionist plans by masquerading as a liberator of the Somali nation'.[4]

Ethiopia claimed that an all-out Somali attack was launched against its territory on 23 July; it spoke of full-scale air and tank battles in which Egyptian and Iraqi pilots were allegedly engaged. Somalia's riposte was to accuse Ethiopia of massing troops along the frontier; the Somali ambassador in Rome, Abdullahi Egal Nour, told a Press conference on 28 July that regular Somali forces had been involved in the fighting for the first time when Ethiopian planes violated Somali airspace. In an interview with the Abu Dhabi newspaper *Al-Ittihad* on 28 July, the WSLF Secretary-General, Abdullahi Hassan Mahmoud, said his forces had liberated 60% of the Ogaden and killed or captured 1,000 Ethiopian troops in two weeks of fighting. The Front claimed that over 100 towns were 'liberated' and flying the WSLF (not the Somali Republic) flag. By this time, Somali officials were admitting privately that Somali troops on leave were being allowed to 'volunteer' to join the WSLF guerrillas. However, Somalia still clung to the official position that its regular forces were in no way involved.[5] Its explanation from the first was that the Somali regular troops engaged in the fighting were all Ogadeni Somalis who had volunteered for the Somali army and who had been given leave to return to fight for the liberation of their 'homeland'.

Following reports that Ethiopian aircraft had bombed towns in northern Somalia on 15 August, Barre alleged that Ethiopia was preparing to invade Somalia. He accused Ethiopia of employing foreign troops and said that Somalia would 'have to get involved' if there were any foreign intervention.

August and September were the months of heaviest fighting. By mid-September the Somali forces had control, even by Ethiopian admission, of 90% of the disputed area and were advancing on Dire Dawa, Harar and Jijiga. The WSLF claimed to have inflicted heavy casualties in a mortar and rocket attack on Dire Dawa on 16 August; but Ethiopia insisted that the attack had been repulsed, with at least 500 dead and 500 wounded among the 'Somali regular forces'. The wreckage of a Somali MiG-21 jet fighter was shown to foreign newsmen by the Ethiopians who claimed that Somalia had already lost 18 of the aircraft.

In September, too, the Somalis intensified their operations along the Southern front, in the Ethiopian regions of Bale, Sidamo and Arssi (Arussi). This region is inhabited mostly by members of the Oromo (Galla) tribe, Hamitic cousins to the Somalis. A Muslim faction of the Oromo Liberation Front (OLF)—which had been fighting against central Ethiopian rule for decades—attached itself to the WSLF as the 'Somali Abo Liberation Front (SALF)'. The first SALF communiqué, on 23 August, claimed that 1,000 Ethiopian troops had been killed in fighting around Ginir and Goba, in Bale.

On 24 August, the Somali Government rejected a statement made three days earlier by the OAU Secretary-General, William Eteki Mboumoua, that the organization considered the Ogaden as part of Ethiopia and did not recognize the WSLF as an African liberation movement. Mogadishu accused Mboumoua of 'ignoring the major interest on which the OAU Charter is based'—that which calls for 'the liberation of African territories still under colonial domination and oppression'. The Minister of Information and National Guidance, Abdulkasim Salad Hassan, called on Ethiopia to initiate a dialogue with the WSLF in order to 'seek a peaceful settlement and to allow the people of the area to exercise self-determination'.

Meanwhile, the WSLF began talking about the right of the Ogadenis to decide their own future. A member of the 15-strong WSLF Executive Committee, Ahmed Hussein Haile, said the Ogadenis would have to decide whether or not they wished to be 'reunited' with Somalia, possibly through 'some kind of party Congress with representatives appointed at village and district level'.[6]

The greatest Somali victory of the war occurred on 13 September, with the capture of Jijiga, a market town and Ethiopian forward tank base to the east of Harar. The town, which has a substantial Somali population, fell after two weeks of fierce fighting, during which it changed hands several times. The Somalis claimed that 3,000 Ethiopians had been killed and seven Ethiopian F-5 jets shot down in the battles. The Somali victory came when the Ethiopian garrison—whose morale in the face of the Somali onslaught had been so low that the Ethiopian leader, Lt-Col Mengistu Haile Mariam, had had to visit the town personally to encourage them to fight—mutinied and retreated through the Gara Marda Pass on the road to Harar. They left behind huge stores of weapons and ammunition and even tanks and other vehicles which were promptly seized and used effectively in coming months by the Somalis.

The WSLF Secretary-General said on 12 September that the Ethiopians were 'entrenched' in Harar and Dire Dawa, and that 'the fighting is going very ferociously in both places'. He added that the Ogaden was now 80% under Somali control and ultimate victory was certain, but 'a great number of towns have yet to be liberated'. Dire Dawa and Harar were by far the most important, he said, but 'Sidamo, Bale and Arssi have still also to be liberated in their entirety'.[7]

The Somali Abo Front said on 10 September that its guerrillas had captured 13 towns and villages in Sidamo, and were besieging the main southern Ethiopian garrison at Negelle. On the same day Somalia accused Ethiopian aircraft of raiding the border town of Tug Wajale and the northern capital of Hargeisa, killing some civilians.

Ethiopia and Somalia were now fully engaged in an open war. Diplomatic relations were severed, and Ethiopia mobilized its civilian reserves. In a broadcast on 13 September, Barre again denied that regular Somali forces were involved in the Ogaden; he called on all African states to make the 'insane' Ethiopian leader Mengistu 'see reason'.

At the end of September, the WSLF took Western correspondents and television crews to Jijiga and beyond it, through the Gara Marda Pass, to Hadew, 20 km further west on the road to Harar. John Darnton, of the *New York Times*, wrote: 'Despite vigorous claims by Addis Ababa that the strategic gateway is still in Ethiopian hands and that a critical battle is raging here, the only signs of an Ethiopian presence are the millions of dollars worth of American-supplied tanks, military vehicles and ammunition the Ethiopians left behind in an apparently panicky retreat into the mountains. . . . The only soldiers seen by the reporters wore the plain green fatigues of the liberation front, and there were not more than several score of them, lending support to the front's claim that the fighting had already moved to the outskirts of the major city of Harar, 60 miles (100 km) away.' He said Jijiga was battle-scarred but relatively intact, although only c. 1,000 of its normal population of c. 20,000 were still living there; these demonstrated their support of the WSLF, shouting 'Victory and the land is ours!' or 'We were slaves yesterday—today we are free.' The WSLF commander at Jijiga, Abdullahi Abdi, claimed that 12,000 Ethiopians were killed, wounded or captured there.[8]

The head of the Ideology Department of the Somali Revolutionary Socialist Party (SRSP), Mohammed Aden Mahmoud, told a Press conference in Rome on 20 September that the WSLF was ready to enter into immediate ceasefire talks with 'democratic forces' in Ethiopia (as opposed to the ruling Dergue), but that the sovereignty of the Ogaden was not negotiable. But four days later, Abdullahi Hassan Mahmoud denied that the WSLF was ready to discuss a ceasefire and said the liberation front would not stop fighting 'until the last inch of their territory is liberated'.

The WSLF concentrated its attacks throughout October on Harar, the walled medieval capital of eastern Ethiopia with a mixed population of Hararis, Somalis and Shoans. The Front claimed to have surrounded the town and to be inflicting heavy casualties on its defenders. The WSLF and SALF published the first issue of their new daily *Danab* (Lighting) on 1 October in Mogadishu. It claimed that 800 Ethiopians had been killed in fighting at two points between Harar and Dire Dawa. Clashes were also reported at Fiambiro and Babile, in the mountains between Harar and Jijiga. On 16 October, Ethiopia finally admitted that its forces had 'temporarily evacuated Jijiga and withdrawn to strategic positions to the west'.

The first trickle of Soviet arms was now reaching Ethiopia. The Soviet ambassador in Addis Ababa, Anatoly Ratanov, declared on 19 October that the USSR had 'officially and formally' stopped the supply of arms to Somalia, its main African military client since a Treaty of Friendship and Co-operation was signed between them in 1974.[9] The USSR, he said, was now providing Ethiopia with 'defensive weapons to protect her revolution'.

Ethiopian warplanes bombed Jijiga on 4 October, killing six civilians and wounding nine—all of them medical personnel—in an apparently deliberate attack on the town's only hospital. A correspondent of the London *Daily Telegraph* who witnessed the attack said the raiders destroyed the hospital with 250-lb bombs, rockets and cannon fire.[10]

The WSLF was reported to have penetrated Harar's defences and entered the city on 23 November and to be engaged in street fighting with the Ethiopian garrison. Somali military sources claimed on 25 November that some units of the Ethiopian Third Division had retreated towards Dire Dawa and that others—which had been trying to contain the WSLF advance at Babile—were cut off and in disarray. By 28 November, the WSLF was claiming 'absolute control of Harar and the surrounding area'. But this was a dubious claim, never verified.

The battle for Harar was the turning point in the war. The WSLF supply and communications lines, based on the northern Somali city of Hargeisa, 225 km to the east, were clearly over-stretched. Its forces numbered c. 20,000. Against them were pitted c. 60,000 Ethiopians with increasing Soviet and Cuban military backing. By the end of November, the Somali forces had probably been forced to withdraw 15–20 km from Harar, while the reinforced and regrouped Ethiopians prepared for their counter-attack.

Somalia again reported several Ethiopian air attacks on northern Somali cities in December: it claimed that ten people were killed in a raid on Hargeisa on 9 December; two children in raids on Hargeisa and the port of Berbera on 27 December; and 13 people in an attack on Tug Wajale on 30 December. But the ground fighting had died down in the Ogaden; only the SALF continued to claim victories in Sidamo and Bale.

Indirectly aided by rising concern in the Arab Red Sea capitals and in Washington about the extent of the Russian and Cuban build-up in Ethiopia, Somalia raised the spectre of an imminent Russian-backed Ethiopian 'invasion' of its country, with the Russians purportedly eager to take revenge for their expulsion from Somalia. The air raids on Hargeisa were seen as evidence of this aggression. Seeking military support to replace Russian aid, President Barre said in Iran on 28 December: 'The invasion of Somalia has begun. . . . We are seeking arms to defend ourselves.' As initial Ethiopian probes drove Somali forces back from their positions around Harar, Somalia scored a propaganda coup by displaying a captured Cuban soldier to the foreign Press. He said his name was Carlos Orlando and that he had been attached to a Cuban artillery unit at Harar.

Early in 1978, Barre began to adopt a harder line in his attempts to secure Western support. On 28 January, he said there was no chance of a negotiated settlement with Ethiopia since control of the fighting had now passed from Ethiopian hands to the Soviet Union, which was 'conducting a war to teach African countries that if they do not obey, they will be punished'.[11]

Finally, in early February 1978, Somalia did what it had claimed it had not done over the previous seven months of war: it committed its regular army to the battle. On 9 February, the Minister of Information, Abdulkasim Salad, told a Press conference in Mogadishu that Somalia's 'people and resources' had been mobilized to counter 'any invasion mounted by the allied Russian and Cuban forces' from Ethiopia. Two days later, the SRSP Central Committee declared a state of emergency and called on former servicemen and civilians to volunteer for duty. To defend itself against the imminent 'invasion', Somalia was 'sending in some of its regular troops' to help the WSLF freedom fighters. 'The Somali Democratic Republic (SDR) believes that the problem of the Horn of Africa would have been alleviated and that a satisfactory solution would have been found if foreign powers had not interfered,' the Central Committee declared. 'The Government of the SDR, having heard the opinions of peace-loving nations and organizations, does not oppose any just and lasting peace. However, the prerequisites of this peace are: a halt to the bloodshed now taking place; the guaranteed withdrawal of foreign troops now taking part in the conflict; and the granting of the right of self-determination to the peoples under Abyssinian colonial domination, which is supported by foreign troops seeking to exterminate the people.'[12]

At a mass rally in Mogadishu's Dervishes Park on 12 February, Barre rejected American calls for a Somali withdrawal from the Ogaden. If anyone were going to withdraw, he said, it would be the 'Abyssinian colonialists', the Russians and the Cubans; the freedom fighters, the rightful owners of the territory, would fight to the last man. The Government reported that by 13 February, 30,000 volunteers, the youngest of them 15, had enlisted for 14 to 60 days' military training. They would then join the defence forces and 'if necessary' go to the Ogaden.

During this upsurge of Somali patriotism, Ethiopia's forces were pushing forward from Harar and Dire Dawa; on 10 February, Addis Ababa urged the Somalis to 'give up the battle or face annihilation'. Ethiopian aircraft had also resumed attacks on Hargeisa and Berbera on 8 February. The WSLF was conceding no more than 'tactical withdrawals' along the mountain road from Harar to Jijiga, and on 7 February still claimed to be holding the Gara Marda Pass. They said they were resisting the Ethiopian armoured attack from Harar and Dire Dawa and had destroyed 43 Ethiopian tanks.

In taking stock of the enemy's capabilities, Mengistu claimed on 14 February that in seven months of war, Somalia had deployed 17,000 troops, 250 tanks, 350 armoured vehicles, 600 artillery pieces and more than 40 aircraft. The Ethiopian commander on the eastern front, Col Mulatu Negash, told Western correspondents in Dire Dawa that Somalia had deployed c. 25 brigades (each of c. 1,200-2,000 men), though this seems a gross exaggeration. He displayed captured Somali weaponry including tanks and armoured cars, heavy and light machine-guns, 122, 85 and 87mm anti-aircraft guns, 106mm anti-tank mortars, hand grenades and ammunition. To the Ethiopian charge that 5,000-12,000 Arab troops were fighting on the Somali side, Mogadishu replied that the Russian and Cuban force in Ethiopia totalled c. 20,000. After failing to elicit arms support from Western countries, Somalia appeared by mid-February 1978 to have amassed a respectable arsenal through its Middle East allies; this included c. 60 West German tanks, hundreds of Soviet-made RPG7 anti-tank missiles as well as Nato surface-to-air missiles, and, according to one report, c. 95 second-hand American helicopters, bought on the international market.[13]

In a seeming half-hearted attempt to sue for peace, the WSLF said on 23 February that it was ready for direct talks with Ethiopia to settle the Ogaden dispute. The announcement, in *Danab*, said peace would depend on Ethiopian recognition of the right to self-determination of the Somali population of the region. Ethiopia rejected the call as a 'smokescreen aimed solely at consolidating an influx of troops and arms from Nato countries and reactionary Arab regimes' to bolster the 'dwindling' Somali morale.

At the end of February, four Somali brigades—c. 8,000 men—waited at Jijiga for the expected Ethiopian thrust along the road from Harar and down through the Gara Marda Pass. The attack had been delayed by heavy rains, but these had not prevented enormous quantities of new Soviet equipment, together with Cuban artillery and infantry units, from being deployed to the north of Jijiga, behind the Ahmar mountain range—a direction from which the Somalis did not expect to be attacked. On 28 February, Cuban mechanized units with armoured vehicles were airlifted to a point near Genasene, 28 km north of Jijiga, and advanced on the Somali garrison. The rains prevented Ethiopian reinforcements being flown in and the Somalis appear to have repulsed the Cuban thrust. A second Soviet airlift, using Mi-6 helicopters each capable of carrying two light tanks, was able to land additional Cuban and Ethiopian units which, with the help of raids by Cuban-piloted MiGs, penetrated the Somali defences within 24 hours. The Somalis scattered in confusion; thousands were killed, wounded or captured. During the battle, the Soviets unveiled a weapon never before tested in combat—the BMP-1, a highly mobile armoured vehicle with a 73mm gun, anti-tank missiles and heat-seeking anti-aircraft missiles. Somali sources described it as a 'moving castle'.[14] By 5 March, Ethiopia had retaken Jijiga, which had been in Somali hands for six months.

Four days later, on 9 March, Somalia as much as admitted defeat. It announced it was withdrawing its regular forces from Ethiopia after receiving guarantees from the 'big powers' that Ethiopian forces would not cross Somalia's frontiers and that other foreign forces would be withdrawn from the area. The Justice and Religious Affairs Minister, Abdisalam Sheikh Hussein, said Somalia had been 'advised by big powers to solve the problem in a peaceful manner'. He added that these powers had guaranteed the safeguarding of the rights of the people of 'Western Somalia', and demanded that they urgently 'initiate the process for bringing about a just and lasting settlement of the conflict in the Horn of Africa'. The withdrawal was announced simultaneously by President Carter; State Department officials said that his Administration had made a 'considerable effort' to bring it about.

Although Somali withdrawal of regulars had in fact begun even before the Ethiopian attack on Jijiga on 5 March, the Ethiopian regime was still not satisfied: it insisted that there could be no peace until Mogadishu permanently renounced its claims to the Ogaden, Djibouti and north-eastern Kenya. No such categoric assurance came from the Barre regime, but on 15 March, Somalia said that all its regular forces had been withdrawn. However, the WSLF leader announced at a Press conference in Mogadishu that the liberation struggle would go on (see chapter on Ethiopia, under The Ogaden Front).

OGADEN: THE DIPLOMATIC FRONT

It was a measure of Somalia's creative foreign policy[15] that President Barre participated in two rival efforts in March 1977 to carve out spheres of influence in the Red Sea area. The first was a secret meeting initiated by President Fidel Castro in Aden on 16 March of Somalia, Ethiopia and South Yemen (PDRY). Castro had visited Mogadishu from 12–14 March and had floated the idea of the Aden meeting with Barre. He had then gone to Addis Ababa to raise it with Mengistu Haile Mariam. He and Mengistu travelled secretly (and apparently separately) on 16 March to Aden. (For a fuller discussion of Castro's initiative, see essay on Cuba's role in Africa.) The purpose of the meeting, as Siyad Barre much later disclosed in an interview with al-Ahram (Cairo, 19 May), was to explore Castro's proposal that the three Red Sea Marxist states should unite in a federation—what Castro called a 'progressive front'—at the mouth of the Red Sea. The front would also eventually include Eritrea and Djibouti, due to become independent in June. While aspects of Castro's plan appeared attractive to Mengistu—it would settle at a stroke both the war in Eritrea and the Ogaden dispute with Somalia, and allow him to get on with consolidating his control over the Ethiopian revolution—it was repugnant to Barre. He supported the Eritrean struggle for reasons of 'Arab' and 'Muslim' solidarity—even though the Eritreans are neither Arab nor wholly Muslim—and also as a means of undermining the Dergue in Ethiopia and therefore of contributing towards the struggle to create a Greater Somalia. In Barre's view, neither Somali

74

nor Eritrean aspirations for self-determination would be satisfied by the Castro plan. He later also maintained that the Aden proposals failed to address themselves to the 'national problem' of the Somalis and Eritreans.

Speaking publicly for the first time about the Aden meeting, on 15 March 1978, Castro said that his aim had been to 'prevent a war [between Ethiopia and Somalia], to prevent an act which was a treason to the international revolutionary movement, to prevent the Somali Government from passing into the hands of imperialism'. He claimed that the Somalis had promised at Aden that they would never invade Ethiopia; but in reality, he said, 'they had everything planned'. According to Castro, the Somali Government had been taken over by a 'rightist faction' in an alliance with 'imperialism'.

The second test for Somali diplomacy came on 22–23 March at a summit meeting at Taizz (North Yemen) attended by Somalia, the Sudan, North Yemen (YAR) and again South Yemen. Though planned for some time and technically initiated by the Sudan, this meeting was strongly backed by Egypt and in particular by Saudi Arabia, which was using promises of generous economic aid to entice Somalia and South Yemen into an anti-Soviet Red Sea alliance. The aim of the meeting was to discuss ways of securing the Red Sea as a 'zone of peace', free of outside (i.e. non-Arab) interference. The four leaders were united in opposing Israeli penetration into the region, something they all perceived in Israel's military assistance to the Dergue.[16] The final communiqué referred to a possible future summit of all Red Sea states to 'discuss' combined defence arrangements'—a prospect which remained unfulfilled.

FOREIGN ALLIANCES: RELATIONS WITH THE EAST

Somalia began 1977 as one of the USSR's best friends in Africa,[17] receiving generous Soviet military assistance and economic and technical aid. However, there was some evidence of Somali concern about Moscow's increasingly friendly attitude to Ethiopia[18] and some friction on an individual level, particularly where Russian school teachers were seen by some Somalis as attempting to undermine the teachings of Islam.[19]

Nikolai Podgorny, then still President of the USSR, visited Mogadishu on 2–3 April 1977 in the course of his African tour, his talks with President Barre ending in 'mutual understanding and success'. The Vice-President and Defence Minister, Lt-Gen Mohammed Ali Samatar, visited Moscow from 25 May. By that time, Soviet arms were beginning to trickle into Ethiopia (for details see chapter on Ethiopia). President Barre answered speculation about Somalia's reaction to this develop-ment in two interviews, both published on 27 June. There was some variation in his replies. To *Newsweek*, he said: 'There will be no conflict between Somalia and the Soviets . . . [but] it's no secret that we don't see eye to eye on Ethiopia.' On a possible break with the Russians, he said: 'We are not thinking in terms of divorce and remarriage'.[20] But he told the Kuwaiti newspaper *al-Yaqza* that Somalia would take an 'historic decision' should the Soviet arming of Ethiopia constitute a threat to Somalia. 'We would not be able to remain idle in the face of the danger of the Soviet Union's arming of Ethiopia.'[21]

These remarks led to more intense speculation that, notwithstanding its protestations to the contrary, Somalia was about to break with Moscow. One particular report in the London *Sunday Telegraph* on 17 July was dismissed by Mogadishu as 'sheer speculation' and a 'baseless lie'. But another report on the same day quoted 'authoritative African sources' in Washington that Soviet military personnel 'in large numbers' were already leaving Somalia.[22] This report coincided with Barre's return to Mogadishu on 14 July from a two-day visit to Saudi Arabia where 'Red Sea security' was discussed.

However, it was the Soviet Union which made the first move to break the alliance An article in *Izvestia* on 16 August referred to the fighting in the Ogaden as an 'armed invasion' of 'Ethiopian territory' by 'regular units of the Somalian army'— three statements guaranteed to arouse Somali ire. The article said that 'even the plausible excuse of implementing the principle of self-determination' did not justify Somalia's action. With relations deteriorating fast, Barre visited Moscow from 30–31 August. On his return (after a stopover in Egypt) on 1 September, the SRSP Central Committee held an all-night session.

While no official statement was made by the SRSP, it had already accepted in early August that the break with Moscow was inevitable. But Barre had told his closer Arab allies through their embassies in Mogadishu that he would not initiate the break himself since this would leave the Russians with no alternative but to increase their military support for the Dergue and then doubtless do everything possible to undermine the Somali regime.[23] He knew this because when Sadat broke with the Russians, they had transferred their military and political support to Libya. Throughout August, the Somalis showed their hostility to the Russians by having no contacts with their ambassador in Mogadishu, by restricting all Russian military personnel to two areas, and by forbidding their advisers any access to government offices. In mid-August, they also briefly detained a Soviet airliner carrying arms to Uganda which made a stopover in Mogadishu without first obtaining permission. Until this friction, Aeroflot had not been in the habit of seeking permission for its transit flights. Somalia's friends—especially Egypt, Sudan, Saudi Arabia, Kuwait and Iran—stepped up their attempts to buy arms for it on the open market, while at the same time increasing their efforts to persuade Washington and London to replace the Soviets as arms suppliers.

During this period—from July to September—the Somali campaign in the Ogaden was at its most successful. By early September, the WSLF was daily expecting the fall of Harar and Dire Dawa, and was planning to declare the unification of the Ogaden with Somalia at a ceremony at Harar on 21 September.[24] Somalia's principal concern in September was to consolidate its victories in the Ogaden before Soviet and Cuban military aid enabled the Ethiopians to launch an effective counter-attack. It also encouraged the Eritrean and Afar liberation movements to increase their pressures on Addis Ababa. The darkened mood of the people was described by one correspondent travelling in northern Somalia: 'The Russians are hated in Hargeisa. . . . Visitors . . . are treated with open hostility until they prove conclusively that they are not the dreaded "Roosh (Russians). . . . "Merykans" (Americans) and "Inkriki" (Britons) are wished a long life.'[25]

In marking the eighth anniversary of the 1969 revolution on 21 October, President Barre warned that Moscow's 'frantic one-sided support' for Ethiopia could jeopardize relations between Somalia and the USSR. Two days before, the Soviet ambassador in Addis Ababa, Anatoly Ratanov, announced that his country had 'officially and formally' ended its arms supplies to Somalia.

The break finally came on 13 November. After a 10-hour meeting, the SRSP Central Committee decided to abrogate the 1974 Treaty of Friendship and Co-operation with Moscow; order all Soviet experts and military technicians out of the country within seven days; abolish all air, sea and land facilities enjoyed by the USSR in the Somali Republic, and reduce the size of the ·Soviet Embassy in Mogadishu to that of the Somali Embassy in Moscow.[26] Additionally, because 'the Government of Cuba deliberately sent its troops into the Horn of Africa to assist colonialism and annihilate a people who are struggling for a just cause', diplomatic

76

relations with Cuba were cut and all Cuban diplomats, staff and experts ordered out of Somalia within 48 hours. There was obvious public approval of this move. Somalis even turned up at Mogadishu Airport to jeer and jostle the Cubans and Russians as they boarded planes to leave. The Soviet Union blamed Somalia's 'chauvinist, expansionist moods' for the rift. According to one account, the Somali decision came after the Soviet Ambassador in Mogadishu delivered a message threatening 'grave consequences for Somali-Soviet relations' unless Somalia ended its 'interference in the internal affairs of Ethiopia'.[27]

In tearing up the Treaty, President Barre warned about 'an imminent joint Soviet-Cuban plan for an all-out military operation from Ethiopia against the SDR'. To his fellow members in the Arab League he said on 20 November: 'We appeal to you to fulfil your historical obligations in siding with your brother who is being devoured, for the time will come when you too will be devoured. Those of you who border the Red Sea: it is your duty and your obligation to side with the Somali nation in defence of its independence and honour against this unholy alliance.'

The expulsion of Russians and Cubans was matched by the withdrawal of 370 Somali students from the USSR and 73 from Cuba. The EEC offered to find places for some of the students and also discussed taking over various Soviet development projects in Somalia.

Despite the military break with the Russians, the Somalis chose to maintain diplomatic relations and some economic links, as well as their unique 'self-help' brand of socialism. Nor did the break mean a sudden pro-Western 'tilt' in Somali foreign policies. An intermediary, Mr Gianni Giadresco, a member of the Italian Communist Party, established a channel of communication between Moscow and Mogadishu in February 1978. The Soviet Union had put forward new proposals, contingent on a Somali withdrawal, which not only offered the resumption of massive Soviet military and economic aid, but revived the idea of a Red Sea 'federation' as well. This time, President Barre, no longer constrained by his plans for an Ogaden offensive, appears to have accepted the deal. The proposals were put to him by the Libyan leader, Col Gaddafy, during a visit to Tripoli by Barre in the last week of February 1978. As sketched out by Arab and Western diplomatic sources, they included: a) the withdrawal of all regular Somali military units from the Ogaden; b) a promise by Somalia to respect Ethiopia's internationally recognized boundaries; c) a formal renunciation of Somalia's claims to Djibouti and Kenya's NFD; d) a regranting of Soviet rights to Somali naval facilities; and e) Somalia's participation in a political grouping with Ethiopia and South Yemen. In return, Somalia would receive a promise of eventual autonomy for the Somali people of the Ogaden, a guarantee that Ethiopia would honour Somalia's border, and a resumption of Soviet military and economic aid. The military aid would presumably be of the type Somalia was receiving before the break with Moscow, which is much more important to it now that its army is shattered. Western military aid would probably be more low-key.

FOREIGN ALLIANCES: RELATIONS WITH THE WEST

It was sheer exasperation with the increasingly violent path being pursued by the rulers of Ethiopia, its traditional ally in the Horn of Africa, that led the US to decide in April 1977, in President Carter's words to his aides, to 'do everything possible to get the Somalis to be our friends'. Relations between Washington and Mogadishu had been all but non-existent for years. The first US move was, from the Somali point of view, hardly a friendly one. A report to Congress by the State Department on 27 April named Somalia—together with South Yemen, Libya and Iraq—as countries which had been actively supporting international terrorists.

Senator Jacob Javits added further charges against Somalia, provoking an angry reply from Mogadishu that 'the righteous struggle of movements fighting against oppression and colonialism was justified and could not be described as terrorism'.

On 26 July, with the Ogaden offensive already under way and with heightened Soviet involvement in Ethiopia, the US announced that it was prepared 'in principle' to supply defensive arms to Somalia to help it protect its 'present territory'. A State Department spokesman said: 'We think it is desirable that Somalia knows it does not have to depend on the Soviet Union'. This was followed by similar offers from Britain and France. The announcement had been preceded by extensive contacts with American allies around the world—from Britain and France to Egypt, Saudi Arabia, Iran and Pakistan—to arrive at a 'consensus' about the desirability of governments joining together to aid Somalia. Putting together such a 'consortium' was an unusual approach which understandably prompted Ethiopia to allege that the US and its allies, despite their disavowals, were channelling arms to Somalia through 'conservative' Islamic states.

By early August, however, US officials were telling a visiting Somali delegation that no American arms would be supplied while fighting continued in the Ogaden. One official said the 'extreme nature' of the Somali-backed campaign had changed President Carter's mind about supplying arms.[28] The State Department line was that 'we have decided that providing arms at this time would add fuel to a fire we are more interested in putting out'. The US also made clear it would not approve the transfer of any American arms supplies to Somalia from third countries. Britain and France joined the US on 1 and 2 September in withdrawing their offers of 'defensive arms', saying that the fighting in the Ogaden would have to stop before the arms supplies could be granted. US officials declared themselves 'shocked' at the scale of the Ogaden fighting.

The Somalis were understandably piqued, charging that the US had misled them. There was even an allegation from Barre himself that it was the prospect of US supplies—and even an indication that Washington 'was not averse to further guerrilla pressure in the Ogaden'—which had prompted Somalia to undertake the Ogaden campaign in the first place. Newsweek reported in September that President Barre's personal physician, Dr Kevin Cahill, an American, had conveyed that impression to him following meetings with US officials in Washington. The report claimed that the US had simply requested that Somalia drop its claims to Djibouti and part of Kenya. Barre checked the US overture with his ambassador in Washington (his son-in-law, Abdullahi Ahmed Abdu), and then received assurances from Saudi Arabia that it was prepared to ship French and British arms to Somalia 'immediately'. Newsweek said President Barre felt 'absolutely confident that he could supply his armies without Soviet help, and kicked off the Ogaden offensive'. However, the US Assistant Secretary of State for African Affairs, Richard Moose, insisted that the US assurances referred to by Newsweek had not been 'of such a nature that a prudent man would have mounted an offensive on the basis of them'.[29] (Also see essay on the US and Africa.)

By the time of the Russians' expulsion from Somalia, the US understood that much of Africa regarded the Somalis as the 'aggressors' in the Ogaden and that Kenya especially was strongly hostile to its being rearmed (see chapter on Kenya). The US took the stance that it could not make arms available to Somalia until the 'territorial integrity' of Ethiopia was 'restored'. While determined to stay out of the conflict, Washington sought through diplomatic means to persuade Moscow and Havana to withdraw; it insisted that full support be given to the OAU to handle what was primarily an African affair (see chapter on Conflict in the Horn of Africa). This policy seems to have been reinforced by a visit to Mogadishu on 17

November by the full Armed Services Committee of the US House of Representatives. Barre deplored the US unwillingness to become involved and told a Press conference on 23 November that the Americans were indifferent to the prospect of a Russian 'takeover' in the Horn of Africa. On a visit to Iran in December, he left behind a letter for President Carter, who was due there shortly afterwards, appealing for Western help.

On 5 December, the US announced plans to resume economic aid to Somalia, cut off in 1971 because Somali flag vessels were trading with North Vietnam (although emergency food aid to drought victims and Ogaden refugees had continued). The new plans called for a $15m five-year agricultural research and training programme and a $10m four-year health care project.

By the time Ethiopia was gearing up for its Ogaden counter-offensive in January 1978, the Western powers were concentrating all their efforts on bringing about a negotiated settlement. President Barre had called in the ambassadors of the US, Britain, France, West Germany and Italy on 16 January to warn of an imminent invasion of Somalia by 'Warsaw Pact countries' backing Ethiopia. On the very next day, however, the US repeated that it would not supply arms to Somalia while the fighting continued.

The US State Department was constantly revising its estimates of the number of Cuban personnel in Ethiopia and the extent of the Soviet arms shipments. The question of whether or not Ethiopia would carry its counterattack across the border into Somalia—something even the most frenzied Ethiopian regime would have been foolish to do, since it would destroy the widespread sympathy felt for Addis Ababa as the 'victim of Somali aggression'—came more and more to dominate Western attitudes towards the conflict.

The five major Western powers met in Washington on 22 January to discuss ways of ending the Ogaden war; they urged a negotiated settlement and reaffirmed their support for OAU peace moves. The US Secretary of State said on 10 February that he had received assurances from the Soviet Union itself that Ethiopian forces would not cross into Somalia; if that promise were not kept, he hinted, the US would have to reconsider its position on arms supplies. On 12 February, Barre told a rally in Mogadishu that there was now no hope of help from the US; Somalia 'stood alone' against Soviet aggression.

President Carter himself announced Somalia's agreement to withdraw its regular forces from the Ogaden on 9 March 1978. This was in response to an undertaking from the Russians and the Ethiopians that there would be no 'invasion' of northern Somalia. On 21 March, the US Assistant Secretary of State for African Affairs, Richard Moose, visited Mogadishu to renew American economic development programmes and to state US terms for future military aid: non-belligerency in the Ogaden in return for American guarantees of Somalia's territorial integrity.

OTHER FOREIGN RELATIONS
RELATIONS WITH BRITAIN
Britain followed the US lead in offering 'modest quantities' of 'defensive' weapons to Somalia in July 1977, but withdrew the offer a few weeks later because of the intensity of the Ogaden fighting and strong protests from Kenya. Britain also participated with its Nato allies in diplomatic contacts aimed at resolving the Ogaden conflict through African mediation. The Government gave a warm welcome to a strongly pro-Somali Labour MP, James Johnson, and to leading British Conservative politicians (including MPs Winston Churchill and Julian Amery) who said after visiting Mogadishu in February 1978 that a Conservative Government in Britain would supply arms to help Somalia resist 'Soviet im-

perialism'. They had no official party endorsement for such a promise.

Somali-British relations were strained early in 1977 when a British woman, Jane Wright, and three South African and European crewmates were detained by the Somalis and accused of espionage after their yacht ran aground along the coast. (Another Briton, Michael Postle-Hacon, an engineer, was arrested in March 1977.) As Ms Wright and her companions awaited trial, a British delegation led by the Foreign Office Under-Secretary, Ted Rowlands, visited Somalia from 22–25 May— the first visit by a British minister since 1960. After a postponement of the trial in May, the National Security Court sentenced the four on 30 June to one year's jail and a fine of SSh 10,000 on charges of illegal entry into the country; they were acquitted of all charges of espionage for lack of evidence. All four were released on 2 July after President Barre reviewed their case and allowed the jail sentences to be changed to additional fines.

RELATIONS WITH WEST GERMANY

A completely unpredictable event created the conditions for greatly expanded relations with West Germany. A Lufthansa airliner, with 87 passengers on board, was hijacked on 13 October 1977 on a flight from Majorca to Frankfurt and ended up at Mogadishu airport four days later. The hijackers, claiming to belong to the Popular Front for the Liberation of Palestine (PFLP), demanded the release of 11 imprisoned Baader-Meinhof terrorists in West Germany, plus a multi-million dollar ransom. The pilot of the aircraft was murdered by the hijackers at Aden. After agreement with the Somali authorities, 60 West German commandos stormed the aircraft at Mogadishu airport on 17 October, killing three of the hijackers and wounding the fourth, a woman. The passengers and crew were released without serious injury. Somalia at first claimed that the raid had been carried out by 'Somali commandos in co-operation of some West German experts', but it later became clear that the Somali authorities had consented to the operation only after Western and Saudi Arabian diplomatic pressure. Bonn thanked the Somalis for their co-operation and promised 'not to forget' it. Both sides denied that any particular deal had been struck beforehand.

In January 1978, West Germany announced a credit of DM 25m for Somalia as part of an expanded economic aid package. The loan was unusual in that it was not 'tied' to a specific development project, and the Ethiopians at once claimed that Somalia would use the money to purchase arms. Bonn said it could not rule this out, although the credit had been specifically extended for use in 'economic and social development'. Shortly afterwards, the West German ambassador was expelled from Ethiopia.[30] The Ethiopian regime also charged on 26 October that a Boeing 707 with the painted-over markings of a West German cargo airline, Condor, had been seen unloading arms supplies at Mogadishu. This later turned out to be one of two planes leased by Condor to an American private airline believed to have been involved in running arms purchased on the international arms market for Somalia's use in the Ogaden war.

West German economic aid to Somalia reached DM 53m, including the untied DM 25m loan, after the signing on 5 February 1978 of an agreement on co-operation in the development of fisheries, irrigation and water resources.

RELATIONS WITH FRANCE

France joined the other Western powers in refusing arms supplies to Somalia during the Ogaden war and in pushing for a Somali withdrawal and a negotiated settlement. A delegation led by Mohamed Aden Shekh, a member of the SRSP Central Committee, visited Paris shortly after the fighting began in the Ogaden. France was anxious not to offend either Somalia or Ethiopia because of its interests in Djibouti. Shortly before Somalia's withdrawal from the Ogaden in February 1978, the French Foreign Minister said that his country was prepared to reconsider its position towards Somalia, but he defended France's 'wait-and-see policy' in the Horn.

RELATIONS WITH CHINA
China managed to maintain a successful policy of neutrality between Somalia and Ethiopia, encouraging the former in its break with Moscow and attacking the Russians (but not the Dergue) for their military involvement in Ethiopia.[31] The main thrust of Chinese involvement in Somalia continued to be economic aid projects. There were two high-level Somali visits to China in 1977 and 1978 which seemed to indicate a further improvement in relations. Vice-President Ismail Ali Abokor led a delegation on a two-week visit to China (and North Korea) in June. Welcoming editorials in the Peking press noted the super-power rivalry in the Red Sea region, citing particularly the role of 'Soviet socio-imperialism' which was described as 'cunning, vicious and voracious'.[32] Information Minister Abdulkasim Salad Hassan visited China in March 1978 to sign agreements on co-operation in the mass media, and said on his return that China supported the Somali cause.

RELATIONS WITH ETHIOPIA
Diplomatic relations between Addis Ababa and Mogadishu were broken off on 7 and 8 September 1977, about six weeks after the beginning of open hostilities in the Ogaden. Whatever attempts the Soviet Union may make to encourage a rapprochement it will be exceedingly difficult to heal the rift between the two neighbours. Official Somali speeches and commentaries made great play of the internal crises of the Dergue. Speaking of the Dergue's use of 'red terror', Barre said: 'Socialism does not oppress people'. The Somalis viewed Mengistu Haile Mariam as the successor to the 'Abyssinian' empire-builders of the past. A Radio Mogadishu commentator said on the eve of the Ogaden war that Somalia 'saw no reason whatsoever to restrain the guns of the Western Somali freedom fighters after the mad, criminal and genocidal regime in Addis Ababa, which has chosen to ignore the calls of those peoples who fell victims to the colonial empire, decided to enforce its will through the barrel of the gun'.[33]

RELATIONS WITH DJIBOUTI
The independence of Djibouti on 27 June 1977[34] was hailed as a victory by Somalia, which became the first country to recognize the new Republic. Vice-President Hussein Kulmiye Afrah, who attended the independence celebrations, described the day as 'the third national day in the history of the Somali people' (the first two being those marking the independence of the former British and Italian Somalilands). He wished 'the other two remaining Somali regions' (the Ogaden and north-eastern Kenya) rapid accession to independence. He said that Somalia stood ready to confront anyone who aspired to attack Djibouti.

President Barre visited Djibouti from 11–12 July and said that the two countries now had equal responsibilities towards each other: 'It is necessary for us to help each other . . . be it for our general interests or in defence against the enemy'—the 'sick regime in Addis Ababa'. Radio Mogadishu said that Siyad Barre was welcomed in Djibouti as the 'father of the Somali nation' and that the trip was 'like the President's visit to a region of the Somali Democratic Republic'. The commentary pointedly continued: 'The fatherly visit to Djibouti of Challe Siyad is an occasion for mutual self-congratulation between separated brothers, for greater Somalia to become free is a just cause and a responsibility of those parts which have achieved their independence. Their unity is entirely a Somali issue which does not concern anyone else. Our goal is the freedom of all Somalis and our objective is to put the white star on the blue flag.'[35] President Barre announced on 1 July that the people of Djibouti would not require passports to enter Somalia.

RELATIONS WITH KENYA

Although Kenyan-Somali relations are not marked by the instinctive animosity of those between Somalia and Ethiopia, Nairobi feared that if the Somalis succeeded in the 'reconquest' of the Ogaden, the next target for 'liberation' would be its own Northern Frontier District (NFD), which is inhabited by c. 250,000 ethnic Somalis. Kenya played a leading role in opposing the sale of any arms by the Western powers to Somalia. When some Somali units passed through north-eastern Kenya on their way to southern Ethiopia in late June, Kenya at once charged that 3,000 'regular Somali troops' had attacked a police post at Rhamu. Mogadishu described the report as 'baseless and unfounded'. Kenya withdrew a complaint to the OAU about the incident and Vice-President Hussein Kulmiye Afrah visited Nairobi from 14–21 July with an official proposal for a federation of the two countries; longstanding suspicions prevented the Kenyans from examining the proposal seriously. However, by September, Kenya was openly siding with Ethiopia over the Ogaden 'invasion'. Following a meeting with Somalia's Minister of Water and Mineral Resources, Hussein Abdulkadir Qasim, in Nairobi on 20 September, the acting Kenyan Foreign Minister, James Osogo, warned Somalia to renounce any claim it might have on part of Kenya.

Relations hit rock bottom in October with Kenyan allegations that Somalia was recruiting Somalis in the NFD to fight against Ethiopia 'and eventually against Kenya' itself. Kenya's Vice-President, Daniel arap Moi, warned on 15 October that Kenya would not tolerate the presence of Somalis with 'divided loyalites'. Foreign Minister Munyua Waiyaki said on 25 October that Kenyan support for Ethiopia was 'purely moral', and that a close watch was being kept on the movements of 'armed Somali groups along the border'. Somalia tried to play down the rift, arguing that it had issued passports to 100 Kenyan Somalis in the previous six months only to allow them to emigrate to Arab countries to work. When President Barre received the credentials of the new Kenyan ambassador in Mogadishu on 9 October, he asserted that relations between the two countries were 'excellent and becoming stronger all the time'.

But in early November, Nairobi reported demonstrations by NFD Somalis against Somali 'expansionism', and President Kenyatta said on 7 November that any threats against Kenya's territorial integrity would be crushed 'by all available means'. Kenya reported that armed Somalis had killed 23 Kenyans in an attack near Moyale, on the Ethiopian border, on 25 January 1978. In February, Kenya forced an Egyptian airliner carrying a clandestine cargo of arms to Somalia to land at Nairobi. It was with great relief that Kenya greeted the withdrawal of Somali forces from Ethiopia, although there was no immediate move towards improved Kenyan-Somali relations (also see chapter on Kenya).

OTHER AFRICAN RELATIONS

The Ogaden conflict drove a wedge between Somalia and much of the rest of Africa, which took the view that Somalia was violating the OAU principles of the integrity of territorial boundaries and of non-interference in each other's affairs. However, Somalia and the WSLF argued that they were upholding the OAU principles of self-determination for all nationalities and liberation of territories under 'colonial rule'. Among OAU member-states, only Egypt could be said to have openly backed Somalia in the war—to the extent of sending arms and technical personnel. Sudan actively shared Egypt's antipathy to the Ethiopian regime (and to Soviet involvement), but refrained from overtly supporting Somalia. President Numeiry visited Mogadishu from 17-20 March' shortly before the Taizz talks on Red Sea security (see above).

In October, Somalia criticized the OAU stand towards the Ogaden conflict as 'unjust', saying that 'African unity will never become a reality as long as African states colonize other African peoples and also as long as individual interests in collaboration with problems inherited from the all-time evil, colonialism, prevail'. A last minute diplomatic offensive in December took three Somali delegations on separate visits to Ivory Coast, Nigeria, Togo, Benin, Cameroon, Ghana, Gabon, Tunisia, Morocco, Algeria, Mauritania, Senegal, the Gambia, Liberia, Guinea-Bissau, Equatorial Guinea and Sierra Leone. In January 1978, Somalia called on the OAU to take a stand against the Russian and Cuban role in Ethiopia and other African countries. An OAU delegation led by Nigeria's External Affairs Commissioner, Brig-Gen Joseph Garba, visited Mogadishu in early February in an attempt to mediate between Somalia and Ethiopia.

RELATIONS WITH THE ARAB STATES

The Somali leadership spent considerable time in 1977 and early 1978 touring the Arab world to enlist support. The Saudi Foreign Minister, Prince Saud al-Faisal, visited Mogadishu on 5 April, reportedly to make $300-400m available to Somalia provided the Russians were expelled. At the same time, the Somali Minister of Culture and Higher Education, Omar Arteh (a former Foreign Minister and Somalia's most polished diplomat) was touring the UAE, Qatar, Bahrain and Kuwait. A 14-man UAE delegation was in Somalia from 1-8 June, and the President himself visited the UAE on 23-24 June for 'urgent discussions on the security of the Red Sea in the light of Djibouti's independence and expected developments in the area'. On 12-13 July, Barre was in Saudi Arabia, where he reportedly also met the PLO leader, Yasir Arafat. Another trip, from 13-15 September, took Barre to Saudi Arabia (for what the Saudi Press Agency described as talks on the 'security of the Red Sea as an Arab lake'), Egypt, Syria (where President Asad was reported to have urged him to avoid an irretrievable breakdown of Somali-Soviet relations), Kuwait, Iraq, the UAE, Qatar and back to Saudi Arabia. Iraq was reported to have made military aid available to Somalia. At first it allowed Soviet aircraft to refuel at Baghdad during the arms airlift to Ethiopia, but quickly rescinded these facilities (see essay, 'Crisis in the Horn').

The Arab League Foreign Ministers meeting in Cairo on 5 September adopted a resolution expressing 'deep concern' over the Ogaden conflict and urging foreign powers to 'stay out and let the peoples of the region reach a peaceful settlement'. But the League stopped far short of endorsing the position of Somalia—an Arab League member since 1974.

The tempo of the Somali diplomatic offensive in the Arab world picked up from October onwards, as the Somali position on the Ogaden battlefront began to slip and as the US wavered in its attitude to Mogadishu. Barre and his ministers were almost constantly on the move around the Arab capitals. However, by the end of January, after visits by Barre to Saudi Arabia and Jordan—when Somalia was beginning to elicit more outright pledges of support from Arab states—its military position was already irretrievable.

Those arms bought in Switzerland and elsewhere in Europe with the help of Arab funds were flown to Mogadishu aboard three Boeing 707 airliners leased to a Miami-based air charter company. The planes had once belonged to the Lufthansa cargo airline Condor, whose markings were still visible under a coat of white paint.

It took c. 30 missions to fly out the 590 tons of Soviet-made weapons (including Kalashnikov rifles and ammunition). The flights stopped to refuel at Jeddah before crossing Yemeni airspace to Mogadishu and were logged as Somali passenger aircraft. When the South Yemenis became suspicious about the number of these flights and ordered one of them to land at Aden, it happened indeed to be a regular Somali Airlines flight. On reaching Mogadishu, the arms shipments were unloaded and the aircraft turned round so fast that one of them arrived in Britain for an overhaul still carrying a case of arms which had been overlooked.

Egypt was also involved in the arms airlift to Somalia—a fact that came to world attention when an Egypt Air Boeing loaded with arms was forced down in Kenya en route to Mogadishu. The value of Egypt's arms aid was put at $30m. Somalia also received limited arms aid (light weapons, such as rifles) from Iran. But the US categorically insisted that its military clients (e.g. Saudi Arabia, Egypt, Pakistan and Iran) strictly observe the restrictions on the re-export of US arms to third countries.

The Arab League agreed on 29 March 1978 to extend military and other assistance to Somalia 'because of the presence of a foreign threat in the region'. Somalia must therefore be aided 'to defend its borders in the event of attack from outside. This would cover all kinds of assistance. It can include arms or money with which to buy arms.'

RELATIONS WITH IRAN·

Iran's eagerness to provide Somalia with substantial material and financial assistance—and, in contrast with some Arab and European countries, to do so openly—stemmed almost entirely from the Shah's concern with Soviet penetration of the Indian Ocean and Red Sea region, and not from any sense of Islamic solidarity. It was during a visit to Tehran in early September that a senior SRSP member, Col Ahmed Mahmud Farah, gave the first indication that Somalia might evict the Russians. He told a Tehran newspaper that if the USSR continued to ban arms supplies to Somalia while supporting Ethiopia with experts and weapons, there would be no further need for Soviet experts in Somalia. A delegation led by the head of national security, Brig-Gen Ahmed Suleiman Abdulle, met the Shah in Tehran in early November, and President Barre himself paid a three-day visit at the end of December.

The Shah announced on 1 January 1978 that he would intervene if Ethiopia invaded Somali territòry: 'Iran will not remain indifferent in the face of any further aggression against the recognized borders of Somalia'. This statement provoked shocked outrage in Ethiopia, Kenya and at the OAU (see essay on 'The Disunited OAU'). The Shah's statement was followed on 15 January by a promise from the Saudi Foreign Minister that his country would also go to Somalia's aid 'if it becomes a target of foreign aggression'. Arms from various sources, made available by Iran, began arriving in Somalia early in January 1978.

RELATIONS WITH LIBYA AND PDRY

The only two Arab states which supported the regime in Ethiopia against Somalia were Libya and South Yemen, although there was some ambiguity in their positions towards Mogadishu. The Middle East News Agency reported on 31 May 1977 that Col Gaddafy had refused to receive the head of the Somali delegation to the eighth Islamic Foreign Ministers' Conference in Tripoli, even though the envoy was carrying a message from President Barre.

South Yemen actively assisted the Soviet arms sea and airlift to Ethiopia, ferrying equipment across the Red Sea from Aden to Assab. The South Yemenis also, on two occasions, forced down Somali civilian airliners which they suspected were carrying arms supplies purchased in Europe.

There was a sudden improvement in Somali relations with Libya at the beginning of 1978. Omar Arteh said after a visit to Tripoli for talks with Gaddafy that the two countries had 'resolved to forget past differences—on the basis of the Somali saying: let anything on this side be swept away by the wind, and that on the other by the flood'. Barre himself was warmly received in Tripoli early in March 1978 when Gaddafy conveyed to him the substance of a Soviet proposal for peace in the Horn of Africa (see Relations with USSR above). At the same time, an official Libyan commentary called for the 'cutting off of non-African connections' with the Horn conflict, returning it from an 'international state' to an 'African state' through African—and the commentary specified Libyan—mediation.

POLITICAL AFFAIRS

The break with the Soviet Union and the bitter anti-Soviet theme of Government propaganda and popular demonstrations led to inevitable speculation that Somalia was about to stray from the socialist path on which it had embarked in 1969. [36] But such speculation resulted largely from a misinterpretation of the highly individualistic attitudes of the Somalis and from misleading conclusions drawn by foreign correspondents covering the Ogaden war, who found Mogadishu's relatively relaxed openness in such sharp contrast to the rigid orthodoxy of Marxist Ethiopia. Speaking in May 1977 to the Democratic Union of Somali Women about the need to 'respect the traditions of Somali family life and to guard against the dangers of imitating foreign culture', President Barre referred to 'the false propaganda spread by imperialists to the effect that Somalia would renounce socialism'. He said that 'our socialism was not negotiable. We would never renounce it, but would pursue an independent policy.' [37]

Nevertheless, in the first year of the one-party state created with the formation of the Somali Revolutionary Socialist Party (SRSP) on 1 July 1976, [38] there were signs of disagreement within the ruling body, particularly over the question of Somalia's relations with East and West. Fidel Castro, reporting in March 1978 about his meeting in Aden a year before with Somali and Ethiopian leaders (see above), claimed that the Somali Government was split between Left and Right, with Siyad Barre representing 'a powerful reactionary Rightist group in favour of an alliance with imperialism, the Arab reactionaries, Saudi Arabia, Iran and others'. [39]

The apparent split came into the open in January 1978 with the defection of the former Ambassador to Kenya, Hussein Haji Ali Dualeh, who claimed that most Somalis were disillusioned with President Barre's 'one-man rule'. Dualeh said he had been recalled to Mogadishu in September 1977 and ordered to join the army at the Ogaden front. He claimed that Barre had ordered him killed for trying to promote peace with Kenya and for opposing the Ogaden offensive.

Dualeh also identified himself with the Somali Democratic Action Front (Sodaf), an opposition organization of former army officers, civil servants, ministers and ambassadors based in Rome. Sodaf's existence had been disclosed in August by three of its founders: Osman Nour Ali, a former Minister of Justice, Labour and Religious Affairs, now Sodaf's secretary-general; Mahmoud Chelle, a former Minister of Industry and Commerce, now Sodaf's 'foreign minister'; and Abderrahman Saleh Ahmed, a former ambassador. The Sodaf leaders accused Barre of stifling all internal opposition by repressive police methods. They also raised the tribal issue, claiming that they themselves represented Somalia's three principal groups—the Isaaq (Issas), Mijertain and Hawiya—while members of Barre's minority Marehan clan (a branch of the Darod tribal family) filled all important

Government, Party and military posts, including 90% of the army troops in the Mogadishu region.[40] Sodaf claimed to have several hundred members, including some in clandestine cells within Somalia, and said it sought to present itself to moderate Arab regimes as an alternative to their efforts to 'buy' Barre away from Soviet influence. Sodaf also pointedly claimed to have a manifesto recognizing the 'territorial integrity and sovereignty' of all states—an intended reassurance to Ethiopia, Kenya and Djibouti.[41] There was no way of judging Sodaf's actual strength within Somalia. Since Sodaf stands to the right of Barre, Castro's allegation that Barre represents the 'reactionary Rightist group' would still leave open the question of who stands for the 'progressive Left'.

PARTY CHANGES
The SRSP Central Committee was reorganized on 27 October 1977 'in line with the purposeful conduct of the affairs of the party and nation during this sensitive period'. The Departments of Health and Social Welfare, Justice, and Education and Sports were merged into a single Department of Social Affairs. The Research and Political Institute Departments became the Bureau for Political Education and Research. The Defence and Security Departments were merged, and the Departments of Finance and Commerce, Agriculture, and Industry were combined into a single Economic Bureau.

A committee was formed to 'plan, administer and collect donations' for the 'Somali liberation movements'. It had Brig-Gen Ali Mattan Hashi as its Chairman, with Ahmed Mohamed Dualeh and Mohamed Ali Warsame as members. However, Gen Hashi, an SRSP Central Committee member, died in Italy on 21 January 1978.

GOVERNMENT CHANGES
A new Ministry of Local Government and Rural Development was formed on 1 October 1977 to answer a need for what the President saw as 'economic development of the regions and districts, co-ordination of political orientation and popular programmes, and the streamlining of the rural development campaign'. Sworn in as Minister was Col Abdirazaq Mahmoud Abubakar, the Ogaden-born former head of the Education and Sports Department of the SRSP.

Mohamed Yusuf Wayra, a member of the SRSP Central Committee and former adviser to the President on economic affairs, was appointed Finance Minister on 20 December 1977, replacing Abdirahman Nuur Hersi, who became the President's economic adviser. Abdirahman Jama Barre was appointed Foreign Minister on 27 July 1977. The Cabinet was reshuffled by the SRSP's Political Bureau on 31 March 1978 'in view of the critical stage the country is passing through' and 'in order to speed up national development'. The reshuffle could also be seen as tightening the loyal inner circle around President Siyad Barre. One of his most devoted aides, the former Foreign Minister Omar Arteh Ghalib became Minister of the Presidency.

Within the SRSP Central Committee, 13 members were appointed to the provinces 'where they will be responsible for the supervision and proper execution of national duties'. It was not clear how these provincial duties affected the assignment of responsibilities under the Committee's reorganization of 27 October 1977, which involved some of the same members.

YOUTH CONGRESS
The Somali Revolutionary Youth Union, a successor to the Somali Youth League— the political party which led the country to independence—held its first Congress at the Mogadishu Military Academy from 10–14 May 1977. Addressing the Congress, Barre said the SRYU was formed 'to defend the gains of the revolution and oppose reactionaries and imperialists'.

DEFENCE AND SECURITY

The toll of the Ogaden war on the armed forces has yet to be fully calculated. Somalia was thought to have thrown 40,000 men and women—its full 25,000-strong army plus 15,000 irregulars—into the conflict. Some of these forces may also have been 'seconded' to the Western Somali Liberation Front, whose strength was estimated at c. 20,000. Casualties were believed to have been severe, particularly in the action around Jijiga in the closing stages of the war. After Jijiga was recaptured by the Ethiopians, the Somali units dispersed in disarray, and hundreds of Somali forces must have been trapped in the mountains between Harar and Jijiga. One estimate is that as much as a quarter of the Somali armed forces was wiped out in the war, but it is impossible to verify this.

Equipment losses were also severe. Even before the Ethiopian counter-offensive gained speed, an Arab military source in Mogadishu estimated that 30% of Somalia's armoured force of 200 T-34 and 50 T-54/55 Soviet-made medium tanks had been destroyed. In one battle in August, 22 Somali tanks were reported knocked out in two hours of Ethiopian air attacks. From the beginning of the war, Ethiopia claimed to have shot down dozens of Somali aircraft, including MiGs from the three Somali fighter squadrons, but much of the Somali air force was grounded anyway because of a shortage of spare parts, and the Ethiopian claims were almost certainly exaggerated. Still, it is clear that Somali losses early in the war were not fully compensated for by the modest infusions of arms from Egypt, Saudi Arabia and Iran. Many of the mostly small arms provided by these sources were in any case destroyed or abandoned in the final stages of the war.

The rebuilding of the manpower and morale of the armed forces together with the re-equipping of the army and air force are now priority items for the Somali Government.

ARMED FORCES

The Army numbers 30,000 and has seven tank battalions; eight mechanized infantry battalions; 14 motorized infantry battalions; two commando battalions; 13 field and ten anti-aircraft artillery battalions. It is equipped with 200 T-34, 100 T-54/-55 medium tanks; 100 BTR-40/-50 and 250 BTR-152 armoured personnel carriers; c. 100 76mm and 85mm guns; 80 122mm howitzers; 100mm anti-tank guns; 150 14.5mm, 37mm, 57mm and 100mm anti-aircraft guns and SA-2/-3 surface-to-air missiles. The 500-strong Navy has three Osa-class guided-missile fast patrol boats with Styx surface-to-surface missiles; six large patrol craft (ex-Soviet Poluchat class); four motor torpedo boats (ex-Soviet P-6 class) and four medium landing craft (ex-Soviet T-4 class). The Air Force numbers 1,000 and has 55 combat aircraft. Formations consist of one light bomber squadron with three Il-28; two ground-attack fighter squadrons with 40 MiG-17 and MiG-15UTI; one fighter squadron with 12 MiG-21MF and one transport squadron with three An-2, An-24/-26. Other aircraft include three C-47, one C-45, six P-148, 15 Yak-11 and two Do-28. There is one helicopter squadron with five Mi-4, five Mi-8 and one AB-204. In all services, spares are short and not all equipment is serviceable. Paramilitary forces number 12,000 and include 8,000 police, 1,500 border guards and 2,500 People's Militia. [42]

THE GOVERNMENT (as at 31 March 1978)

SRSP Political Bureau
*Secretary-General of the SRSP
and President of the Somali
Democratic Republic*   Maj-Gen Mohamed Siyad Barre
Vice-President   Maj-Gen Hussein Kulmiye Afrah

Vice-President and Minister of Defence	Lt-Gen Mohamed Ali Samatar
Vice-President and Assistant Secretary-General of the SRSP	Brig-Gen Ismail Ali Abokor
Head of the National Security Service	Brig-Gen Ahmed Suleiman Abdulle
Ministers:	
Foreign Affairs	Abdirahman Jama Barre
Commerce	Brig-Gen Mohamed Ibrahim Ahmed
Labour and Social Affairs	Mohamed Burale Ismail
Industry	Brig-Gen Mohamed Sheikh Osman
Land and Air Transport	Kenadid Ahmed Yusuf
Ports and Sea Transport	Brig-Gen Mahmud Jele Yusuf
Health	Col Musa Rabile Gode
Sports	Abdulkasim Salad Hassan
Education and Public Instruction	Aden Mohamed Ali
Information and National Guidance	Abdisalam Sheikh Hussein
Justice and Religious Affairs	Ahmed Shire Mahmud
Agriculture	Col Ahmed Hassan Musa
Livestock and Forestry	Yusuf Ali Osman
Fisheries	Osman Jama Ali
Public Works	Mohamed Hawadle Madar
Water and Mineral Resources	Hussein Abdulkadir Qasim
Local Government and Rural Development	Maj-Gen Jama Mohamed Ghalib
Post and Telecommunications	Abdillahi Osoble Siyad
Finance	Mohamed Yusuf Wayra
Presidency	Omar Arteh Ghalib
Culture and Higher Education	Ahmed Ashkir Botan
Provincial Responsibilities:	
Central and Lower Juba	Omar Salah Ahmed
Gedo	Col Mohamed Omar Jays
Bay	Salah Mohamed Ali
Bakol	Col Abid Warsama Isaak and Mohamed Abdi Dunkal
Lower Shebelle	Ahmed Mohamed Dualeh
Central Shebelle	Abdarrahman Aydeed
Hiran	Brig-Gen Mohamed Ali Shire
Galgadud and Mudug	Col Ahmed Mahmud Farah
Nugaal	Col Abdillahi Warsama Nur
Sanaag and Bari	Mohamed Ali Warsama
Togdheer	Col Abderazzaq Mahmud Abubakar
North-West	Col Farah Wais Dulle
Special committee on purchasing, contracts and economic development:	Maj-Gen Abdulla Mohamed Fadil Abdirahman Nur Hersi Ahmed Mohamed Mahmud Brig-Gen Mohamed Nur Galal

SOCIAL AFFAIRS
TRIBALISM
Somalia's superficial linguistic, social, cultural and religious cohesion—remarkable in Africa—belies a strong sense of clan-consciousness among the c. 15 major groupings and dozens of sub-groups which make up the Somali nation. Tribalism was legally abolished years ago, but SRSP leaders continue to draw attention to its destructive and divisive effects. The Party's approach is to substitute neighbourhood communities for the kinship-based traditional social structure. This change is promoted through 'orientation centres' in each district where, for example, all marriages must now be contracted (rather than in a traditional clan setting).

RESETTLEMENT SCHEMES

The bold experiment in settling c. 5% of Somalia's nomadic population in farming and fishing schemes has continued to produce success stories as well as disappointments. The aim is to reduce pressure on grazing areas which accentuated the suffering caused by the 1974–75 drought in which c. 20,000 nomads, 1m cattle, 5m sheep and 30,000 camels died. By the end of 1976 c. 112,000 nomads in the relief camps had been persuaded to give up their traditional life and join seven farming and fishing resettlement schemes.[43] Because the authorities were caught unprepared for the opportunity which the devastating drought presented to tackle the problems of nomadism, the major resettlement was undertaken with a minimum of study and few firm financial commitments.[44]

The scheme now involves c. 120,000 people, including 15,000 in fishing settlements on the Indian Ocean—a remarkable accomplishment considering the herdsmen's distaste for eating fish. Boats and equipment were supplied by Russia and Sweden. Some irrigation works have been completed and planting begun in the agricultural settlements. Schools and health clinics have been built and political orientation classes organized. However, most of the settlements still rely on food donated by the UN World Food Programme. The attrition rate has been less than 10%. A number of international agencies, including the IDA, the African Development Bank, the European Development Fund and various Arab funds, have made long-term financial commitments.

LEGAL AFFAIRS

Hassan Warmahaye Birie and Arab Osman Buraleh were executed by firing squad in Boramo on 22 April 1977, after being found guilty of espionage and banditry by the National Security Court in the north-west region.

A teacher, Yusuf Ali Barre, was sentenced to 10 years' imprisonment by the National Security Court on 17 June for being in possession of political documents criticizing Government policies.

Amnesty International drew attention in July 1977 to the case of the former commander of the police force, Mohamed Abshir Musse, who had resigned in early 1969 in protest at alleged electoral malpractices. He was arrested after the Revolution later that year and except for the period April-June 1973 has been detained ever since. Musse was reportedly held in Lanta Bur prison, west of Mogadishu, and in poor health. The former Prime Minister, Ibrahim Egal, who had been released in 1976 and rearrested soon afterwards, was also still in detention.

THE PRESS

Construction of a national television station is to begin in 1978; this will cover the Benadir region in its initial phase. The Director-General of Information and National Guidance, Osman Awes Nuur, said on 'Mass Media Day', 21 January 1978, that the news media were expected to play an active role in the 'orientation and politicization' of society. He added that the departure of Russian technicians in late 1977 had not had any unfavourable impact on the running of the country's radio transmitters.

The African Development Fund agreed to lend $1.7m to the State Printing Agency to renovate its equipment and increase its publishing capacity. The Agency also receives technical assistance from West Germany.

The state-run Somali National News Agency (Sonna) signed a co-operation agreement with its Sudanese counterpart (Suna) in September 1977, and was accepted as a member of the Federation of Arab News Agencies in November.

EDUCATION
The number of students enrolled in the 844 primary and 39 secondary schools (1976 figures) was estimated at 350,000 in September 1977. The withdrawal of Soviet experts meant a drastic reduction in the number of teachers, particularly in secondary schools and the university. The EEC was approached for educational assistance to compensate for the loss of Russian aid. An IDA credit of $8m is to be used to build, expand and renovate schools.

HEALTH
According to an announcement by the US National Centre for Disease Control, the world's last known centre of smallpox is in southern Somalia, where 3,203 cases were reported in the first nine months of 1977.

TRADE UNIONS
The first Congress of the Somali Federation of Trade Unions was held from 27–30 April 1977 in Mogadishu. The Congress adopted a 32-article Constitution, changed its name to the General Federation of Somali Trade Unions, and adopted as its emblem a red flag with the five-pointed white Somali star in the centre, together with a rising sun, a hoe and a wheel. A Central Committee of 86 members and an Executive Committee of 13 were elected by delegations from all regions and districts as well as representatives of the six trade unions in government establishments. President Barre urged the GFSTU to be allied to the peasants, intellectuals, armed forces, youth, women and the rest of society.

The members of the Executive Committee include: Mahmud Ali Ahmed (a member of the SRSP Central Committee), chairman; Abdillahi Mohamed Mireh, first vice-chairman; Abdillahi Mohamed Shegow, second vice-chairman; Abdiweli Adan, foreign relations; Hawa Afrah Hirabe, relations between workers and social organizations; Abdillahi Musa Yusuf, mobilization, ideology and information; Abderrahman Osman Rageh, justice and workers' welfare; Mohamed Ali Hirsi, finance; Abdi Mohamed Amin, sports and culture; Yusuf Mohamed Hassan, education and training and Omar Mohamed Handule, grievances. An additional Inspection and Supervision Committee is composed of Mohamed Farah Issa, Ali Sheikh Adan and Sahra Sheikh Mohamed.

LOCAL GOVERNMENT
The town of Adad, in Galgudud region, was designated a district on 8 February 1978. The districts of the region now comprise Dusamareb, Adad, El Dere, El Bur and Abudwaq.

POPULATION
The 1977 population was estimated at 3.33m (cf 3.18m in 1975). Average annual birth rate is 45.9 per 1,000; death rate, 24.0 per 1,000. In 1975, the economically active population was estimated at 1.085m, including 893,000 in agriculture.

ECONOMIC AFFAIRS (12.0 Somali shillings = £1 sterling)
Just as the development programme was beginning to show impressive results, earning Somalia praise for its 'bootstrap' spirit from such agencies as the World Bank, the Ogaden war intervened to cause a serious drain on economic and human resources. The effects were multiple: public finance was diverted to purchase arms and prepare the home warfront; manpower (and womanpower) was channelled into the military, with a mass call-up in early 1978; and energies which would have gone into development projects were consumed by the war effort. It was probably due as

much to these economic strains as to the deteriorating military position that Somalia eventually agreed to pull back from the Ogaden: President Barre calculated that a withdrawal would enhance his chances of attracting more sizable infusions of Arab and Western aid.

The Five-Year Development Plan (1973–78), involving the investment of SSh 839m in 1976 alone,[45] had seen the creation of a fishing industry, the opening up of thousands of acres of newly irrigated land to cultivation, and the establishment of 25 new industries, with ten more due to come on stream in 1977–78.

The country, however, remains one of the world's 25 poorest, with an estimated 1976 GNP of $370m (or $110 per capita). The economy is heavily dependent on foreign assistance (see below) and the trade deficit in 1976 was SSh 44.2m. If anything, the trading picture deteriorated in the first half of 1977: exports, which had been SSh 87.8m in the first half of 1976, were down to 65.1m. The trade deficit by mid-1977 was already SSh 42.9m, only SSh 1.3m less than the deficit for all of 1976. Thanks to infusions of foreign capital, foreign exchange reserves were quite healthy, standing at $88.7m at the end of November 1977. However, one of the first indicators of the cost of the war was that two months earlier those reserves had stood at $101m.

The cost of living index for Mogadishu was 171 at the end of 1976 and 184 at the end of September 1977 (1970 = 100); the index for food items was 190 and 209 respectively.[46]

AGRICULTURE AND FISHERIES

Although agriculture began to show signs of recovery, there were lingering after-effects from the 1974–75 drought. Harvests of maize and sorghum improved from 42,000 tons in 1974 to c. 180,000 tons in 1977. But the country is still a long way from self-sufficiency and had to import c. 40,000 tons of food in 1977.

One of the main efforts towards self-sufficiency centres on sugar. The Government awarded an £88m contract in August 1977 to Booker Agriculture International, a subsidiary of Booker McConnell of the UK, to design and manage an irrigated sugar project on 11,400 hectares at Jelib in the Juba valley. The production targets are 40,000 tonnes a year by 1981 and 70,000 tonnes by 1984, yielding a surplus for export. Another Booker subsidiary, Fletcher and Stewart, is to supply £18m worth of sugar-processing equipment; five other British firms will be involved in building the factory and other works. The sugar project will be funded by Arab finance, half the total cost by the Abu Dhabi Fund for Arab Economic Development. The Saudi Arabian Fund for Development agreed to lend $70m towards the project in November 1977.

Development of the fishing industry continued to show considerable promise. Annual production reached c. 5,000 tonnes in 1977 (cf 2,222 tonnes in 1975 and 1,246 tonnes in 1974). The Minister of Fisheries announced in October 1977 that the eventual production target was 40,000 tonnes a year. The fishing community has been augmented by c. 15,000 former nomadic herdsmen who deploy a fleet of 500 motorboats and 18 trawlers. Iraq, which established a joint fishing company with Somalia in July 1976, sent eight trawlers to participate in the June 1977 catch.

INDUSTRY

The SSh 15m tannery at Kisimayo was inaugurated in April 1977 with an initial capacity of 200 skins a day, rising eventually to 500–1,500. It will employ c. 150 people and joins the tannery at Hargeisa (capacity 7,000 treated skins a day), and a third planned for Mogadishu (capacity of 500 sheepskins a day). Exports of hides and skins, 80% of which go to Italy, accounted for 4–5% of Somali exports.

The oil refinery being built at Halane with finance from the Iraqi External Development Fund is to have an annual capacity of 150,000 tonnes of petrol, diesel oil and aviation fuel. The cost of the refinery has been estimated at SSh 173m.

MINING

The Government was reported in May 1977 to be considering a joint venture with Westinghouse Corporation (US) to exploit a potentially large uranium deposit in Mudugh district, north of Mogadishu. The Government signed an agreement with the Arab Mining Society on 28 January 1978 for investment in uranium and cobalt prospecting.

AGREEMENTS WITH USSR

The departure of the Russians left several co-operative ventures and agreements in doubt. Before the break, on 20 April 1977, Somalia signed an agreement with the Soviets to draw up the next development plan for 1979–83. Another agreement, signed on 16 August, provided for co-operation in agriculture, cartography and marine affairs. Another project in doubt was an irrigation scheme developed with Soviet technical assistance at Fanole involving creation of two state cotton plantations on 45,000 hectares. Somalia and the USSR also signed an agreement on 4 October for water exploration in several regions.

COMMUNICATIONS

The new port of Mogadishu, financed by loans from the EEC and IDA, was inaugurated on 20 October 1977. It is the Republic's largest harbour and, with four berths for ships of up to 40,000 tons and a fifth for those over 50,000, ends the era of transferring cargo to shore by lighter.

The Government began studying a plan to build a new international airport c. 20 km from Mogadishu at a cost of c. $100m. [47]

Somali Airlines began weekly (Sunday) flights to the Seychelles on 3 July 1977. In June it purchased a Fokker F-27 from the Netherlands at a cost of Ssh 26m, bringing its fleet to 12 aircraft.

The 228-km Galciao-Garowe section of the Beleduen-Burao highway, built with Chinese assistance, was completed on 19 October 1977. The first 362 km of the projected 970 km highway had been completed in 1976.

FOREIGN AID

Arab Governments and Funds continue to be the major source of overseas finance, but there is now also the prospect of greatly increased assistance from the West, particularly from the US, UK and West Germany. Two new loans totalling $24m were provided by the Kuwait-based Arab Fund for Economic and Social Development (AFESD) for road construction, and a third by the United Arab Emirates for $8m towards the construction of ten schools. The African Development Fund lent $5.5m towards the Hargeisa-Boroma road project, to be financed in conjunction with the IDA and the Islamic Development Bank. The ADF also provided a loan of $1.7m for educational projects.

The US announced on 5 December 1977 that it would resume economic aid to Somalia. Congress was asked to approve a $15m agricultural research and training programme over five years, due to begin in 1978, as well as a $10m four-year health care programme. An agreement was signed in March 1978 for a $7m loan to enable Somalia to buy American food supplies; the US had previously agreed to provide $6m worth of food aid. The first 10,000 tons of a US gift of 23,000 tons of food and cereals arrived in Mogadishu on 31 January 1978.

The EEC agreed in February 1978 to help with manpower training—one of Somalia's greatest economic weaknesses.

On 21 March 1978, Britain's Ministry of Overseas Development announced a £1m grant and an expansion of its technical co-operation programme, which includes a £650,000 training school for employees of the Juba valley sugar project. The grant will enable Somalia to buy British commodities and equipment.

QUARTERLY INDICATORS OF ECONOMIC ACTIVITY (million Somali shillings, unless otherwise stated)

	1976				1977		
	1 Qtr.	2 Qtr.	3 Qtr.	4 Qtr.	1 Qtr.	2 Qtr.	3 Qtr.
Prices (monthly averages)							
Cost of Living: Mogadishu							
all items 1970 = 100	155	166	170	171	178	180	184
food 1970 = 100	168	184	189	190	200	202	209
Money and Banking (end of qtr)							
Currency in circulation	434.5	386.4	417.0	413.9	453.1	445.9	470.3*
Demand deposits:	393.2	417.7	469.3	464.8	487.2	498.4	562.1*
commercial banks							
Advances: commercial	947.0	870.2	811.8	880.9	870.4	874.7	891.3*
Foreign Trade (monthly averages)							
Exports, fob	52.6	35.2	45.3	45.2	38.9	26.2	—
of which: live animals	32.2	14.1	32.6	30.2	25.5	13.8	—
Imports, cif	59.3	63.7	53.1	46.4	50.2	57.8	—
Exchange Holdings (end of qtr.)							
Foreign exchange (m $US)	51.3	80.6	67.7	75.0	76.5	79.5	101.0†
Exchange Rate							
Market rate (Ssh/$)	6.295	6.295	6.295	6.295	6.295	6.295	6.295

*End of July.
†Figure at end November $88.7m.
Source: Central Statistical Department, Ministry of Planning and Co-ordination.

MONETARY SURVEY (million Somali shillings at end of period)

	1975	1976	1977 (first half)
Foreign Assets (Net)	500.4	515.2	595.0
Domestic Credit	803.5	1,110.8	1,047.4
Claims on Government (net)	−238.2	124.4	46.4
Claims on Official Entities	107.1	105.5	126.3
Claims on Private Sector	934.6	880.9	874.7
Money	825.8	994.9	1,022.2
Quasi-Money	179.3	205.1	220.8
Other Items (net)	298.9	426.0	399.4
Money, Seasonally Adjusted	794.0	956.6	1,042.0

Source: IMF, International Financial Statistics.

INTERNATIONAL LIQUIDITY (million US dollars at end of period)

	1975	1976	1977 (first half)
International Reserves	68.5	85.0	90.1
Gold	0.1	0.1	0.2
SDRs	5.1	5.0	4.9
Reserve Position in IMF	5.0	4.9	5.5
Foreign Exchange	58.3	75.0	79.5
Fund Position			
Quota	22.2	22.1	22.2
Payments Agreements Assets	1.7	3.4	2.9
Commercial Banks: Assets	36.7	22.3	26.7

Source: IMF, International Financial Statistics.

BALANCE OF PAYMENTS (million US dollars, minus sign indicates debit)

	1973	1974	1975	1976
A Goods, Services and Transfers	-38	-51.7	—	-69.2
Exports of Merchandise, fob	57.1	64.0	88.6	81.0
Imports of Merchandise, fob	-97.5	-133.7	-141.1	-153.1
Exports of Services	16.0	20.6	26.6	30.7
Imports of Services	-42.9	-54.2	-76.4	-68.7
Private Unrequited Trans. net	2.7	3.5	1.9	1.2
Govt. Unrequited Trans. net	25.9	48.2	100.3	39.7
B Long-Term Capital, nie	26.1	61.0	52.8	69.6
C Short-Term Capital, nie	11.8	-1.3	-24.9	12.6
D Errors and Omissions	—	-.6	-1.3	.7
Total (A through D)	**-.8**	**7.3**	**26.6**	**13.7**
Reserves and Related Items	.8	-7.3	-26.6	-13.7

Source: IMF, *International Financial Statistics.*

SECTORAL INVESTMENT ALLOCATIONS UNDER THE FIVE-YEAR DEVELOPMENT PROGRAMME 1974–78 (thousand Somali shillings)

Sector	Total allocation	per cent
Livestock	162,084	4.2
Other agriculture	1,124,506	29.1
Forestry	51,153	1.3
Fisheries	77,990	2.0
Water Resources	139,552	3.6
Mining	45,683	1.2
Electricity	136,540	3.5
Manufacturing industry	588,257	15.2
Transport and communications	944,697	24.5
Education	191,065	4.9
Health	77,721	2.0
Housing	156,982	4.1
Labour	11,319	0.29
Tourism	12,590	0.3
Information	37,116	1.0
Cartography and statistics	106,099	2.7
Total	3,863,357	

Source: Ministry of Planning and Co-ordination Five-Year Development Programme, 1974–78. *Africa Research Bureau*, 15 July–14 August 1977.

DIRECTION OF TRADE (million US dollars)

	1970	1974	1975	1976
Major Suppliers				
Italy	13.29	39.57	45.80	34.37
Kuwait	—	—	11.93	15.79
Soviet Union	3.00	15.68	15.68	15.68
United Kingdom	2.81	5.04	9.21	11.15
United States	3.57	3.16	0.22	10.56
China (PR)	0.79	8.98	8.98	8.98
West Germany	4.12	4.75	8.78	8.41
Thailand	—	4.85	13.67	7.76
Kenya	2.37	6.86	9.26	6.24
Japan	3.36	3.63	11.70	5.02
Total (including others)	**45.10**	**129.40**	**196.52**	**164.72**
Major Purchasers				
Saudi Arabia	16.72	35.19	52.78	63.34
Italy	8.04	6.33	8.96	14.32
Guatemala	—	—	—	6.07
Yugoslavia	—	—	0.36	4.28

Soviet Union	—	3.37	3.37	3.37
China (PR)	—	2.40	2.40	2.40
Kuwait	—	—	4.57	2.38
UAE	—	—	2.33	2.36
Total (including others)	**31.34**	**62.05**	**87.46**	**114.59**

Source: IMF, *Direction of Trade, 1970–76.*

NOTES

1. See *Africa Contemporary Record (ACR)* 1976–77, pp. B325, B330.
2. *Ibid*, pp. B330–2.
3. For full statement and reactions, see pp. C80–85.
4. See chapter on Kenya in this volume.
5. *Financial Times*, London; 26 July 1977.
6. Interview with the *Emirates News*, Abu Dhabi, 27 August 1977.
7. Interview with the *New York Times*, 13 September 1977.
8. *New York Times*, 29 September 1977.
9. See *ACR* 1974–75, p. B275.
10. *Daily Telegraph*, London; 6 October 1977.
11. Interview with West German television, 28 January 1978.
12. Radio Mogadishu, 11 February 1978.
13. United Press International from Mogadishu, 17 February 1978, and *Daily Telegraph*, 5 February 1978.
14. *Sunday Times*, London; 19 March 1978.
15. See *ACR* 1976–77, p. B330.
16. See Ethiopia chapter: Relations with Israel, in this volume.
17. See *ACR* 1976–77, p. B332.
18. *Ibid.*
19. For a discussion of this, see 'The Model Socialist State that Prays Five Times a Day', in the *Economist*, London; 14 May 1977, p. 65.
20. *Newsweek*, New York, 27 June 1977.
21. Interview with *al-Yaqza*, Kuwait; 27 June 1977, quoted by Qatar News Agency.
22. *Washington Post*, 18 July 1977.
23. Statements to Colin Legum by diplomats in Mogadishu.
24. NSLF statement to Colin Legum in Mogadishu, 12 August 1977.
25. *Daily Telegraph*, 8 October 1977.
26. See note 3 above.
27. *Afrique-Asie*, Paris; 28 November 1977.
28. *Washington Post*, 1 September 1977.
29. *Newsweek*, 26 September 1977.
30. See chapter on Ethiopia in this volume.
31. See essay, 'Soviet and Chinese Policies in Africa', and p. C85.
32. *People's Daily*, Peking; 19 June 1977.
33. Radio Mogadishu, 12 July 1977.
34. See chapter on Djibouti in this volume.
35. Radio Mogadishu, 12 July 1977.
36. See *ACR* 1969–70, pp. B174ff.
37. Radio Mogadishu, 28 May 1977.
38. See *ACR* 1976–77, p. B325.
39. Radio Havana, 15 March 1978.
40. *International Herald Tribune*, Paris; 31 August 1977.
41. *Ibid.*
42. *The Military Balance 1977–78* (London: International Institute for Strategic Studies).
43. See *ACR* 1976–77, p. B327.
44. *Financial Times*, 19 April 1977.
45. See *ACR* 1976–77, p. B334.
46. Because of the war, the price of bread and meat rose in Mogadishu by 50%; at the same time subsidies were cancelled on imported staples such as flour, sugar and rice. Cooking gas, normally imported from Kenya, could be obtained only on the black market at four times its official price.
47. *Marchés Tropicaux et Méditerranées*, Paris; 26 August 1977.

Republic of Djibouti

Even in the most favourable of circumstances, the prospects for the tiny Republic of Djibouti in its first year of independence would not have been optimistic. One of Africa's smallest and least populous states, it is virtually devoid of natural resources and seethes with ethnic rivalry between its two main population groups, the Afars and Issas. The ethnic factor stems not so much from the fact that these Islamic-Hamitic cousins vie for jobs and social opportunities and political influence at home, as the fact that they are each merely a part of larger clans with roots deep inside Djibouti's two powerful neighbours, Ethiopia and Somalia. Moreover, Djibouti's accession to independence came at the same time that Ethiopia and Somalia, traditional enemies, were fighting a war which would determine the future of the entire Horn of Africa region. Nor did independence in any way reduce the new Republic's dual importance to its neighbours. To Somalia, it is still one of the three 'lost' territories involved in the long-dreamed-of ingathering of all Somali clans in a 'Greater Somalia'; to Ethiopia, the port of Djibouti has long been the main outlet to the sea, linked with Addis Ababa by a 784 km railway which in recent years has carried as much as 60% of Ethiopia's external trade. Somalia's involvement in the Ogaden in 1977 (see chapter on Somalia) underscored its determination to recover the three 'lost' territories (the third is Kenya's Northern Frontier District). Although Somalia has pledged to respect Djibouti's sovereignty, some leaders in the young Republic (especially among the Afars) remained deeply suspicious. The fact that the rail link to Addis Ababa was out of action for most of 1977 because of sabotage by either Somali or Afar insurgents brought the port of Djibouti to a standstill and emphasized the new state's economic dependence on Ethiopia. As if all this were not enough to expose the Republic's vulnerability, the fragile Afar-Issa coalition put together at independence finally collapsed at the end of 1977 under the strain of ever-widening ethnic divisions. It was all a far cry from the relative harmony that had prevailed a year earlier as the *Territoire français des Afars et des Issas* (TFAI) had set off on the road to independence.

POLITICAL AFFAIRS
PRE-INDEPENDENCE DEVELOPMENTS
The first signal that France was preparing to pull out of the TFAI, after having possessed the former 'French Somali Coast' for some 114 years, came at the end of 1975, when France announced that a timetable was to be worked out for independence.[1] There followed months of jockeying between the ruling National Union for Independence (UNI) of the Gaullist chief minister, Ali Aref Bourhan, and the opposition African People's League for Independence (LPAI), the vehicle for rising nationalist sentiments stemming from grievances about the conduct of French colonial rule. As the departing French manipulated these sentiments to create a favourable climate for independence, Aref was abandoned by most of his UNI supporters and was eventually forced to resign.[2] In December 1976, France confirmed that a referendum on independence would be held in the territory.

A 'round-table' conference on the future of Djibouti was convened in Paris on 28 February 1977, involving four political factions: the LPAI, the Parliamentary Opposition (the UNI members who had bolted from Ali Aref), a second dissident UNI faction, and the Somali-backed Front for the Liberation of the Somali Coast

(FLCS). Those not invited to the Paris conference were Ali Aref and his remaining UNI supporters, the Ethiopian-backed Djibouti Liberation Movement (MLD), and a Marxist-Leninist Afar group, the Djibouti Popular Liberation Movement (MPL).

The conference decided on 19 March that a referendum and simultaneous elections for a new 65-member Chamber of Deputies would be held on 8 May. Independence would follow on 27 June. France would sign co-operation agreements with the new state, covering monetary support and cultural and military assistance. French financial aid would be maintained at the level of the pre-independence subventions (c. $120m in 1976). The optimism which prevailed after the announcement of these decisions was expressed by LPAI spokesman Ahmed Dini: 'Up to now, elections in our territory have constituted a factor of division. Now, they will permit us to unite.'[3]

A United Patriotic Front of five main political groupings was in fact formed in five days of talks, from 28 March-2 April in Accra (Ghana), held under the aegis of the OAU. Participating were the Afar parliamentary group led by Abdallah Mohamed Kamil (who had succeeded Ali Aref as President of the Council of Government); an LPAI delegation; the Marxist MPL, and the rival 'liberation' movements—the Somali-backed FLCS and the Ethiopian-backed MLD. While agreeing in principle to form 'a political organization embracing all the present political parties in the country', the Accra conference was not felt by observers to have sunk once and for all the differences among the groups over the results of the Paris round-table talks.

The TFAI Chamber of Deputies was dissolved by decree on 31 March, and a single list of 65 candidates agreed by the round-table participants was posted. France informed the OAU that its role would be limited to sending just six observers to monitor the referendum. The Arab League, to which Djibouti was expected to apply for membership after independence, was also planning to send observers.

The elections would be the first application of liberalized laws governing one of the most contentious issues in Djibouti, that of nationality. A law adopted in 1963, when France was trying to create conditions for an Afar 'majority' in the TFAI, restricted the eligibility for French nationality to persons born after 1942. This law was abolished in 1976, and those previously denied nationality were permitted to appeal. By the end of 1976, the number of people possessing French identity cards—a requirement for voting—had risen from 45,000 to 105,000.[4]

The two 'consultations'—the referendum and the elections—passed without incident. On the referendum question 'Do you wish the French Territory of the Afars and Issas to become independent?' the French Government reported the following results:

Registered voters	105,962
Votes cast	81,981 (77% of total)
YES votes	81,108 (98.7%)
NO votes	205
Spoilt ballots	668

Official results showed that 92.5% of electors voted in the (mostly-Issa) town of Djibouti itself; 99.3% of them voted 'yes'. In the mostly-Afar country areas, the turnout was down to 62.6% and the 'yes' vote to 97.7%, a faint indicator that enthusiasm of Afars for independence might be less than that of Issas.

The results of the legislative elections showed that 81,549 voters—76% of those eligible—cast ballots: 75,295 (92%) voted in favour of the single list of 65 candidates; 6,254 ballots were spoilt. The blank or void ballots were thought to represent supporters of the two Afar parties, the MPL and UNI, whose leaders charged after the voting that they had been intimidated. Of those elected, 33 were Issas, 30 Afars and two Arabs.

The last TFAI Council of Government was formed on 18 May under Hassan Gouled (61), president of the LPAI. The 16 portfolios (including three—Defence Justice and Foreign Affairs—for which France would hold nominal responsibility until independence) were distributed among eight Issas (including a member of the Gadabursi, a related Somali clan), seven Afars and one Arab.

COUNCIL OF GOVERNMENT OF THE TFAI (formed 18 May 1977)

President, in charge of Co-operation	Hassan Gouled Aptidon (Issa)
Planning and Development	Abdallah Mohamed Kamil (Afar)
Interior	Moumine Bahdon Farah (Issa)
Public Works	Omar Kamil Warsama (Gadabursi)
Rural Economy	Idris Farah Abaneh (Issa)
Education	Mohamed Ahmed Issa (Afar)
Civil Service	Hassan Mohamed Moyale (Afar)
Health	Ahmed Hassan Liban (Issa)
Labour and Vocational Training	Ibrahim Harbi Farah (Issa)
Finance	Ibrahim Mohamed Sultan
Commerce, Industry, Arts and Crafts	Mohamed Djama Elabe (Issa)
Industrial Administration	Ahmed Hassan Ahmed (Afar)
Youth, Sports and Culture	Hussein Hassan Banabila (Arab)
Ministers of State	
Defence and National Service	Djama Djilal Djama (Issa)
Justice and Prison Affairs	Ismail Ali Youssef (Afar)
Foreign Affairs	Ali Mahamade Houmed (Afar)

From 18 May, it was clear that Hassan Gouled would emerge as the Djibouti Republic's first President; he was thought to be a leader in the right place at the right time. Born in Djibouti in 1916, he had little formal education and once worked as a transport contractor. A career diplomat, Gouled represented Djibouti in the French Senate from 1952–58 and in the National Assembly in Paris from 1959–62. He returned to serve as Minister of Education under Ali Aref, but broke with him in 1967 to lead the campaign against French rule on the occasion of the French-run referendum in the TFAI. Gouled grew up with the LPAI and has been its president since 1972. A gentle-looking man who usually wears a white cap over his grey hair, he suffers from cataracts and fatigue.

Gouled was elected by acclamation by the Djibouti Chamber of Deputies on 24 June to be the first President of the new Republic.

The relative calm prevailing during the run-up to independence was briefly shattered on 21 June by an incident at Loyada, on the border with Somalia. Some 300 armed partisans of the FLCS, coming into Djibouti from Somalia for the independence celebrations, were stopped at the frontier by a French patrol. Two FLCS deputies in the Djibouti National Assembly went to Loyada to try and persuade the militants to disarm. Three days of negotiations ensued. At one point, shots were fired at the two MPs—Aden Robleh Awaleh, former FLCS secretary-general, and Ahmed Mohamed Hassan; both were seriously wounded. Finally, when the FLCS supporters agreed to take off their uniforms and give up their arms, they were allowed into the country. However, one of their leaders, Ali Guelle Dirir, known as 'Jannaleh', was found dead on the beach at Loyada the next day. An FLCS statement later said 'this accident could only have a political interpretation'.

(It was at Loyada on 3 February 1976 that FLCS guerrillas had hijacked a busload of French schoolchildren and clashed with French troops sent to rescue them.)[5]

The FLCS—dressed in uniforms similar to those of the new national army—were allowed to take part in the march-past during the independence celebrations; they had the additional pleasure of seeing the FLCS flag unfurled as the banner of the new Republic of Djibouti. This features two horizontal bands of green and blue, with a white triangle at the hoist, bearing at its centre a red five-pointed star.

INDEPENDENCE DAY, 27 JUNE 1977

The new flag was unfurled at 12.01 a.m. on Monday, 27 June 1977 accompanied by festive singing and dancing that went on through the night. Fifteen countries, including Ethiopia and Somalia, were represented at the ceremony, but none at Head of State level; some delegations had to be politely asked to stay away because of a shortage of accommodation. Among the participants in the celebrations were representatives of the MPL and UNI opposition. A long-time Afar leader, Chehem Daoud—a former associate of Ali Aref—served as master of ceremonies.

In a message marking the accession to independence of France's last mainland African possession, President Giscard d'Estaing said: 'For 20 years, France has conducted the decolonization of Africa south of the Sahara in a context of peace and dignity. 15 sovereign states have emerged out of this decolonization, the only one to have been carried through peacefully from beginning to end. . . . While renouncing all sovereignty, France is not abandoning Africa. True, decolonization is over and done with. True, France is not tempted by imperialism in any form. But we have powerful reasons for working together. The first is our knowledge of each other, which stems from living together. . . . The answer to this knowledge is co-operation; in other words, the joint endeavour to solve the difficult problems which confront you: education, health, agriculture, development. . . . I should like this complementarity between Europe and Africa to be expressed one day for all to see in a pact of solidarity setting the seal on the task of decolonization and opening the era of solidarity. It would lay down the rules of political and economic co-operation between Europe and Africa, as well as the principles of your continent's security, founded on respect for independence and on the right of each of its peoples to choose for itself the form of its political and social organization. Africa could thus avoid becoming the pawn of outside confrontations and being drawn into a ruinous armaments race. Those Arab states who wished it could become associates in this pact.'[6]

POST-INDEPENDENCE ACCORDS WITH FRANCE

Independence Day was also marked by the signing of a treaty, two accords, a protocol and three conventions regulating future co-operation between France and Djibouti. These included: 1) a treaty of friendship and co-operation; 2) accords on economic and financial co-operation; and 3) a provisional military protocol. The protocol established that France would maintain c. 4,500 troops at Djibouti and would have the right to intervene militarily, at the request of the Djibouti government, 'if the Republic of Djibouti was the victim of aggression and in the case of legitimate defence'.[7] French forces would be withdrawn gradually from the country, as its own defence force, drawn from the native ranks of the French forces, were developed. The first French units to leave would be the gendarmerie and the 13th half-brigade of the Foreign Legion, whose behaviour had frequently caused resentment in Djibouti.[8] It was agreed that, in the future, French forces would not take part in 'operations for the maintenance or restoration of order'.

The bigger question—crucial to the survival of the new Republic—was the level at which France would provide economic aid (see below). Still unanswered also was the outlook for the estimated 6,900 non-military French residents of Djibouti, whose presence created employment for tens of thousands of Djiboutians. There seemed to be no rush among them to leave. One French shipping agent who had lived there for 15 years said: 'To the individual Frenchman, it makes little difference whether he stays or goes because he never really had any commitment here, he never put down any roots.'

The French troops in Djibouti were placed briefly on alert on 2–3 July as a 'precaution' against reports of troop movements in Somalia. Sources in Paris said the military moves appeared to be related to Somali border tensions with Ethiopia and Kenya.

On 12 July, President Gouled named as his Prime Minister Ahmed Dini Ahmed (45), an Afar and former associate of Ali Aref (see below). This appointment laid to rest speculation that Gouled might exercise both top posts, and gave the first republican government of Djibouti a flavour of Afar-Issa collaboration. Under a decree promulgated on 27 June, Djibouti was to have a presidential regime, with the President acting as Head of State and head of government.

On 15 July, President Gouled named what was officially called a 'transitional government' which would have the task of 'determining budgetary needs and limiting expenses within the bounds of political austerity and financial equilibrium'. The Government comprised ten Issas or representatives of related clans (including the President himself and one member each of the Gadabursi and Issak clans), six Afars and one Arab. It also made a gesture to political balance by including, in addition to partisans of the ruling LPAI, a member of the FLCS (Aden Robleh Awaleh), a representative of UNI (Ahmed Youssef Houmed), and a former member of the MPL (Hamad Abdallah Hamad).

THE GOVERNMENT (as at 15 July 1977)

President	Hassan Gouled Aptidon (Issa)
Prime Minister, in charge of Territorial Administration, and the Creation of New Resources	Ahmed Dini Ahmed (Afar)
Port	Aden Robleh Awaleh (Issa)
Interior	Moumine Bahdon Farah (Issa)
Defence	Ahmed Hassan Ahmed (Afar)
Finance and National Economy	Ibrahim Harbi Farah (Issa)
Justice and Prison Affairs	Ismail Ali Youssef (Afar)
Foreign Affairs	Abdallah Mohamed Kamil (Afar)
Commerce, Transport, Tourism and Civil Aviation	Mohamed Djama Elabe (Issa)
Civil Service	Ahmed Hassan Liban (Issa)
Agriculture and Animal Production	Idris Farah Abaneh (Issa)
Industrial Administration	Ali Mahamade Houmed (Afar)
Public Works	Omar Kamil Warsama (Gadabursi)
Public Health and Social Affairs	Ahmed Youssef Houmed (Issak)
Youth and Sports	Hamad Abdallah Hamad (Afar)
National Education	Hussein Hassan Banabila (Arab)
Labour and Social Services	Djama Djilal Djama (Issa)

THE NEW GOVERNMENT

Fourteen of the 17 ministers had been members of the government formed in May, but this did not include Ahmed Dini Ahmed who had last been in government, as

Minister of Interior, in 1972. This Afar from Obock—described by *Le Monde* as a 'combative and intransigent nationalist'—had entered politics as a protégé of Ali Aref, whom he served as Minister of Production in 1962–64. He broke with Aref in 1965 and helped to form the Afar Democratic Union (UDA), which bitterly opposed Aref's 'collusion' with the French. During the 1967 referendum—when Afars and Issas were divided over the future of the territory—Ahmed Dini again rallied briefly to Aref and became Interior Minister. But he broke with him, this time for good, in 1970 and by 1972 was one of the most active leaders of the LPAI, serving as its official spokesman.

Another Afar minister who would become instrumental during the first troubled year of independence was Abdallah Mohamed Kamil (41) who had served as the last pre-independence head of government. Also from Obock and a former member of the UDA, he likewise had rallied to Ali Aref in 1967, only to break with him later, particularly over Aref's policy of rapprochement with Ethiopia. Married to an Issa, Kamil had served as secretary-general of Aref's last administration, replacing his old rival as President of the Council of Government on 31 July 1976. He was described as a quiet, capable and honest administrator, and almost an apolitical one who, 'while never having made a secret of his Afar patriotism, had acknowledged that Djibouti, an Issa town, could not be governed without the tacit agreement of Somalia'.[9]

Together with the appointment of the government, President Gouled announced the creation of an Economic and Social Development Planning Bureau and a Bureau of Information and Culture.

The new Minister of Finance and National Economy, Ibrahim Harbi Farah, died in hospital in Paris on 22 November 1977, aged 38.

FROM UNITY TO DISSOLUTION
Despite the relative harmony achieved in Djibouti's first Government and its serious efforts to deal with daunting economic problems, the Republic became a hostage within the first six months of independence to the crisis raging all around it. The fighting in eastern Ethiopia was to place an intolerable burden on Djibouti's meagre resources: the severance of the Addis Ababa-Djibouti rail line by Afar or Somali guerrillas in May (see Economy, below) totally disrupted the transit trade through the port of Djibouti and along the railway to Ethiopia, on which the majority of Djiboutians depended for employment. The war in the Ogaden sent c. 10,000 Somali refugees streaming into Djibouti (see Social Affairs, below). Moreover, the ethnic tensions between the Ethiopian regime and the Afars living in Ethiopia on the one hand, and the Somalis of the Ogaden on the other, were mirrored within Djibouti's divided Afar and Somali Issa communities.

Soon after independence, militants of the FLCS (now legalized in Djibouti by the inclusion of five FLCS deputies in the new Chamber of Deputies) discreetly opened training camps along the frontier with Ethiopia in readiness to join their 'brothers' fighting against the Ethiopians in the Ogaden. At the same time, and no doubt in response, militant Afars in Djibouti were rallying with their kinsmen across the border in Ethiopia in a striking new display of Afar solidarity. Outraged by the Gouled regime's soft line on the FLCS, Djibouti Afars sought to ship arms to a faction of Ethiopian Afars who were helping in the Ethiopian campaign against the Somalis in the Ogaden. In fact, most Ethiopian Afars have been alienated from the Dergue since a series of punitive attacks on Afar settlements in May and June of 1975. An Afar Liberation Front, with one wing based in Riyadh under the leadership of Ali Mirreh, the exiled former Sultan of Aussa (the hereditary Afar

101

homeland in eastern Ethiopia), and another in Mogadishu under his son Hanfare, has mounted persistent guerrilla action against Ethiopian road and rail routes crossing Afar country between Addis Ababa and the Red Sea.[10] But a minority of 'progressive' Afars, mostly from the Adoimara clan, have opted to collaborate with the Dergue, in exchange for guarantees of regional autonomy. They established links with the Marxist MPL in Djibouti, largely due to their common distrust of the Somalis.

Afar dissension in Djibouti surfaced on 16 October when two gunmen, identified as militant Afars, took over a Twin Otter aircraft of Air Djibouti on the runway at Tadjoura airport, in the mostly-Afar north of the country. The French pilot was shot dead, as was one of the ten passengers—the mother of Justice Minister Ismail Ali Youssef. Several others were wounded. The fate of the hijackers is not known. The attack was clearly aimed at Youssef, an Afar, who a short while before had acted to prevent the delivery of a consignment of Soviet-made Kalashnikov sub-machine guns destined for the anti-Somali Afar faction in Ethiopia. Officials identified the hijackers as members of a 'pro-Ethiopian' Afar faction. The question of the arms deliveries had created considerable tension between Prime Minister Ahmed Dini, also an Afar, and ministers who favoured Ethiopia against Somalia.

Another incident on 29 November reflected the spill-over of regional tensions into Djibouti. A French teacher was killed at Galafi, near the Ethiopian border, by a group of Afars armed with Kalashnikovs. The Government then ordered 25 French *coopérants* living in the hinterland to return to the capital.

President Giscard d'Estaing had previously expressed French anxiety about Djibouti's capacity to withstand the rising tide of conflict in the Horn of Africa. Receiving the credentials of Djibouti's first ambassador in Paris, Ahmed Ibrahim Abdi, on 1 September, Giscard said: 'The troubles afflicting its huge neighbours are already harming the fragile nascent economy of Djibouti. The French Government views with sympathy the efforts of President Hassan Gouled to maintain the new state amidst these regional quarrels.'

Djibouti's tense calm was shattered on the night of 15 December when two grenades exploded at Le Palmier en Zinc (the Zinc Palm Tree), one of the capital's most popular cafes. Six people, several of them French, were killed and 30 injured. The Government's reaction was immediate: President Gouled blamed the Popular Liberation Movement, ordered the MPL banned and its leaders arrested. He also warned all governments, especially Ethiopia, against 'receiving or training these criminal elements', and announced that 'vigilante groups' would be organized in all towns, quarters and villages to complement the security forces.

But on the day after the attack, an even greater crisis developed when the President was faced with the resignation of his Prime Minister, Ahmed Dini, and four other Afar Ministers—Ahmed Hassan Ahmed (Defence), Ahmed Youssef Houmed (Public Health and Social Affairs), Ali Mahamade Houmed (Industrial Administration) and Hamad Abdallah Hamad (Youth and Sports). They accused the Government of 'savage tribal repression' against the Afar people, 'bringing with it arbitrary rule and endangering national unity'. Ahmed Dini said he would rather 'suffer with [his] people' than be Prime Minister. Some 600 Afars were arrested in the aftermath of the attack at Le Palmier. In extensive searches made in Afar quarters and towns, a cache of grenades, rifles and pistols was uncovered.

The Djibouti authorities appeared to suspect Ethiopia of using dissident Afars to foment insecurity in Djibouti in order to weaken the French-backed Government's position. Increased Ethiopian influence in Djibouti would be useful to the Dergue in helping to ensure access to the port of Djibouti in the event of Massawa and Assab being totally denied to them by the Eritrean liberation forces. It would also be a source of leverage against both the Eritreans and the Somalis.

Ethiopia's reply to Gouled's charge of its involvement in the Palmier attack was forthright: 'At a time when the new Republic of Djibouti is trying to stand on its feet, certain external forces, like the so-called Front for the Liberation of the Somali Coast, which is a puppet of the Mogadishu regime, are weaving plots and conspiracies to disrupt the normal and peaceful development of Djibouti and to create chaos which will be conducive for foreign forces with expansionist aims to intervene and annex the Republic.'[11] The Voice of Revolutionary Ethiopia also broadcast a statement on 20 December from the 'Djibouti information office in Paris' expressing 'surprise' at the Government's 'hasty decision' in banning the MPL. The Ethiopian Foreign Ministry went further (according to a Tass report on 23 December) by 'denouncing the Djibouti Government's repression of the MPL'.

Somalia, for its part, accused Ethiopia of infiltrating terrorists into Djibouti, on which it had always had 'black designs'. It accused the Soviet Union of being behind a conspiracy to set up a pro-Soviet puppet regime in Djibouti as part of a projected pro-Moscow federation of states in the Horn of Africa.

The authorities on 28 December published the photographs of 17 people arrested in connection with the grenade attack, and listed ten people, all Afars, held principally responsible. On 29 December, it was announced that the key perpetrators of the attack—two Afars named Daoud Banoita Tourab and Mohamed Daoud Abada—had been arrested. They were said to have had six accomplices, all Afars. Arms had been discovered in the homes of seven other Afars, including a gendarme and a police inspector.

In response to the government crisis, President Gouled decided not only to reallocate ministries, but also to rule by decree. He formed a Special Commission of Afars, headed by the Foreign Minister, Abdallah Mohamed Kamil (one of only two Afars remaining in the Government). It also included three Afar deputies and the prominent Afar political figure, Senator Barkat Gourat, former leader of the Parliamentary Opposition group which had earlier broken away from Ali Aref. The Commission presented a list of grievances to Gouled on 5 January 1978, including the 'inequality' in Cabinet posts held by Afars and Issas and in the distribution of posts in the army, police and civil service. They also requested the release of Afars detained after the Tadjoura airport incident.

There was some consolation for President Gouled when the four ministers who had resigned with Ahmed Dini agreed to return to the Cabinet. The Government formed on 5 February 1978 was headed by Abdallah Mohamed Kamil, who in addition to the Premiership, retained his Foreign Affairs portfolio and acquired Defence as well. Secretaries of State were appointed to assist him in the two latter portfolios; the outgoing Defence Minster, Ahmed Hassan Ahmed—one of those who had resigned—was reappointed Secretary of State for Defence. The ethnic balance of the new Government was six Issas, six Afars, one Somali and one Arab.

If Africa's newest state was not exactly disintegrating less than nine months after its independence, it was evincing signs of strain that posed very real threats to its existence, particularly in view of the turmoil swirling around it. Djibouti's experiment in co-operative bi-nationalism had not so far succeeded. The Afars, perhaps 40% of the population, clearly felt that the supremacy they had enjoyed in the latter days of French rule was being replaced by Issa domination. They resented the alleged 'repressive' measures taken against them, especially while the Government sanctioned the clandestine actions of the FLCS. Ironically, these developments together with the larger ethnic dispute between the Ethiopians and Somalis,

103

have driven the Afars of Djibouti into an unofficial alliance with the very Ethiopian regime which had suppressed and alienated its own Afar population.

THE GOVERNMENT (as at 5 February 1978)

President	Hassan Gouled Aptidon (Issa)
Prime Minister, Foreign Affairs and Defence	Abdallah Mohamed Kamil (Afar)
Ministers:	
Justice and Prison Affairs	Ismail Ali Youssef (Afar)†
Port	Mohamed Ahmed Issa (Afar)
Industrial Administration	Ali Mahamade Houmed (Afar)†‡
Interior	Moumine Bahdon Farah (Issa)†
Youth and Sports	Hamad Abdallah Hamad (Afar)†‡
Finance and National Economy	Abdelkader Waberi Askar (Issa)
Agriculture and Animal Production	Idris Farah Abaneh (Issa)†
Labour and Social Services	Djama Djilal Djama (Issa)†
Civil Service	Ahmed Hassan Liban (Issa)†
Public Works	Omar Kamil Warsama (Gadabursi)†
National Education	Hussein Hassan Banabila (Arab)†
Public Health and Social Affairs	Ahmed Youssef Houmed (Afar)†‡
Secretaries of State:	
Foreign Affairs	Aden Robleh Awaleh (Issa)
Defence	Ahmed Hassan Ahmed (Afar)‡

†Held same position in previous Cabinet
‡ One of four ministers to resign

SOCIAL AFFAIRS
POPULATION, HEALTH AND EDUCATION

Djibouti gained independence with only rudimentary educational and health services for its estimated 220,000 people. Of these, 120,000–150,000 live in Djibouti town, while the rest lead a mostly nomadic existence. There were fewer than 100 physicians (one per 2,730 people), and fewer than 2,000 hospital beds (117 people per available bed). The illiteracy rate is estimated at 90%. There are 32 primary and secondary schools with an enrolment of c. 10,444 pupils. The birth rate is estimated at 42 per 1,000; the death rate at 7.6.

REFUGEES

President Gouled predicted on the eve of independence that the country's first major problem would be the influx of hundreds of refugees from Ethiopia. He was proved right, as the Ogaden war drove c. 10,000 refugees into Djibouti. At Dikhil and Ali-Sabieh near the border, camps were set up and administered by the UN High Commissioner for Refugees, which made $200,000 available and received additional assistance from international relief organizations. The refugees severely taxed the resources of Djibouti, which has to import all fresh food supplies for its own people.

FOREIGN AFFAIRS

The first countries to recognize Djibouti's independence, apart from France, were Ethiopia, Somalia, Egypt, Kuwait, Iraq, North Yemen, Tunisia and China. Britain, the Soviet Union, Saudi Arabia and the United States quickly followed.

The new Republic became the 49th member-state of the OAU and the 22nd member-state of the Arab League. (Only a tiny minority of its people are actually Arabs, but almost all are Muslim.)

RELATIONS WITH FRANCE
The former colonial power promised to continue to serve as a lifeline for the new state under the economic and military agreements signed on 27 June 1977 (see above). In addition to an annual economic grant equivalent to its colonial sub-vention, France was to maintain a force of c. 5,000 troops in Djibouti, 500 serving as instructors and advisers to a new national army. The French units comprise two regiments of ground forces, three combat companies, four maritime police patrols and an air detachment operating 12 F-100 aircraft.

RELATIONS WITH ETHIOPIA
Ethiopia officially welcomed the independence of Djibouti, declaring on 26 June 1977 that it was 'ready to safeguard the security and unity' of the new state. Accusing Somalia of continuing to claim Djibouti as part of its territory, the Ethiopian regime warned that the policies of 'the expansionist Government of Somalia not only place Djibouti's newly-won independence in serious jeopardy, but also worsen the already grave situation in the region'. [12]

RELATIONS WITH SOMALIA
Somalia's President Siyad Barre said in the week before Djibouti's independence that 'Somalia owes it to itself' to protect the new state's independence. He was later reported to have said that the Djibouti people should consider themselves to be natives of Somalia, and that Somalia would not require passports or travel documents of them. The ascendancy of the Issas in Djibouti's first nine months of existence and President Gouled's tough line against both his own Afars and alleged Ethiopian interference were obviously heartening to Somalia, which continues to nurture the hope of reclaiming this 'lost territory'. In welcoming Djibouti's independence, Mogadishu radio said it 'paved the way for the complete freedom of the Somali nation as a whole'.

RELATIONS WITH THE ARABS
As Djibouti sees in the Arabs its primary source of economic and diplomatic support, both Hassan Gouled and Abdallah Kamil were frequent visitors to Arab states during the year. Kamil said after Djibouti's acceptance into the Arab League that his country needed $300–500m in investment and technical aid. He described Djibouti's foreign policy as 'an Arab policy with regard to everything that was in the interest of the Arab nation—particularly where Red Sea security was concerned. Several Arab technical missions visited Djibouti to explore areas for investment and assistance. In September 1977, the President appealed to the Arab states to 'save Djibouti from economic catastrophe'. Saudi Arabia was reported to have con-tributed significant economic assistance in the state's first year of existence. The Arab League pledged $1m in financial aid; other assistance came from Iraq and Libya (see Economy, below).

RELATIONS WITH ISRAEL
To Israel, Djibouti's independence meant not only the installation of yet another 'Arab' state along the Red Sea, but also the possible loss of a major entrepot for its goods bound for Ethiopia.
At independence, Ahmed Dini confirmed that 'our policy toward Israel will be that of the Arab League. I would think that Israel cannot go on operating out of the port.' [13] It was estimated that 15 vessels of the Israeli shipping line Zim normally called at Djibouti each month; in 1976, Israeli traffic represented 5% of the tonnage

handled by Djibouti. *Le Monde* observed that the 'closure' to Israel of the Strait of Bab el-Mandeb—between Djibouti on the African side and South Yemen on the Arabian side—would be as serious as the closure of the Strait of Tiran, the access route from the Israeli port of Eilat to the Red Sea. As a precaution, Zim removed all its movable equipment from Djibouti.

ECONOMIC AFFAIRS (330 Djibouti francs = £1 sterling)
Djibouti's leaders expressed the hope after independence that the country would become a Hong Kong style 'free port' for its neighbours. It was necessary to harbour such hopes in order to evince the slightest optimism about the infant state's economic prospects. Starting off with virtually no economic resources (either agricultural or industrial), with an unemployment rate of 40%, with an artificial economy dependent on subventions from abroad and the spending of foreign nationals in the country, Djibouti proceeded to independence under the following additional handicaps: its only economic asset, its port, had declined in importance as Red Sea traffic increasingly bypassed it in favour of Aden or Jeddah; the port's primary function, as a trans-shipment point for goods bound to and from Ethiopia, became redundant after the Djibouti-Addis Ababa railway was put out of action by guerrilla attacks at the end of May 1977; another of the port's main customers, Israel, ceased to call after Djibouti joined the Arab League (see Foreign Affairs); and unemployment was expected to rise to as much as 80% with the gradual French withdrawal.

The number of ships using Djibouti (1,773 in 1976) fell from an average of 143 a month in the first six months of 1976 to 100 in the same period of 1977. Receipts fell in the same period from 750m Djibouti francs (DjF) to DjF 500m. Furthermore, it was only in the second half of 1977 that the impact of the railway's closure would be felt. With Ethiopian traffic halted (and c. 10,000 tons of Ethiopia-bound goods tied up on the quayside), the drop in port receipts was expected to be closer to 50%. Due to the continuing insurgency problem in eastern Ethiopia, from both Somali and Afar guerrillas, the completion in March 1977 of a road link to Addis Ababa, running roughly parallel to the railway, was not expected to have much effect.

The cessation of Ethiopian traffic meant unemployment at the port, which in its prime provided jobs for 2,500 Djiboutians—the territory's largest single employer. Jobs also dried up on the railway. This came at the same time as the new Government was seeking to 'rationalize' the ethnic balance of employment. Before independence, most dock and railway workers were Afars brought in from outside Djibouti town (a mainly Issa city), and the Government had promised to open up opportunities for employment of Issas. In anticipation of this, Somali workers were actually arriving in Djibouti from Somalia—pushing the number of jobless to c. 18,000. Most of Djibouti's workers are unskilled and, like their counterparts across the Red Sea in North Yemen, could conceivably find jobs in the Gulf states, but the Government's policy was to prevent the attrition of skilled and unskilled labour alike. On 21 July 1977, the Interior Minister said that passports would be granted only to politicians on official assignments, businessmen and those travelling for education or health purposes. 'If jobs turn up tomorrow and staff is not available, this will retard the country's development,' he explained. In order to increase local productivity, the Government also sought to ban the import (mostly from Ethiopia) and consumption of the stimulant *qat*. The President estimated the cost of *qat* consumption at DjF 4m a day, approximately a third of the Government's Budget.

Djibouti was all but totally dependent on external aid, primarily from France, Saudi Arabia and Iraq. The total annual French contribution is estimated at $140m a year. This includes grants and expenditures by the c. 10,000 French citizens in Djibouti, which amount to c. DjF 7,000m ($40m).

The UN Development Programme approved aid worth $850,000 in June 1977. Libya agreed to send experts to 'Arabize' the educational programme, rebuild schools, improve clinics and train police.

Exports in 1975—mostly live animals, hides and skins—earned c. $15m. Imports were worth c. $135m. The 1977 ordinary Budget was DjF 5,900m ($35m), compared with DjF 5,713m ($34m) in 1976. By the end of 1977, the Budget deficit was estimated at DjF 2,000m ($12m). In August, France contributed $22m to support the Djibouti franc and another DjF 172m in guarantees for currency in circulation.

Livestock and fishing are the only economic activities engaging the rural population of Djibouti; both are carried out in rudimentary fashion. Industry consists only of a liquid oxygen plant, a small construction materials company, two abattoirs, a meat processing plant, and a Coca-Cola and Pepsi-Cola bottling plant. There is no tourist infrastructure, with only six hotels offering combined accommodation of 118 rooms. Surveys of geothermal and mineral resources in the hinterland have proved disappointing.

1978 BUDGET

The 1978 Budget, presented to the National Assembly on 28 November, amounted to DjF 9,650m, 2.8% to be spent on debt servicing, 51.09% on staff, 25.02% on material and 3.2% on upkeep. Ahmed Dini said staff salaries were not high but the number of employees in the administration was excessive owing to arrested or substantially reduced activity in some economic sectors. For example, the building sector and the railway services were 'completely paralysed' so the Government had to try to find paid employment for the affected people. No new administrative posts were created except in national education and health. For remaining services, the 1977 allocations applied. The taxes created during the 1977 budgetary period (DjF 1,200m) covered part of the new expenses resulting from independence. Indirect taxation was substantially increased, except for the surcharge on *qat* (DjF 600m) which was abolished. [14]

TRADE WITH EEC COUNTRIES (thousand EUAs)

	1974	1975	1976
Source of Imports			
West Germany	23,314	939	1,162
France	19,198	30,447	20,692
Italy	1,047	872	1,759
Netherlands	1,455	1,706	2,215
Belgium-Luxembourg	788	915	1,124
United Kingdom	5,076	7,066	8,118
Ireland	148	1	64
Denmark	449	321	671
Total	**51,475**	**42,267**	**35,805**
Destination of Exports			
West Germany	25	106	1
France	389	4,127	583
Italy	645	379	413
Netherlands	19	34	6
Belgium-Luxembourg	101	—	—
United Kingdom	1,912	2,380	61
Ireland	—	—	—
Denmark	—	—	—
Total	**3,091**	**7,026**	**1,064**

Source: Statistical Office of the European Communities, *Monthly External Trade Bulletin.*

FOREIGN TRADE (million US dollars)

	1972	1973	1974	1975	1976
Exports	7	13	18	33	30
Imports	46	63	111	104	103

Source: IMF, *Direction of Trade, 1970–76.*

EXPORTS BY COMMODITY IN 1976 (in tonnes)

	Tonnage	%
Total of which:	**230,435**	**100**
Livestock	5,745	2.5
Pulses	29,397	12.8
Oil seed	4,298	1.9
Oil cake	7,477	3.3
Sugar	9,080	3.9
Molasses	20,283	8.8
Wax	300	0.1
Coffee	34,880	15.1
Other agricultural products	2,262	1.0
Skins and Hides	3,261	1.4
Miscellaneous	113,452	49.2

IMPORTS BY COMMODITY IN 1976 (in tonnes)

	Total	TFAI	Via Somalia	Via Ethiopia
Total of which:	**279,915**	**114,751**	**53**	**165,111**
Agricultural products	63,237	28,990	9	34,238
Food and Drink products	52,395	37,664	6	14,725
Petroleum products	8,595	7,892	—	703
Paper and textiles	32,205	6,222	3	25,980
Mineral products	18,177	14,806	1	3,370
Metal products	18,453	2,860	13	15,580
Electrical goods	11,705	3,004	6	8,695
Vehicles and transport equipment	14,007	4,373	1	9,633
Chemical products	52,389	4,277	13	48,099
'Special transactions'	8,752	4,663	1	4,088
of which: Arms	2,464	2,349	—	115

Source: *Marchés Tropicaux,* 24 June 1977.

NOTES

1. See *Africa Contemporary Record (ACR)* 1976–77, p. B427.
2. *ACR* 1976–77, p. B432.
3. *Le Monde,* Paris; 20 March 1977.
4. For a full discussion of the nationality question, see *ACR* 1976–77, pp. B434–5.
5. *ACR* 1975–76, p. B410.
6. *Le Monde,* 28 June 1977; also press release from French Embassy in London, 28 June 1977.
7. *Marchés Tropicaux,* Paris; 1 July 1977.
8. *ACR* 1976–77, p. B428.
9. *Le Monde,* 31 July 1977.
10. For a fuller discussion, see *Conflict in the Horn of Africa,* by Colin Legum and Bill Lee (London: Rex Collings, 1977). Also, chapter on Ethiopia.
11. Radio Voice of Revolutionary Ethiopia, 17 December 1977. (For details of this station, see *Press and Information* in chapter on Ethiopia.)
12. *Ibid,* 21 December 1977.
13. *Washington Post,* 29 June 1977.
14. *Africa Research Bulletin,* December 1977.

Democratic Republic of Sudan

By no means uncharacteristically for the Sudan, 1977 produced a number of quite unexpected developments—notably the return of Said al-Saddiq al-Mahdi, the former Prime Minister and leader of the Ansari Muslims, from exile in London. Then, when everything seemed to be set fair for a return to national reconciliation and stability, a major political upset occurred in the elections in the Southern Sudan in February 1978, which brought the downfall of Abel Alier's government there. While the new government is unlikely to change its relations towards the North, there were further unexpected developments in Khartoum. The early honeymoon with Said Saddiq had not gone as well as hoped, and he returned to London for a time in February 1978, but went back to Khartoum after a month.

Meanwhile, by early 1978 the Sudan appeared to have undergone another swing of the pendulum, reverting to many of the less satisfactory features of the political period before the 1970 military coup. These included the re-emergence of the politically divisive sectarian politics of the two Islamic groups, the Ansari and the Khatmia, as well as the official recognition given to the formerly clandestine Islamic Charter Front. Very little of the Left-wing revolutionary character of President Gaafar Numeiry's Revolutionary Command Council (RCC) appeared to have survived the changes of 1977.

Sudan came very close to the brink of war with Ethiopia in·July 1977, but by December an agreement was signed between the two neighbours setting them on the road to reconciliation. However, General Numeiry continued to pursue a policy of extreme hostility towards the USSR over its role in the conflict in the Horn of Africa, and generally to consolidate those trends in foreign policy established after the abortive 1973 coup: closer ties with Egypt and Saudi Arabia, a pro-Western and strongly anti-Soviet orientation. The year also saw major adjustments in economic policies and the beginning of a new Six-Year Development Plan.

The interdependence of these domestic, foreign and economic issues was specially marked during 1977. There was a growing realization that political stability cannot be maintained in the face of continuing economic difficulties, persistent outside pressures and internal opposition. The rapid economic development envisaged in the Six-Year Plan cannot be achieved without the uninterrupted flow of foreign investment, which in turn cannot be guaranteed unless stability is maintained. Equally, outside challenges and pressures—particularly from hostile pro-Soviet neighbours—cannot be effectively met or resolved without assistance from the West and pro-West Arab countries, and without the consolidation of the internal front and the economic base. Hence the mounting emphasis in 1977 on national unity, on the 'opening to the West' and on the economic 'big push'.

POLITICAL AFFAIRS

The most dramatic event of 1977 was the national reconciliation between President Gaafar Muhammad Numeiry and opposition elements led by Saddiq al-Mahdi. In many ways it was as unexpected and dramatic as Sadat's spectacular visit to Israel. Like Sadat's visit too, the issue of national reconciliation raised a whole series of new questions. Was it a desperate act on President Numeiry's part to try to consolidate his internal position at a time of serious external challenges and pressures by Libya, Ethiopia and, as he saw it, the Soviet Union? or was it a shrewd tactical move by him to sow division and discord within the opposition forces of the National Front? On the other hand, could it have been a tacit admission by Saddiq that armed and underground resistance to Numeiry's regime was no longer viable after the experience of 2 July 1976?[1] Or was it a preliminary move in an attempt to infiltrate the regime and undermine its institutions from within? Perhaps there were outside pressures for a reconciliation in order to maintain the kind of internal stability most conducive to economic growth and foreign investment. Or perhaps there was a secret deal between Numeiry and Saddiq to share power. If so, what would be the impact of such an agreement on their respective allies and supporters? To what extent, in fact, was it a natural coming together of two groups politically opposed in terms of the exercise of power, but whose class interests have nevertheless remained identical? More specifically, what kind of repercussions would the 'reconciliation' have on the delicate situation in Southern Sudan? Before examining how and why the move towards reconciliation took place, it is necessary to review the course of events that preceded it.

1977 began, like any other year, with the celebrations of Independence Day during which there was no let-up in the continuing denunciation of 'the treacherous Libyan invasion' of 2 July 1976. In his anniversary speech, Numeiry roundly condemned 'those agents who sold themselves to the devil in an attempt to come back and rule the people again'.[2] More surprising was a statement published in the local press by Ahmad al-Mahdi, Saddiq's uncle, in which he denounced 'the suspicious criminal moves aiming at the destruction of the Sudan and its people' and hailed 'the sincere efforts of President Numeiry to realize the welfare and progress of our country'.[3] At the time, many were puzzled by the attitude of Ahmad al-Mahdi. Few believed he had undergone a genuine conversion to the regime. The more likely explanation was that he was motivated to preserve whatever was left of the interests and welfare of the Mahdi's family. With Saddiq in exile—sentenced to death *in absentia*—it might have become incumbent on his uncle (who had been a political rival of his nephew in pre-1969 days) to assume the leadership of the Ansari Muslims in Sudan and to arrive at some sort of *modus vivendi* with the regime.

On 25 January, the 2,000-delegate Second National Congress of the ruling Sudan Socialist Union (SSU) convened in Khartoum. Officially, the function of the Congress was to participate in reorganizing the political machinery, to choose the Executive Bureau and the SSU Central Committee and, more important, to elect the President of the SSU for a six-year term—a position which automatically leads to nomination as Head of State. Numeiry, who was the sole nominee, was unanimously re-elected.

Although the main theme of the Congress was unity, it had hardly disbanded when news came of yet another 'coup attempt' in Juba, capital of the Southern Region. In the early hours of 2 February, mutinous members of the Air Defence Force occupied Juba airport for several hours before loyal troops recaptured it. Nine Sudanese soldiers and one American civilian pilot were killed.[4] The abortive mutiny came at an embarrassing time and seemed to be in sharp contrast with the atmosphere of national solidarity and unity which had emanated from the Second National Congress. The Government, however, lost no time in identifying those behind it. Abel Alier, Vice-President and Chairman of the High Executive Council for the Southern Region, declared that 'the Juba conspiracy was motivated by foreign powers'. The President was more specific; he pointed an accusing finger at 'the tripartite alliance of Saddiq al-Mahdi, [Philip Abbas] Qabush, and their sources of finance and planning in Tripoli'.[5]

In an interview in April 1977, Numeiry played down the 'Juba incident'. What had happened in Juba, he said, could not be described as an attempted coup or even a mutiny; 'it was simply an attempt at sabotage and disruption by an isolated few.

Their aim was to mar the celebrations of the fifth anniversary of Unity Day and thus to cast doubts on Sudan's national unity and stability.' This time, however, the President accused two of the exile National Front leaders, Sharif Hussain al-Hindi and Qabush, with Libya and Ethiopia behind them, of masterminding the attempt.[6] He emphatically denied that these repeated coup attempts indicated instability or even some basic flaw or malpractice in the political system. On the contrary, he argued, they were an indication that Sudan was moving in the right direction. When Sudan was 'the sick man of Africa' nobody bothered about it; but with its emergence as 'a dynamic force' in the continent, its enemies could no longer afford to ignore it.[7]

Nevertheless, the 'Juba incident' came as a rude reminder to the regime of potential dangers at a time when it had not yet recovered from the events of 2 July 1976. The regime seemed too readily anxious to explain away disturbances and setbacks in terms of 'conspiracies' hatched abroad. No serious mention was made of possible involvement of disaffected Anyanya guerrillas and/or diehard Southern separatist politicians who opposed the peace settlement. Instead, the regime readily linked what happened in Juba—which could very well have been a local and isolated affair—to a wider regional conspiracy involving Libya, Ethiopia and, indirectly, the Soviet Union. In any case, no concrete evidence was ever presented on the complicity of outside powers, or even of the Opposition leaders. Indeed, one would have thought that the South (a particular stronghold for the government whose people have no particular love for the politicians of the old regimes) would be the last place where they could attempt to stage a come-back to power.

The President announced another Cabinet reshuffle on 11 February 1977. The Prime Minister, al-Rashid al-Tahir Bakr, and most Ministers retained their posts. However, four senior Ministers—among them Mamoun Bihairi, the Minister of Finance, and Badr al-Din Suliman, the Minister of Industry—were removed. Notable among the new arrivals were Abd al-Wahab Ibrahim, who became Minister of Interior while still retaining his job as head of Public Security; and Dr Mansour Khalid, who returned to the post of Foreign Minister which he had first held from August 1971 to January 1975. Dr Mansour's reinstatement was widely interpreted as an indication of the government's determination to continue the policy of strengthening Sudan's relations with the West, especially with the US. The local verdict was that 'the reshuffle represented essentially a change in the executive and not a change in policy'.[8]

The national referendum on General Numeiry's second term as President was held in mid-April 1977. According to official figures, of 5,769,342 registered voters 5,672,507 went to the polls; of these 5,620,020 voted in favour and 48,377 against. The President's candidature was thus endorsed by a 98.3% vote.[9]

In May, the regime made a move towards decentralization in government. The President decreed the dissolution of the Ministry of People's Local Government and the splitting of the Ministry of Transport and Communication. In addition, a new Ministry of Energy and Mining was formed. In place of the dismantled ministry, a new office was created in the Presidency charged with ensuring greater participation in government at the local level. In August, the People's Local Government Act was amended to facilitate the process of decentralization, and during September, a series of 'enlightenment campaigns' were conducted to generate popular enthusiasm for the decentralization drive.

Despite the massive endorsement of the President in the April referendum (which opponents found too overwhelming to be entirely convincing), it was evident that the regime recognized the need not only for stronger political organization, but also for asserting its own legitimacy more positively so as to make a repetition of the all-too-frequent coup attempts less likely in the future.

It was in his inauguration speech in May that Numeiry made his first conciliatory gesture to the Opposition. He declared that the Sudan had decided 'in response to the efforts and good offices of friendly governments and individuals to welcome back all those who have been misled into committing crimes against their country'.[10] The gesture went almost unnoticed at the time. Few realized that it was directed specifically at the leadership of the National Front, including Saddiq; fewer still thought that Saddiq, who had only recently called Numeiry a 'mass murderer' and vowed to overthrow him, would be inclined to respond positively. In an interview in June, Numeiry stated that Saudi Arabia and other countries were behind his call for reconciliation. He asserted that he made his move from 'a position of strength and self-confidence', and hinted that 'some important personalities' in the Opposition had responded to his call for unity.[11]

Then in his monthly 'Face the Nation' television and radio address on 18 July, Numeiry announced that he had met Saddiq al-Mahdi on 12 July in Port Sudan. He asserted that he saw himself as 'the symbol of national unity', as 'the President not of a faction of the Sudanese people but of them all'. He was prepared to 'meet the devil himself' to make that unity materialize; his duties and responsibilites made it imperative to consolidate the unity of all Sudanese.[12]

From his exile home in London, Saddiq al-Mahdi confirmed his meeting with Numeiry. 'In politics', he said, 'there is nothing permanent.' With this confirmation, the question arose as to what an agreement between the two leaders would likely entail, or as one commentator put it, 'whose political funeral is it going to be'?[13]

Speculation was rife in Khartoum. According to one theory, Numeiry's reasons for taking this initiative were his dissatisfaction with the functioning of the SSU and his disappointment in the performance of some of his top political associates. At the time, one of the leading figures of the regime, Abu al-Qasim Muhammad Ibrahim—who was reportedly out of favour with the President even before the issue of national reconciliation arose—was outside the country; his absence was readily interpreted as a sign of his fall from grace. Some even claimed that he was in self-imposed exile in protest against the regime's reconciliation with the National Front.

Left-wing opposition forces had their own explanation for the moves towards national reconciliation. In a clandestine pamphlet dated 31 August, the Sudanese Communist Party (SCP) stated that 'there is no basic contradiction between the ruling authorities and the circles of capitalist development in the country. The Right-wing opposition aims at a limited change at the top confined to the removal of Numeiry and his clique while retaining the basic pillars of the social system.' The pamphlet attributed the move to internal and external factors, namely: the growing isolation of Numeiry's regime; the setbacks and strains sustained by the Right-wing opposition after 2 July 1976; and the economic and political pressures exercised by Saudi Arabia, directly and indirectly (through the Cairo-Riyadh axis), in co-ordination with American policy and the 'big monopolies' investing in Sudan.[14] In view of the changed balance of forces created by the move of the National Front from a position of opposition to one of negotiation, the SCP advocated the creation of a 'democratic front' open to 'all parties, organizations and personalities' to continue the struggle for democracy, basic human rights and 'the overthrow of dictatorship'.[15]

When the General Amnesty Act of 1977 was announced on 7 August, more than 1,000 political detainees were released. The Act offered amnesty to any Sudanese 'provided that he consents to submit to the provisions of the permanent Constitution of the Democratic Republic of the Sudan . . . and provided further that such a person agrees to return to the Sudan if he has been living abroad'.[16] Lists containing the names of 30 Opposition leaders who came under the Amnesty Act were published on 14 August. They included not only Saddiq al-Mahdi and Sharif Hussain al-Hindi, but also leading members of the underground SCP and of the Muslim Brethren.[17]

Despite, or perhaps because of, the persistent speculation and rumours, official pronouncements and newspaper editorials continued to strike reassuring notes. On 27 July, al-Ayam commented that the President's call for the people to rally around the SSU indicated that 'the revolution continues and we must carry on with the struggle for freedom, democracy and socialism'. Commenting on Libyan and Ethiopian broadcasts that reconciliation was conditional on certain concessions, al-Ayam declared on 1 August: 'The May Revolution stands on such solid ground that it is impossible for its enemies to change its direction or to deflect its objectives'. However, rumour and speculation persisted, fuelled no doubt by uncertainty about the nature and scope of 'national reconciliation'. Some of the regime's supporters, both northern and southern, openly voiced their concern at the risks involved in dealing with such seasoned and ambitious politicians as Saddiq al-Mahdi and Sharif Hussain al-Hindi. In August, an editorial in the official monthly, edited by the Minister of Information (a Southerner), called on Saddiq al-Mahdi and Sharif Hussain to 'reassure us' of their public recognition of the legitimacy of the May Revolution, and reminded them that they were welcome only as individuals: 'To do or to think otherwise would be to seek the legitimacy of the illegitimate and . . . the recognition of the illegal'.[18]

On 10 August, Dr Hassan al-Turabi, Secretary-General of the banned Islamic Charter Front, and Dr Ja'far Shaikh Idris, another Front leader, were appointed to the committee set up to revise the laws of the Sudan in conformity with Sharia law.[19] Both men were prominent leaders in the National Front and had only recently been released from imprisonment. There were also two other significant appointments to the committee—Ahmad al-Ahmadi and Said Ahmad al-Mirghani, the two sons of the famous old religious leaders who had for so long led the Ansari and Khatmia sects in bitter political hostility. To many it seemed that the return to the centre of politics of the scions of the Islamic sects might end the hope that religious sectarian politics (one of Numeiry's most striking achievements) had been permanently ended. Although Ahmad al-Mahdi is the uncle of Said Saddiq, the two had been strong political opponents in the old UMMA party. These appointments seemed to indicate the regime's intention to emphasize the role of Islam in the political system—a move which both Saddiq and the Muslim Brethren strongly advocate, and which the Saudis were bound to look upon approvingly.

Numeiry made another surprising move on 16 August by announcing the resignation of Muhammad al-Bagir 'for reasons of ill-health' from the post of First Vice-President, and the appointment of the controversial and supposedly self-exiled Abu al-Qasim Muhammad Ibrahim in his place. Abu al-Qasim was also to retain his powerful position as Secretary-General of the SSU.[20] The President's announcement was preceded by an angry attack on 'those with sick imaginations who spread malicious rumours and misleading lies'. He insisted that he made his move from a position of strength. His objective was not 'national reconciliation'; nor was it the building of 'national unity': it was to reinforce the potential of an already existing unity.[21]

Far from clarifying the situation, these developments seemed to confound an already confused public and to send speculation running in all directions. The exponents of a secret-deal 'theory', who had just been denounced as 'rumour-mongers', continued to argue that the deal was still on and that Abu al-Qasim had merely been 'kicked upstairs' in advance of being stripped of his powerful position as Secretary-General of the SSU. Others speculated that the deal, assuming there was one, was now definitely off; therefore Numeiry had to mend his bridges with the old guard and reassert emphatically, as he did, that he had made no concessions. In reality, the Government itself was largely to blame for the prevalent atmosphere of rumour and counter-rumour. For instance, during Abu al-Qasim's absence abroad in mid-July, there was a virtual black-out of news about his trip in the government-controlled Press, lending credibility to rumours of his imminent downfall. With his unexpected elevation to the post of First Vice-President, news about him immediately dominated the headlines, thus indicating a sudden change of attitude.

More seriously, the regime's insistence, underlined by the President's angry remarks of 16 August raised serious questions as to what exact role the Opposition leaders were expected to play upon their return to Sudan. Saddiq himself stated in London that his sole condition for meeting Numeiry was the release of political prisoners and the guarantee of civil and human rights in the Sudan. He also indicated that both parties had agreed to discuss 'substantive' topics and to find 'a new political formula to accommodate his proposals, the views of the Ansar sect as well as Numeiry's sytem of government'.[22] Saddiq endorsed the Addis Ababa Agreement (which had ended the civil war with the South)[23] and agreed that the pre-1969 multiparty system should not be resurrected. He suggested, however, that there was a need to increase Muslim influence in the South through intensified 'cultural intercourse' and to strengthen Islamic institutions in the country.[24] Such views seemed to coincide with the increasing Islamic orientation of the regime, underlined both by the establishment of the committee to adapt existing laws to the Sharia and by the inclusion of leading opposition elements in its membership.

The President sprang yet another surprise on 10 September when he sacked some of his leading Ministers, including Dr Mansour Khalid, the Foreign Affairs Minister, and al-Sharif al-Khatim, Minister of Finance and National Economy. Al-Rashid al-Tahir was removed from the Premiership and assigned instead to the Foreign Affairs Ministry. Numeiry himself took over the Premiership and the Finance portfolio.[25] The 'rumour-mongers' could hardly have been blamed if they saw in the removal of these two powerful Ministers, and in the demotion of Rashid al-Tahir, a confirmation of their 'theories'. The President's move clearly suggested the Premiership and the Finance Ministry were being kept vacant for Saddiq and al-Hindi respectively, posts which they had held in the pre-1969 period.

On the eve of his departure for home, al-Mahdi said in an interview that the July coup had taught both his National Front and Numeiry's SSU several important lessons.[26] The Front learnt that it could not topple Numeiry as easily as it had assumed, and Numeiry learnt that the opposition forces were stronger than he had allowed for. Both sides had come to realize that their policies of violent confrontation could be continued only by attracting external support, which resulted in strengthening foreign involvement in the Sudan's internal affairs. It had also taught all Sudanese that a society like theirs could only prosper under a system that allowed for adequate democratic participation by all the major political forces in the country. He concluded that the time had therefore come for Sudan to develop a new political system which would make non-violent political change possible. He disavowed any idea that he shared the aspirations of the Muslim Brothers, claiming that he himself rejected the notion of a theological state. He envisaged his own role as that of a leader providing ideas about how a new political system suitable for Sudanese needs might be evolved.

Saddiq al-Mahdi returned home to a hero's welcome by his supporters on 27

September. He reiterated his support of Numeiry's policies and called for the consolidation of unity through 'a genuine and unified stance towards democratic practices, basic human rights, Islamic legislation and real participation by all the Sudanese people at all levels in the task of national reconstruction'.[27] This new emphasis on the role of Islam increasingly became a source of grave concern—not only among non-Muslim Sudanese—that Islam might be accorded a special status in the political system.

In an interview in December 1977, Saddiq declared that Numeiry's initiative for reconciliation was 'realistic and I would not like to attach any value judgement on it'.[28] In order to resolve political differences, a 'consensus' had become imperative—a consensus which would better serve the cause of stability, development and non-interference by third parties. According to Saddiq, it is possible to construct a system based on consensus without necessarily allowing a multiplicity of political parties. But in working for such a consensus-based system, Islam has a significant role to play—'a role which can be ignored only at the risk of wasting a major social force'. Saddiq expressed his conviction that Islam could be revived and made to apply in modern society 'without impairing the religious autonomy of non-Muslims'.[29] Numeiry emphatically asserted that Saddiq's return would not constitute any deviation from the declared objectives of the regime. But what about Islamic legislation? According to the President, making Islam the major source of legislation would not mean the enforced conversion of non-Muslims. 'We are giving them what in Islamic law is good for the people here.'[30]

However, the increasing religious orientation of the regime, particularly in setting up the committee to review Sudanese laws in conformity with the Sharia, aroused some fears about the implementation of the Islamic constitution. In an editorial in *Sudanow*, Bona Malwal, a Southerner and Minister of Information and Culture, wrote: 'The recent addition of a few extremist names to the membership of the committee, although welcomed as part of the national reconciliation effort and therefore necessary, has complicated the public view of the committee's work, and may indeed have reinforced some people's fears.' The editorial called on the committee to ensure the operation of the principle of 'religion to the individual and the country to all'.[31] In another article published in *Sudanow*, Dr Abdullahi al-Na'im, a Muslim Northerner and lecturer in the Faculty of Law, University of Khartoum, called for the immediate dissolution of the committee because it was likely to be exploited by sectarian and extreme Right-wing elements. He argued that traditional Sharia could not be reconciled with modern constitutional government since most of its detailed rules were based on three fundamental inequalities: political, economic and social. 'Anyone who maintains otherwise is either unfamiliar with the basic principles of traditional Sharia or is playing a huge political confidence trick.'[32] Joseph Lagu, the former leader of the Anyanya rebels and Commander-in-Chief in Southern Sudan, said in an interview that the adaptation of Sudan's laws to the Sharia was being viewed 'with great concern' in the South, and that to give any religion priority in Sudan would cause 'discomfort'.[33]

Thus, as 1977 drew to a close, fears about the Islamic orientation of the regime and uncertainties surrounding the whole issue of national reconciliation remained unresolved. The situation was further complicated when, in an interview with the Lebanese newspaper *al-Nahar* in November, Sharif Hussain al-Hindi ruled out the possibility of his early return to the Sudan, and hinted strongly that the regime had reneged on its agreement with the Opposition. He gave a pessimistic appraisal of the country's economic situation and made his return conditional on some drastic changes in certain policy aspects related to the joint defence pact with Egypt, the existing security laws, and the foreign and economic orientation of the regime.

The President announced the dissolution of the People's Assembly on 14 December, with elections for the new Assembly scheduled for January 1978. The election rules stipulated that every candidate had to secure endorsement by the SSU and refrain from campaigning along party or sectarian lines. However, there appears to have been an understanding that none of the prominent SSU or National Front personalities would contest the elections. This made it difficult to analyse accurately the significance of the results announced in February 1978. However, it was immediately clear that many of those elected to the new Assembly were prominent old traditionalists like the Chief of Dongola and two of his sons who had remained carefully in the background during the radical years of the RCC.

It is, perhaps, characteristic of 1977 that the year ended with renewed speculation that the move towards national reconciliation had come to a dead end; that the Muslim Brethren faction in the National Front had definitely defected to the regime; and that Saddiq seemed to be unhappy with the existing state of affairs.

By early 1978, with Said Saddiq's role still unclarified, it appeared that the task of effecting a reconciliation was perhaps more difficult than either of the two leaders had foreseen. Nevertheless, neither seems to have been daunted. In March, there was a report that a Council on Policy was to be set up on which both Numeiry and Said Saddiq would serve, together with a number of their prominent supporters.

SOUTHERN SUDAN
1978 REGIONAL ASSEMBLY ELECTIONS

The elections held early in 1978 for the Southern Sudan Regional Assembly turned the political situation almost upside down. Seven of the 15 Regional Ministers in Abel Alier's High Executive Council were defeated, causing Alier himself to resign as chairman, though still remaining a Vice-President of the Sudan. Prominent among those defeated were Hilary P. Logali, the Speaker of the Regional Assembly and an Assistant Secretary-General of the SSU; Mading de Garang, Information and Culture; Ali Tamim Fartak, Youth and Sports; Dr Gamma Hassan, Agriculture; Lubari Ramba, Public Service; and Dr Oliver Albino, Housing. A number of the most outspoken critics of the Alier administration (some of whom had been in detention) were elected. They include Clement Mboro, Joseph Oduho, Benjamin Bol and Ezboni Mundiri. Mboro, who had been Minister of Interior in Said Saddiq's government, became the new Speaker.

An initial analysis suggests that the results were caused by at least three factors. First, a sense of frustration over the relative lack of development which was blamed on insufficiently militant leadership in forcing greater concessions from Khartoum. Second, some disillusionment over nepotism and alleged corruption in the administration. Third, a successful assertion by the Dinka group associated with the Sudan African National Union (SANU), formed by the late William Deng, which was one of the two wings of the Anyanya liberation movement. It seems that the former commander of the Anyanya and later chief of the Southern Sudan Military Command, Gen Joseph Lagu, was closely identified with the swing against Abel Alier's leadership. Lagu himself (who is on close terms with General Numeiry), succeeded Alier as chairman of the new High Executive Council. While the election outcome is likely to result in greater Southern pressures on Khartoum for higher development fund allocations, it seems most unlikely that the basic relations between the North and the South will change, especially as Gen Lagu is a strong protagonist of unity. Nor is it likely to affect the position of prominent Southerners in the Government such as the Minister of Information and Culture, Bona Malwal Madut Ring, or Minister of State for Foreign Affairs, Dr Francis Deng.

FIVE YEARS OF AUTONOMY

'The eagle with the broken wing' was the description of the Sudan used by one of the earlier generation of Southern politicians, Buth Diu. The broken wing was the South; without it, he argued, the great Sudanese bird could not fly. That truth finally brought the 17-year old civil war to an end and produced the Addis Ababa Agreement of 23 February 1972[34] which allowed a considerable measure of regional autonomy to the three Southern provinces—Upper Nile, Equatoria and Bahr al-Ghazal—with their capital in Juba. (These were sub-divided in 1976 to create three additional provinces: Lakes, Jonglei and Western Equatoria.) The anniversary of the first five years of the new South's autonomous relationship within a federal Sudan was a time for celebration and stocktaking on 23 February 1977.[35] President Numiery said the trial period had shown the value of building unity 'on the basis of diversity which enriches it, and makes regional self-government the pillars of unity'. The Vice-President of the Republic and Chairman of the South's High Executive Council, Abel Alier, recalled how his new government began five years earlier with only one borrowed car, eight civil servants and one office; now the Regional Government has 1,054 heavy duty vehicles and small cars and 16,460 employees; a new block of government offices is almost completed at New Juba. Two of the major tasks, he said, had been to re-establish the value of 'tilling the soil'— in which even the 'man in the necktie' and the *effendiat* had set an example; and to get people to abandon their old traditions of living far apart. In Western Equatoria, the habit had been to move to new land every time a husband or wife died; in Eastern and Western Equatoria and Bahr al-Ghazal, it was because people were haunted by fear of being poisoned by their neighbours; while in Bahr al-Ghazal, Jonglei and Upper Nile, people would not settle near their in-laws 'for fear of being exposed and·shamed by their actions and social weaknesses'.

While the consensus of the stocktaking was that the new constitutional experiment was living up to expectations, most Southerners still felt that the two continuing weaknesses were the inadequate flow of funds from Khartoum and poor communications. Although an ILO report had recommended that a minimum of £S 70m be spent annually in the South, in fact an average of only £S 10.8m was provided in the first five years. However, the new Six-Year Plan proposes to spend £S 180m during the period in development funds alone. Meanwhile, local self-generated revenue provides only 20% of the Region's present total expenditure.

OPPOSITION ELEMENTS

Opposition elements in the South continue to criticize the Northerners for parsimony and lack of goodwill; they accuse the more influential Southern leaders of failing to use their positions more effectively to compel Khartoum to give a better deal to the South, especially since it has become a vital power-base for President Numeiry's regime.

During the past five years, opposition has come from diverse sources. There were pockets of localized opposition, as in Nuer in 1973–74, where five *kujurs* (prophets)—Kai Riek, Ruei Kuic, Goni Yut, Matai and Tut Kuac—sought to establish their local power. Kai Riek was shot by the army in 1974, and the others surrendered. Some elements among the former Anyanya have also mutinied—most seriously in Wau in February 1976. Two former Anyanya political leaders, Gordon Mortat and Aggrey Gadein, refused to accept the Addis Ababa Agreement and remained in exile; but Gadein finally relented and returned home in 1977. An attack by well-armed Bagarra Arab tribesmen on a Dinka settlement in March 1977 has not yet been properly explained. The incident occurred just north of the regional border and resulted in 300 Dinka men, women and children being killed; the official explanation was that it was simply a tribal vendetta. The Bagarra Arabs are mostly members of the Ansari sect. An exile group which calls itself The Serving Movement for the National Independence of the Immatong Republic, declared itself in favour of the South's complete independence.[36]

An attempt was made in 1975 to get the Assembly to pass a motion of no confidence in Abel Alier's government; this was led by four prominent political leaders—Joseph Oduho, Clement Mboro, Benjamin Bol Akok and Philip Pedak Lieth. The former two were arrested and were in detention up to the elections; the latter two fled to Ethiopia from where they are believed to have had a hand in the insurrection of February 1977 (see above). 'We in the South want nothing less than independence', Lieth declared in a statement in 1977.[37] The alleged leader of the plot, Sergeant Paul Deng, and 98 others were brought to trial in July 1977 accused of attempting to overthrow the Government and Constitution, but their trial was adjourned.

Southerners showed signs of being worried in 1977 by Numeiry's new commitment to strengthening the role of Islam throughout the country—a source of historic suspicion as the Southerners are mainly Christian and animist. These tensions are discussed above.

Another potential source of conflict is the ambitious Jonglei project (see below), although Abel Alier remains a vigorous champion of the great benefits which he believes will accrue from it to the people in the Sudd.[38]

The new University of Juba, which opened with 120 students in October 1977, was criticized in some quarters in the South as being no more than 'a glorified technical school' since it is heavily oriented towards vocatiohal training. This view was strongly condemned by Bona Malwal as failing to recognize the contribution it could make to the real needs of the South for reconstruction. He also saw the university as important in the development of a two-way flow of intellectual life between the North and the South.[39]

DEFENCE AND SECURITY

On 12 May 1977, the Sudan finally broke off all its military ties with the USSR which over the previous seven years had supplied the bulk of its military equipment and training. Arms procurements now come mainly from the West, with considerable economic support from Saudi Arabia, Abu Dhabi and Kuwait. Sudan expects to buy $500m worth of Western arms. Britain, which supplies some military trainers, offers an open market for Sudanese military purchases; the US has agreed to provide the country with arms aid as well as the right to buy aircraft and other requirements. In December 1977, Washington agreed to supply 12 Northrop F-5 fighters in addition to the previously agreed sale of six Lockheed C-130 transport planes at a cost of $74m, to be paid for by Saudi Arabia. US arms deals are expected to reach $80m by the end of 1978. (For arms purchases from France, see below: Foreign Affairs.)

Following the establishment of the Sudan-Egypt-Syrian Joint Military Command, the Sudan joined the Arab Military Industries Organization based in Cairo (see also chapter on Egypt).

THE ARMED FORCES

Total armed forces number 52,100; military service is voluntary. The Army, which numbers 50,000, has two armoured brigades, seven infantry brigades, one parachute brigade, three artillery regiments, three air defence artillery regiments, and one engineer regiment; 70 T-54, 60 T-55 medium tanks; 30 T-62 light tanks (Chinese); 50 Saladin, 45 Commando armoured cars; 60 Ferret scout cars; 100

BTR-40/-50/-152, 60 OT-64, 49 Saracen armoured personnel carriers; 55 25-pounder, 40 100mm, 20 105mm, 18 122mm guns and howitzers; 30 120mm mortars; 30 85mm anti-tank guns; 80 Bofors 40mm, 80 Soviet 37mm and 85mm anti-aircraft guns. (AmX-10 armoured personnel carriers are on order). A force of 1,000 is deployed in the Lebanon with the Arab Peacekeeping Force. The 600-strong Navy has three patrol boats (ex-Iranian), six large patrol boats, six small patrol craft (ex-Yugoslav) and two landing craft. The Air Force, numbering 1,500, has 27 combat aircraft, one interceptor squadron with ten MiG-21 MF, and one fighter, ground-attack squadron with 17 MiG-17 (ex-Chinese). Armaments include five BAC-145 and six Jet Provost Mk 55, three Pembroke (in storage), one transport squadron with five An-24, four F-27, one DHC-6, and one helicopter squadron with ten Mi-8. 15 Mirage fighters, six C-130H, four DHC-5D transports and ten Puma helicopters are on order. A total of 3,500 paramilitary forces are deployed as follows: 500 National Guard, 500 Republican Guard, and 2,500 Border Guard.[40]

THE GOVERNMENT (as at 1 March 1978)

President, Minister of Finance and Economy	Gen Gaafar Muhammad Numeiry
First Vice-President and SSU Secretary-General	Abu al-Qasim Muhammad Ibrahim
Vice-President and Minister of Foreign Affairs	Al-Rashid al-Tahir Bakr
Vice-President	Abel Alier
Ministers:	
Interior and Chief of Public Security	Abd al-Wahab Ibrahim
Energy and Mining	Mamoun Awad Abu Zayd
Irrigation and Hydroelectric Power	Yahia Abdul Majid
Trade and Supply	Haroun al-Awad
Co-operation	Dr Muhammad Hashim Awad
Defence and Commander-in-Chief	Lt-Gen Bashir Muhammad Ali
Industry	Dr Bashir Abbadi
Social Affairs	Dr Fatma Abd al-Mahmud
Public Service and Administrative Reform	Karamallah al-Awad
National Planning	Nasr al-Din Mustafa
Youth and Sports	Zein al-Abdin Abdul Gadir
Transport and Communications	Abdul Rahman Abdalla
Education	Dafalla al-Haj Yousif
Religious Affairs and Waqfs	Dr Awn al-Sharif Gasim
Health	Khalid Hassan Abbas
Agriculture, Food and Natural Resources	Prof Abdalla Ahmed Abdalla
Culture and Information	Bona Malwal Madut Ring
Presidency	Dr Baha al-Din Mohamed Idris
Construction and Public Works	Muawia Abu Bakr
Attorney-General	Dr Hassan Omer
Ministers of State:	
Egyptian Affairs in Sudan	Izzel Din Hamid
Finance and National Economy	Osman Hashim Abdul Salam*
Foreign Affairs	Dr Francis Deng
Culture and Information	Dr Ismail al-Haj Musa
Youth and Sports	Ali Shummu
Education	Hassan Ahmed Yousif
in the Presidency	Khalid al-Kheir

*Appointed Finance Minister in March 1978, relieving the President of this portfolio.

HIGHER EXECUTIVE COUNCIL OF THE SOUTHERN REGION (as at 1 March 1978)

Chairman of the Council	Joseph Lagu
Deputy Chairman and Regional Minister of Administration, Police and Prisons	Samuel Arou
Regional Ministers:	
Agriculture, Irrigation and Mineral Resources	Benjamin Bol Akok
Finance, Planning and Economy	Lawrence Wol
Trade, Industry and Supply	Ezekiel Kadi
Tourism	Samuel Tot
Rural Development and Co-operation	Simon Mori
Communications and Transport	Joseph James Tonbara
Health and Social Welfare	Pacifico Lolik
Youth and Sports	Daniel Kot Mathews
Public Service and Administrative Reform	Mathew Yor
Housing and Public Utilities	Barnaba Dumo
Council Affairs	Father Niro Larib
Legal Affairs	Samuel Lupai
Whip (Raid), Regional Assembly	Philip Yona

SOCIAL AFFAIRS

LIVING STANDARDS

The official cost of living index prepared by the Department of Statistics shows a rise of c. 20% a year since 1970. A report by the economic committee of the Sudan General Federation of Trade Unions, prepared in early 1977, examined the movement in prices of essential commodities for the years 1974–75 and 1975–76. It reveals that sesame oil has increased from 10pt to 20pt a pound, wheat from 40pt to 80pt a ruba, and waika (dried okra) from £S 1.20 to £S 2.00 a ruba. Though the price of some commodities—notably dura and sugar—remained relatively stable, the overall impression is of real rises far in excess of the official figures. The report also points out that transport costs have risen between 100% maximum and 10% minimum, according to area, over the same period. Rents, too, have risen by up to 50% since 1973. The Trade Unions conclude that if present prices are compared with those existing before July 1974, the ratio of increase is 98%. Since the maximum increase in wages is 17%, the actual decrease in workers' incomes is 81%. The statutory minimum wage in Sudan in 1977 was £S 16.50—unchanged since 1975, although wage rates prevailing in the market are difficult to assess. Public sector wages are paid in seven bands ranging from £S 16.50 a month for a newly-employed unskilled man to a maximum of £S 70.05 a month. To reach the top end of the scale, a worker must have special training in a particular skill and at least 20 years service according to an official from the Labour Department.

When President Numeiry returned from the OAU summit in Gabon in July, he launched a serious attack on the problem of rising prices. In his 'Face the Nation' programme broadcast on 19 July, he devoted a great deal of time to explaining how the difficulties arose, and what measures were being taken to stop price rises in sugar, bread, petrol, salt and meat. He argued that shortages 'are mainly caused by defects in the distribution system' which allowed profiteers to sell at high prices on the black market. Certainly, since ex-factory prices are controlled, it is in the wholesale and retail areas that price additions are most easily made. In August, the First Vice-President Abu al-Qasim went further, suggesting that high prices and shortages were artificially created by black marketeers hoarding commodities. He urged citizens not to pay black market prices, and to report any deviation from the official price. The President also pointed out that many people were making excessive profits on imported goods. There are strict controls on such transactions; the invoices and selling prices have to be presented to the authorities. But loopholes still exist. [41]

EDUCATION
Two new universities were opened during 1977—at Gezira and Juba (see Southern Sudan above). The University of Khartoum adopted a new two-semester year, with examinations held at the end of each semester. However, pressure for university places continues to be a major problem. This is relieved to some extent by rigorous standards in marking examination papers for the school-leaving certificate. Of 35,157 higher secondary school students who sat their examinations in 1977, only 16,723 were passed. Failure in Arabic or two other subjects meant disqualification.

There has been considerable public debate over the value of students training abroad, with complaints that much of their education fails to equip them for suitable employment. [42] Britain provides 80-100 education grants annually; West Germany 70; the USSR 35; Japan 25; East European and EEC countries between 5-20 each.

STUDENTS ABROAD 1976-77 [43]

WHAT THEY STUDIED

Engineering and industry	300
Agriculture, Irrigation, and Veterinary Sciences	269
Medicine	135
Economics	74
Journalism, TV and Radio	61
Law	42
Public Administration and Personnel Management	29
Geology and Mining	24
Business Administration	15
Others	630
Total	1,579

WHAT LEVEL

Technical training	257
University degree	40
Post graduate	1,282
Total	1,579

WHO PAID

Government scholarships	938
Foreign grants	641
Total	1,579

PRESS
The Council of Ministers established a Journalists' Union by a special Act, with the aim of raising the standard of journalism and promoting members' rights. A registration committee will decide who is entitled to qualify as a journalist; newspapers and news agencies will in future only be allowed to employ those registered. It remains to be seen whether this proposal will be used negatively to disbar certain journalists from seeking employment.

FOREIGN AFFAIRS
Sudan's foreign relations in 1977 were closely linked to domestic developments. In his address on the anniversary of Independence Day, the President denounced 'the repugnant role of some neighbouring regimes' in harbouring and encouraging 'elements hostile to the Sudan', and threatened to use Ethiopian and Eritrean refugees to 'export unrest and problems to Ethiopia'. [44] Early in January 1977, an

Ethiopian army unit of 96 men took refuge in Sudan after it ran out of supplies. On 8 January, the Ethiopian government officially asked for their repatriation, claiming that they were not engaged in any hostile activity against the Sudan. [45] Khartoum's reaction was to refer again to continued hostile action by Ethiopia and Libya, and to remind both countries that the joint defence pact between Egypt and Sudan[46] 'embodies and confirms the shared belief that the security of the two countries is a joint responsibility'. [47]

There was official concern in Sudan over the riots and disturbances which took place in Cairo in late January 1977. Numeiry condemned 'subversive designs' against Egypt, blamed Libya for them, and appealed to the Arab countries to offer material aid to Egypt.

The Soviets' growing support for Libya and Ethiopia led to increasingly antagonistic statements by Numeiry on Russian involvement in Africa. The official view in Khartoum was that events in and around Sudan were interrelated: they were part of a co-ordinated strategy by the Soviet Union to undermine the Sudanese and Egyptian regimes which constituted a barrier to Soviet expansionism.

In late February 1977, President Sadat and President Asad of Syria arrived in Khartoum for a tripartite summit in which they agreed to create a Unified Political Command. The joint communiqué issued after the meeting stated that the three Presidents focused their discussion on issues related to the Arab world and to the security of the Red Sea, and emphasized their keenness to keep the area outside great power pressures and manoeuvres. [48]

The Khartoum mini-summit could also be seen as fitting into the emerging pattern of the 'moderate' Arab states establishing formal alliances for political and economic co-operation, and to act as counterweights to the 'militant' Arab camp. For Sudan, membership of this new alliance came at a critical time when the country appeared isolated in the region and was facing internal opposition backed by Libya and Ethiopia. [49]

The origins of Sudan's problems with Libya and Ethiopia can be traced not only to domestic factors but to the wider context of Arab politics. For one thing, the quarrel with Gaddafy began when Sudan refused to endorse his pan-Arab line and opted out of the Tripoli Charter. The Libyan leader might have been concerned with the defection of a country that, in his view, could have been the bridgehead of Arabism in Africa. It is more likely, however, that he was mainly interested in Sudan as 'a kind of soft underbelly in an operation essentially aimed at Egypt, the pivot of the Arab world'. [50]

The difficulties with Ethiopia originated basically from the Eritrean problem—a running sore in bilateral relations. The situation was compounded by the emergence of new patterns of alignments in the Horn of Africa, and by Moscow's active support of the Addis Ababa military regime. Moreover, the Eritrean insistence that the Israelis have bases on the islands of Halib and Fatma, south of the port of Assab, has helped to link the question of Red Sea security to the Arab-Israeli conflict. According to David Greig, 'unified Arab control of the waterway would obviously strengthen their negotiating hand at the proposed Geneva conference. . . . and deter the Israelis from any pre-emptive strike on the Arab front-line states.' [51]

The situation in the Horn of Africa, particularly in Ethiopia, became (as one high-ranking source in Khartoum put it) 'a pivotal point in Sudan's foreign policy'. Obviously, the Sudan was directly affected both by the constant flow of Eritrean and Ethiopian refugees (more than 150,000 during 1977), and by the presence of Sudanese opposition elements (estimated at more than 2,000) in training camps in Ethiopia. But Khartoum stressed that developments in the Horn had now become an Arab concern rather than a strictly Sudanese one. Accordingly, the emphasis of Sudanese policy was on Red Sea security which Khartoum believed could not be regarded separately from the security of the Indian Ocean and the Mediterranean.

President Numeiry made a tour of Gulf and Red Sea littoral states in March 1977; on his initiative, the Presidents of the People's Democratic Republic of Yemen (PDRY) the Yemen Arab Republic (YAR), Somalia and Sudan, met in Ta'izz and agreed on the need to convert the Red Sea into 'a lake of peace'. The objective behind the Sudan's Red Sea initiative was to construct a Pan-Arab policy and a united Arab bloc, backed by Saudi Arabia, that would guarantee the Red Sea area against super-power involvement and Israeli infiltration. For Sudan, such a formidable bloc would have special advantages: not only would it act as a counterweight to the 'militant' camp of Arab regimes, but it would also make external aggression and/or internal subversion against the Sudanese regime less likely.

Numeiry's Red Sea diplomacy included an invitation to Somalia to join the Joint Political Command of Egypt, Sudan and Syria—a not too subtle attempt to wean the Somalis away from the Soviets; they were then still receiving Russian military support, but were already beginning to be worried about Moscow's shift to Ethiopia. Somalia's later active involvement in the Ta'izz conference was therefore important. President Siyad Barre praised Sudan's initiative and endorsed his call for a united Arab strategy.[52]

In April, Ethiopia sent a strongly-worded message accusing the Sudan of 'invading Ethiopian territory' and of providing military support to internal dissidents. Khartoum denied the accusation, claiming that it represented 'a futile attempt to cover up the repeated internal defeats sustained by the regime in Addis Ababa'.[53] It was an open secret, however, that the Sudanese regime was giving active support to the Eritrean Liberation Front and the Ethiopian Democratic Union.

In mid-April, Khartoum was anxiously awaiting the outcome of the fighting in Zaire's Shaba province. In Numeiry's mind, the events in Zaire were not seen as a local or isolated occurence; certain parallels were readily found between the 'Shaba invasion' and the Libyan-backed coup attempt in Sudan in 1976. During his visit to the US in April, Foreign Minister Mansour Khalid implied a possible Libyan-Ethiopian-Soviet involvement when he stated that if Sudan was unable to aid Zaire militarily, it was because Sudan was defending itself against the same forces that were trying to overthrow President Mobutu.[54] There were fears in Khartoum that if the 'invasion' succeeded, it would add a third hostile neighbour on the sensitive Southern border—the others being Uganda and Ethiopia. This is what Numeiry had in mind when he declared that 'any danger to Zaire has a direct impact on Sudan's security and national unity'. In Cairo, too, the events in Zaire were seen as an ominous sign of what could happen in Sudan: any pressures to undermine the Sudanese regime would weaken the Egypt-Sudan axis and so expose Egypt's southern flank.

The strain in Soviet-Sudanese relations became more evident in May when the Sudan abruptly terminated the contracts of Soviet military experts and drastically reduced the size of the Soviet embassy staff. According to the official explanation, these experts were no longer needed since the Sudanese army was phasing out the use of Soviet equipment—for which it had not, in any case, received spare parts.[55] As if to underline the break with the Soviet Union, Numeiry left for a week's visit to China early in June.

Sudan's efforts to find alternative sources of arms in the West corresponded with the shifts in regional alignments. In Khartoum, it was hoped that Sudan's increasing identification with the moderate and pro-West Arab regimes—as well as its mounting condemnation of Soviet intervention in Africa—would encourage the

West to provide alternative sources of arms. One objective of Numeiry's visit to France in May 1977 was to negotiate the purchase of French arms. Military sources in Paris had indicated that France would supply the Sudan with 15 Mirage fighters, 10 Puma helicopters and a number of armoured personnel carriers at a cost of $85 to be paid by Abu Dhabi.[56]

Britain, too, announced its readiness to supply the Sudan with arms, and in March 1977, one of Britain's leading counter-insurgency experts was engaged by the Sudanese army. This came at a critical time for Numeiry's regime which 'faced internal subversion backed by two hostile neighbours, Libya and Ethiopia, who are negotiating military deals with the Soviet Union and Cuba'.[57] President Carter had agreed in April to the sale of six Lockheed C-130 transport planes (the bill was paid by Saudi Arabia). Since then the Americans have strongly hinted at the possibility of supplying loans for military aid (see above: Defence and Security).

Sudan's anti-Soviet stance was dramatically and emphatically asserted at the OAU Summit Conference at Libreville, in July 1977, where Numeiry angrily denounced 'the new socialist imperialism' of the Soviet Union which was 'threatening to turn the continent into a vast area of conflict'.[58] According to the London *Daily Telegraph*, many of the delegates were visibly shocked by the force of the attack. This Tory paper noted with satisfaction that 'many independent observers now see the Sudanese leader . . . as the most powerful single influence in Africa against Soviet encroachment'.

The OAU Conference also heard Addis Ababa's complaint that the Sudan was encouraging the disintegration of Ethiopia with the support of 'imperialism and reactionary Arab countries'. Col Mengistu described their combined support of Eritrean secessionist forces as amounting to 'an Arab war . . . against an African Ethiopia'. The Sudan's answer was that the Eritrean problem could not be described as internal; nor did Sudan's involvement in it constitute a case of interference as interpreted in the OAU Charter. For one thing, the refugees had Africanized, if not internationalized, the problem. 'Any settlement must bear in mind their effect on the Sudan as a country of refuge, where they are undoubtedly a constraint on development. The settlement must enable all the Eritreans to return to their homeland, and Mengistu's military solutions are therefore unacceptable.' Moreover, it was the Ethiopian government in 1952 which had unilaterally abrogated a UN resolution on Eritrea—an abrogation which the Eritreans have since then contested.[59] The OAU Conference referred the Sudan-Ethiopia dispute to a mediation committee under the chairmanship of Sierra Leone.[60] Nigeria urged the OAU to set up a special body with powers to stop conflicts between African countries.

Such conflicts were not lacking during 1977. In July, the protracted war of words between Libya and Egypt erupted briefly into actual fighting in which the Egyptians claimed to have 'taught the Libyans a lesson'. Since Egypt had the upper hand, the Sudan (which under the joint defence pact was pledged to come to Egypt's aid) did not intervene militarily.[61]

The close nature of Sudanese-Egyptian relations was again highlighted in late October when members of the Sudan People's Assembly held a joint session in Cairo with their Egyptian counterparts. The emphasis was on unity built through step-by-step integration in the economic, political and military fields. The final communiqué of the joint parliamentary meeting put Sudanese-Egyptian relations in the wider context of Afro-Arab co-operation. 'This strategic depth in our nation, in the heart of the African continent and in a huge region stretching from the equator to the Mediterranean . . . makes our historic meeting an event the repercussions of which are not limited to our two states, but extend to the rest of the Arab and

African states which are interested in the security and stability of the region.'[62]

The reconciliation with Saddiq al-Mahdi seemed to remove a major source of conflict with Libya; indeed, Numeiry declared that there was no longer any reason for continued hostility. During the Arab Foreign Ministers' Conference in Tunisia in November, the Egyptian and Sudanese Foreign Ministers met with their Libyan counterpart and agreed to resume diplomatic relations. The Sudanese Foreign Minister, al-Rashid al-Tahir, expressed the hope that 'this step would consolidate the struggle of the Arab nation for unity and progress'.[63] (As it turned out the hope was premature: Egyptian-Libyan relations were almost immediately ruptured over the issue of Sadat's visit to Israel.)

The pattern of alignments in the Red Sea area again shifted when Somalia ended its 1974 Treaty of Friendship and Co-operation with the Soviet Union and broke relations with Cuba. Numeiry called on Moscow to pull out of Africa or 'face forcible expulsion as happened in Somalia and, before that, in other states'. Exports of arms, said the President, constituted 'an assassination of the principles of peace, justice and non-alignment'.[64]

The tug-of-war in the Horn of Africa was approaching its most crucial stage at the end of 1977; on 13 December, President Stevens of Sierra Leone appealed to Ethiopia and Sudan to show 'flexibility, maturity and an attitude of mutual accommodation', and to avoid recourse to 'the distracting influences of external forces in settling their differences'.[65] The OAU mediation committee which met in Freetown in December to deliberate on the Ethiopian-Sudanese dispute recommended 'normalization' of relations between the two countries, and called on them to resolve peacefully their political differences, particularly the Eritrean problem. Sudan announced its readiness to 'work seriously for the resolution of the problems affecting relations between the two countries'.[66]

President Sadat made his dramatic and controversial peace mission to Jerusalem on 19 November. In the face of the mounting and bitter opposition of the 'rejectionist' states, it was now Numeiry's turn to come to the aid of his Egyptian ally. Sudan was among the first, and very few, Arab League states to openly endorse Sadat's action. The Sudanese Cabinet and party leadership publicly praised Sadat's speech to the Israeli Knesset. In Cairo, Numeiry hailed Sadat's initiative as 'a bold courageous step' and added: 'I believe those who oppose this step understand nothing of what is going on in the Arab region. We hope they will understand, we hope they will rejoice soon for what they are rejecting now.'[67]

Sudan's growing ties and closer identification with Egypt were bound to cause concern among both Right and Left-wing elements in Sudan. For one thing, the traditional animosity of the Ansar towards Egypt has never really changed. In a December interview, Saddiq al-Mahdi discussed Sudan's relations with neighbouring countries: 'As to Egypt, there are now no Egyptian troops in the Sudan'.[68] The underlying implication was that their departure was one of the conditions of his return, or at least an act of which he strongly approved.

The same interview revealed other differences on foreign policy between Numeiry and Saddiq. Saddiq acknowledged the President's concern about 'some of the excesses of Soviet arms policies in Africa'. But he pointedly added: 'However, we should also be in a position to tell the US that it is wrong, for instance, to arm South Africa and Israel. This is the meaning of being independent and neutral'.[69] The clear implication was that Numeiry was being too pro-American. Saddiq also indicated that Western policy in the Horn of Africa needed to be changed, for it was based on wrong premises: 'I strongly question the assumption that, if the [Mengistu] regime is overthrown, a pro-Western regime will be restored. The alternative to the present regime could be even more Left-wing.'

The view of the Left-wing opposition, as expressed in SCP clandestine publications, was that the Numeiry regime, through both its domestic and foreign policies, had tied itself to Western strategies in Africa and the Arab world. The objective of American policy was to build a Saudi-Egyptian-Sudanese alliance as a striking force for Western interests in Africa and the Middle East. The support that this bloc gave to Zaire during the Shaba rising, and its involvement in 'the military encirclement' of the Ethiopian revolution, were seen as indications of the total commitment of Numeiry's regime and the Cairo-Riyadh axis to Western policies and interests.[70]

The SCP denounced Sadat's visit to Israel as 'an act of treason'. According to *al-Midan*, the underground organ of the SCP, Numeiry had no right to support Sadat in the name of the Sudanese people, whose freedom of expression he had in any case confiscated: Numeiry could only speak for himself and his clique for whom support and commitment to 'treason' was no new thing.

What was perfectly clear at the end of 1977 was the completeness of President Numeiry's commitment to an anti-Soviet pro-West stance—a commitment in which both Egypt and Saudi Arabia are likely to continue to play crucial roles. Unless opposition elements, either Right or Left, come to exercise a significant influence on Sudan's foreign policy—at present an unlikely event—this trend will certainly continue to characterize the country's policy in the future.

ECONOMIC AFFAIRS (0.68 Sudanese pounds = £1 sterling)
The Sudan's long-term economic potential is extremely promising provided that the political stability of the country is sustained long enough to overcome very serious short-term problems. Having abandoned the Numeiry regime's earlier phase of wholesale nationalization and rigidly doctrinaire socialism, the Sudan embarked on a new course in 1973–74. While still maintaining the basis of a mixed economy, the regime has opted for a three-pronged approach to rapid development. First, in seeking to establish a partnership between the Sudan, the Arab world and the West, it is opening up its considerable land and other resources: out of 200m acres of arable land, only 10% is effectively cultivated, while 60m acres of pasture land could carry 40m head of cattle. Second, it is attracting large-scale Arab economic resources, both for investment and in partnership arrangements, for industrial and agricultural development projects. Third, it is seeking Western technology and investment. The overall aim is to convert the Sudan into 'the breadbasket for the Third World'.

GDP, which had been averaging 8.5%, leapt to 39% in 1973–74—a figure distorted by inflation. It has now stabilized at c. 18%. Since 1973, public and private investment has quadrupled. The new Six-Year Development Plan, launched in July 1977, aims at a real annual growth rate of 7.5%. Total investment for the six-year period is set at £S 2,670m, of which £S 1,570m will come from the public sector and the rest from private sources.

The public sector deficit (current and development expenditure) rose to £S 130m in 1976. At the end of June 1977, Sudan's foreign exchange position had declined alarmingly to minus £S 53m. The country had a serious cash flow problem, which has been eased only through Arab loans.[71]

AGRICULTURE
Agricultural production showed up well in 1977. The 1976–77 cotton crop increased markedly—up to 700,000 bales from 450,000 in the previous season. Since demand for cotton on the world market is reported to be growing, cotton exports are ex-

pected to reach high levels in the near future. Cotton experts in Europe speak of good prospects for Arab cotton-producing countries which mostly deliver long-staple fibres, the highest grade of cotton.[72]

There was again a sharp rise of 48% in gum arabic sales; figures released in July 1977 showed that 48,700 tons, worth $60,191,585, were sold (cf 33,000 tons valued at $40,449,410 in 1975-76). The rise in sales is attributable to the fact that Sudan, which supplies 70% of the world's requirements of gum arabic, had reduced its export price in 1975, thus making its produce more competitive in the world market.[73]

The first phase of the Rahad agricultural project was completed in December 1977.[74] The project aims at the development of irrigated agriculture on an area of c. 300,000 feddans on the east bank of the Rahad River, using water pumped from the Blue Nile. Principal benefits of the project will be the production of cotton and groundnuts from irrigated farmland, which was formerly unproductive and semi-arid.[75]

Controversy over the Jonglei project erupted again—this time in a desertification conference in Nairobi in September 1977.[76] The Jonglei canal, originally proposed by the British in 1904, aims at eliminating water losses in the Sudd region of Southern Sudan and increasing the White Nile flow for agricultural use. The extent of agricultural and ranching area potentially affected is estimated at 3.75m feddans. The total cost of the Jonglei Canal itself is estimated at £S 70m, to be shared equally by Sudan and Egypt. However, a report by a group of environmentalists claimed that the project would destroy the nomadic tribes' way of life in the area. Sudanese scientists and development officials condemned the report as inaccurate, although some of the ecological worries are in fact acknowledged. The Sudanese are currently spending £12m on research projects on various aspects of the scheme and will eventually spend £30m on development projects for the affected tribes.[77]

PROGRAMME AGAINST DESERTIFICATION
The desert is estimated to be moving forward at the rate of 5-6 km annually, which is especially affecting agriculture in Kordofan province; a farmer there needed five times more land in 1973 than in 1961 to produce 73,000 tons of groundnuts. The government has launched a S£ 26m programme under its Desert Encroachment Control and Rehabilitation Programme.

DEVELOPMENT
Concern over planning and development was again emphasized by Numeiry when he opened the new Juba University in October. The university started its academic activities with a first intake of 120 students and 50 academic staff. The orientation of the university will be towards development, natural resources and environmental studies.

THE SIX-YEAR DEVELOPMENT PLAN
Sudan has been described, perhaps unkindly, as living on its potential and never realizing it.[78] But in 1977, at least the prospects for the future were better than before; the year also saw the introduction of the Six-Year Plan, the first phase of a highly ambitious 18-Year Plan to turn the Sudan into the 'breadbasket' of the Third World. (The plan was reviewed in some detail in the *Africa Contemporary Record 1976-77*, pp. B119ff.) Principally, the Plan aims to 'achieve an accelerated and balanced growth in the Sudan economy combining development with social equity'. More specifically, its target is an annual growth rate of 7.5%, with agriculture

continuing to be the pivot of productive development.[79] Although the emphasis is firmly on agriculture, the Plan recognizes the organic unity between this sector and others. Industry in particular is to be developed as a complementary sector to agriculture, with priority given to agro-industries and import substitution. Basic infrastructure will be consolidated and expanded, particularly in the field of transport and communications, power resources, marketing and storage facilities. The Plan envisages the provision of more social services of a higher standard.

The balance of payments position is expected to be improved through expansion of exports and production of import-substitutes. The private sector, both foreign and local, is to be encouraged to play its role fully and effectively in development. Public and private savings are to be increased and mobilized. The Plan's strategy aims to 'base central development firmly on regional planning so as to ensure that development programmes and projects reflect the potentialities and needs of every region. This would, at the same time, engender balanced development within and between regions within a framework of regional specialization and complementarity.' It is expected that 48% of the Plan's investment will be financed from domestic sources and 52% from external sources, of which £S 556m has already been secured. External resources for the private sector would consist partly of private foreign investment, mainly in the form of joint ventures, and partly of foreign loans.

External finance will be a crucial element in the success of the Plan. The gross inflow of external capital is expected to be £S 1,785m, out of which c. £S 400m is estimated to be used for debt servicing, leaving a net inflow of £S 1,385m for financing development. (See also Tables at the end of this chapter.)

FOREIGN INVESTMENT

During 1977, Sudan intensified its efforts to create the ideal atmosphere for private investment in the country's development. The rehabilitation of private business continued and the year saw a phase of rising private investment, both domestic and foreign. Incentives for private investment range from concessions facilities and guarantees against nationalization, to generous tax exemptions, substantial relief from import and excise duties and full freedom for investors to repatriate all profits accruing from the investment of any foreign capital. The principle of no discrimination between domestic and foreign capital, and between private and public investment, is also upheld.

There was a steady stream of foreign businessmen arriving in Khartoum during 1977. Since the President's visit to the US in June 1976, there have been great expectations of heavy American investment in agriculture and industry. The President established an inter-ministerial committee under the chairmanship of Dr Mansour Khalid to assess the results of American-Sudanese contacts and facilitate investment and trade between the two countries, especially the expansion of technical and economic co-operation.

The USAID office in Khartoum has been planning several projects in road building, agriculture extension, manpower development and health. But final approval by Washington has still to be secured. In an interview with the *Journal of Commerce* (New York) in April, Dr Khalid expressed Sudan's interest in a substantial increase in the current low level of development aid and trade: 'We are very satisfied with the speed and effort shown by US companies investing in Sudan. We would like to see a similar rapid response from the US government.'[81]

Sudan signed a letter of intent with Tenneco Inc in April 1977 as the first step in a development programme to exploit the potential of 775,000 acres over a 15-year period at an estimated total cost of c. $1 bn.

Sudan's growing economic ties with Western Europe also became more evident in 1977. The EEC provided the Sudan with consultancy expertise for the 1978 Khartoum International Fair. France has promised to contribute FF 400m to offset part of the rising costs of the Kenana sugar project and to provide FF 26m for the transporting and digging equipment of the Jonglei Canal. The French also agreed to provide technical aid and to establish a joint committee to organize and co-ordinate co-operation between the two countries. Britain has committed £28m in capital aid and technical co-operation.

The Sudan has also strengthened its economic ties with West Germany. Many of the German investment and aid programmes focus on developing the necessary infrastructure required for industrial and agricultural development. The Germans are particularly interested in development schemes in the Southern region and, apart from direct aid and investment, they are committed to providing Sudan with loans.

A delegation of top Japanese businessmen visited Khartoum in October 1977 and met the President. They expressed interest in investing in agriculture and were investigating the possibility of establishing a pilot farm near al-Duiem. Japan granted a $1.7m loan towards starting an experimental rice farm at Abu Qabash in the Blue Nile Province.

During the President's visit to China in June, the Chinese renewed their commitment to provide development aid to the Six-Year Plan, which would include the construction of a new bridge over the Blue Nile at Sennar, as well as an extension to the rice scheme at Malakal in Southern Sudan. Sudanese exports to China in the first half of 1977 reached £12.27m sterling and included cotton, sesame and gum arabic. China's exports in the same period were £7.5m sterling, mainly in rice, textiles and light manufactures.

South Korea also agreed to provide development aid. A South Korean company, DAE-WOO, which started operations in Sudan in 1976, was expected to win the construction contract for a 400,000 ton per year cement project at Marsa Arakiyai on the Red Sea near Port Sudan. It is perhaps indicative of the growing economic ties between Sudan and South Korea that diplomatic representation was elevated to ambassadorial level in June 1977.

ARAB INVESTMENT

Outside observers believe that development finance is not expected to constitute any serious constraint on Sudan's ambitious development plan since Arab funds are steadily flowing into the country. According to David B. Ottaway, Arab countries (mostly Saudi Arabia and Kuwait) have drawn up a £5.7 bn investment programme for Sudan. 'The oil powers of the Arabian Peninsula', he wrote, 'are becoming daily more committed to uplifting Sudan as part of their own long-term economic survival strategy, particularly in food production.'[82] The first step in realizing this strategy was taken when the Arab Authority for Investment and Agricultural Development was set up in April 1976 to finance agricultural development in Arab countries, beginning with Sudan. The Arab strategy to make Sudan the primary source of food for the whole Arab world has also the advantage of creating an alternative source of investment to the industrial West for surplus Arab petrodollars. According to this plan, it is projected that by 1985 Sudan will be able to supply 42% of the vegetable oil consumed by Arab countries, 58% of their food-stuffs and 20% of their sugar needs.[83]

Since such an economic transformation calls for considerable capital investment, some questions naturally arise about Sudan's ability to absorb a large influx of foreign capital. Moreover, certain problems still remain to be surmounted, such as the inadequate transportation system and limited port facilities, the chronic shortages of unskilled labour, and the growing scarcity of skilled workers. These are obviously the kinds of problems experienced by many developing countries. What is perhaps more serious in Sudan's case is the tendency of some Arab countries and multinational companies participating in investment and management of projects to become engaged in internal rivalries and power struggles and manipulate their positions in order to gain immediate advantage.

As a result of such activities, some projects under construction during 1977 were meeting long delay and generating serious cost overruns. A case in point is the Kenana sugar project, a joint venture between Sudan Development Corporation, Kuwait, Kuwait Foreign Trading Contracting and Investment Company (KFTCI), Japan and Lonrho. [84] In October 1973, the feasibility study for the multinational project, conducted and paid for by the London-based Lonrho, put the total capital outlay of the project in the order of $150m. In December 1974, the figure was revised to $180m. When the final agreement was signed with Sudan in February 1975, the cost of the project was given as $250m. By September 1976, the figure had risen to $350m. Two months later the figure again climbed to $475m, and the Ministry of Industry announced that the project was still short of $260m. [85] This escalation was blamed on three main factors: the delay in the payment of Kuwaiti contributions; the lack of infrastructure which caused contractors' bids to be higher than expected; and finally, world inflation. It was apparent, however, that many of the problems arose from differences and conflicts of interest between Lonrho, the managing company of the project (with a 5.5% share) and KFTCI, the 80% government-owned Kuwaiti company (with 23% of Kenana shares). Lonrho's inaccurate cost estimates might have been a source of friction; so too the Kuwaitis' desire to wrest the lucrative management contract for themselves.

There was heavy criticism in the People's Assembly in April 1977 of a $2.5m loan agreement between Sudan and KFTCI to provide additional funds for the project. The agreement was very peculiar indeed and its terms seemed exorbitant. It did not allow for a period of grace, and any delay in the payment of an instalment of principal or interest would incur an extra 1% of the interest which, at 9.5%, was exceptionally high. There was also a charge of $50,000 for the conclusion of the agreement and 1% charge as administrative commission. [86] However, the Assembly had no alternative but to ratify the agreement since it transpired that the loan had already been made and, presumably, spent. (This of course raises the question of why anyone bothered to bring the agreement before the Assembly at all.)

Lonrho's management services contract was terminated in May 1977 by a shareholders' meeting in Khartoum which was under heavy Kuwaiti pressure. *The Kuwait Times* hailed the decision as 'the realization of a dream that Arabs have in managing their own affairs. . . . The way is now clear for the raising of additional finance for the project.' It was also clear that the Kuwaitis were not above using economic muscle to get their way, although perhaps not to the advantage of the Sudanese. The uncertainties created by Kenana's complex financial and political situation still remain. Observers now question the foreign exchange earning ability of the project, particularly in view of the continual fall in the world price of sugar. But if Kenana can become operational in 1978, it will go a long way towards meeting local demand, thus easing the burden on hard currency purchases abroad. [87]

Another project which faced difficulties and delay was the Port Sudan-Khartoum oil pipeline, which finally became operational in September. The 821-km pipeline was originally due to open in 1976, but suffered a number of setbacks. When the pipeline was completed in 1977 by the Kuwaiti group, Kuwaiti Metal Pipe industries, it was discovered that large sections were not functioning and needed relaying—a task which was costly and time-consuming. The opening of the pipeline did not prevent the government from imposing an unexpected and unexplained 22% increase in the price of petrol at service stations (from 45 to 55 piasters per gallon).

Another controversial deal is a proposed Sudanese-Kuwaiti agreement under which Kuwait will take over the 32,000 sq metres of the Mogran area in Khartoum. The People's Assembly refused to endorse the agreement in July 1977 and returned it to the Council of Ministers for redrafting. (This time the Assembly was not presented with a *fait accompli*.) The Assembly objected that the proposed terms did not precisely specify whether the area was being 'sold' or merely 'leased' to the Kuwaitis, and no specification was made of Kuwait's contribution towards clearing the area. Nor did tax-exemption for Kuwaiti development in the area for six years seem a very satisfactory arrangement. [88]

The Kenana crisis—and certain aspects of the proposed Mogran deal, not to mention the intricacies of the pipeline saga—raise certain misgivings about the dangers inherent in internal squabbles of multi-national ventures, about questionable financial practices and deals, and about persistent under-estimates of project costs. In commenting on the controversial Kuwaiti loan agreement to provide additional funds for the Kenana project, *Sudanow* lamented in May 1977: 'The end will justify the means even where the means include loan agreements with terms as crippling as these, and the only end so far attained is the project's prestige. Until production starts in November 1978, Kenana's sugar will remain bitter.' [89]

The Arab commitment to help uplift Sudan economically and turn it into the 'breadbasket' of the world, is an ambitious, far-sighted and mutually beneficial strategy; but if not checked, short-term, narrow-minded not to say selfish considerations could kill the goose before it has laid any golden eggs at all.

COMMUNICATIONS

The World Bank granted a $12m third-window loan and an $8m credit to Sudan Railways—the fourth such loan—to enable it to meet expansion needs required under the Six-Year Plan. The IDA provided a $17m loan towards the $38.2m Savannah Development project which *inter alia* seeks to open up presently blocked stock routes for the annual migration of livestock owners. The Saudi Fund has contributed $8.5m towards the project, with the balance to come from the Sudan government.

Planning has also begun to provide a new all-weather road from the Southern Sudan to Kenya, by-passing the present route through Uganda.

BUDGET FOR 1977-78

The Budget presented in June 1977 provides £S 307m for Development (cf £S 254m in the previous year), with the largest allocations going to agriculture, transport and communications. The Current Budget provides for expenditure of £S 489.4m and revenue of £S 552.7m—an increase of 23% over the previous year. The Foreign Exchange Budget shows a considerable rise from £S 210m to £S 270.6m, due to higher cotton export earnings. Anticipated inflow of foreign capital for 1977-78 is estimated at £S 293m.

PLANNED GROWTH RATES AND SECTORAL CHANGES (%)

	1976–77 %	1982–83 %	Annual Growth Rate %
Agriculture	39	37	6.5
Manufacturing and Mining	9	10	9.5
Electricity and Water	1	1	8.0
Construction	4	5	9.0
Transportation	6	6	7.5
Commerce, Finance and Real Estate	24	24	8.0
Government and other services	11	11	7.5
GDP at market prices	100	100	7.5

FINANCING OF INVESTMENT DURING 1977–83 (million Sudanese pounds)

	Public Sector Amount	% of Total	Private Sector* Amount	% of Total	Total Investment Amount	% of Total
Total Gross Investment	**1,570**	**59**	**1,100**	**41**	**2,670**	**100**
Financed by:						
I. **Domestic Resources**	**735**	**28**	**550**	**20**	**1,285**	**48**
Public Savings	450	17	—	—	450	17
Private Savings	—	—	550	20	550	20
Deficit Financing	285	11	—	—	285	11
II. **External Resources**	**835**	**31**	**550**	**21**	**1,385**	**52**

*Including the semi-private sector financed jointly by the Arab Authority, the Sudanese private Sector and the Government of Sudan.
Source: Ministry of National Planning, April 1977.

PRODUCTION TARGETS FOR SELECTED KEY ITEMS (thousand tonnes)

	1972–73	1985	2000	% increase in production 1973–85	% increase in production 1973–2000
Cotton	555	1,250	3,100	225	560
Cereals	1,700	3,700	11,600	220	680
Wheat	150	860	1,530	570	1,000
Rice	5	60	160	1,200	3,200
Oil Seeds	810	2,020	6,550	250	810
Fruit and Vegetables	925	1,830	6,100	200	660
Sugar	110	810	2,700	740	2,500
Mutton	400	810	1,500	200	375
Fish	23	57	200	250	870

Source: African Research Bulletin, June–July 1977.

MAJOR EXPORTS (million Sudanese pounds)

	1972	1973	1974	1975	1976
Cotton	72.8	84.3	43.3	70.2	97.8 (50.7%)
Groundnuts	9.7	12.9	18.2	34.4	39.0 (20.2%)
Sesame	9.2	10.7	16.5	11.9	17.4 (9.0%)
Gum Arabic	9.1	7.5	14.3	7.6	11.2 (5.8%)
Cake and meal	4.4	7.9	2.2	4.1	5.0 (2.6%)
Others	19.2	28.9	27.5	24.3	22.6 (11.7%)
Total	**124.4**	**152.2**	**122.0**	**152.5**	**193.0**

PRINCIPAL IMPORTS (million Sudanese pounds)

	1972	1973	1974	1975	1976
Machinery and spare parts	15.7	20.0	30.2	59.0	110.6
Transport equipment	13.4	25.4	33.7	64.4	43.0
Chemical and pharmecutical					
products	14.3	19.0	27.2	40.3	33.5
Crude materials	1.5	1.5	33.9	28.1	31.8
Textiles	17.0	16.2	24.0	43.2	21.8
Sugar	10.3	14.7	33.4	39.6	21.8
Other foodstuffs	10.0	12.1	14.1	14.4	17.4
Others	35.7	42.9	51.0	70.9	61.5
Total	**117.9**	**151.8**	**247.5**	**359.9**	**341.4**

Source: Bank of Sudan, *Seventeenth Annual Report, 1976.*

SUDAN'S DIRECTION OF TRADE by value (million US dollars)

Suppliers	1972	1973	1974	1975	1976
EEC	115.6	163.9	215.0	388.4	450.8
of which:					
UK	*61.7*	*78.6*	*81.9*	*158.1*	*199.5*
W. Germany	*22.5*	*28.5*	*46.4*	*87.8*	*82.9*
Italy	*7.6*	*15.3*	*32.6*	*67.3*	*75.9*
France	*12.0*	*18.3*	*27.8*	*24.3*	*36.2*
USA	13.8	33.2	63.6	88.2	92.1
Iraq	—	—	0.3	50.5	75.5
Other Europe	35.7	43.4	48.1	82.0	70.6
Japan	13.6	26.1	37.5	104.8	64.1
India	—	—	—	—	54.8
Kuwait	2.0	9.7	20.5	24.9	37.6
P.R. of China	25.3	29.4	64.8	46.5	27.8
Other Middle East	21.3	18.9	123.4	52.6	26.0
USSR	15.3	26.0	6.9	4.6	18.1
Others	96.0	85.5	130.6	190.9	62.9
Total	**338.6**	**436.1**	**710.7**	**1,033.4**	**980.3**

Customers	1972	1973	1974	1975	1976
EEC	117.0	158.5	138.2	180.4	235.2
of which:					
Italy	*33.3*	*48.4*	*44.5*	*57.6*	*109.0*
France	*13.0*	*26.6*	*36.3*	*55.3*	*36.8*
W. Germany	*33.2*	*39.8*	*23.4*	*27.0*	*36.5*
UK	*13.5*	*15.7*	*12.0*	*15.9*	*15.8*
Other Europe	34.2	40.4	25.7	45.8	52.9
Japan	29.0	48.5	12.4	18.7	41.6
Yugoslavia	7.0	2.7	2.6	20.2	30.1
P.R. of China	35.8	65.3	33.9	37.5	24.2
India	65.8	25.5	13.1	6.5	23.6
OPEC states	11.8	23.6	40.2	31.7	22.1
USA	10.6	8.4	19.8	9.6	21.7
Egypt	20.2	16.6	10.7	30.6	18.8
USSR	1.4	—	4.7	10.5	18.0
Others	25.1	47.2	49.1	47.9	66.0
Total	**357.9**	**436.7**	**350.4**	**439.4**	**554.2**

Source: IMF, *Direction of Trade.*

SUDAN'S FOREIGN TRADE

	1972	1973	1974	1975	1976
Exports (US$ millions)	357.9	436.7	350.4	439.4	554.2
Annual growth rate (1972 = 100)	100	122	98	123	155
Imports (US$ millions)	338.6	436.1	710.7	1,033.4	980.3
Annual growth	100	129	210	305	290
Trade balance (exports-imports)	**+ 19.3**	**−0.6**	**−360.3**	**−594.0**	**−426.1**

Source: International Monetary Fund, *Direction of Trade*.

NATIONAL ACCOUNTS (million Sudanese pounds; Year beginning 1 July)

	1972	1973	1974
Exports	151.3	167.1	183.5
Government consumption	168.5	180.5	207.8
Gross fixed capital formation	95.2	140.2	214.4
Increase in stocks	10.0	89.1	50.6
Private consumption	611.0	846.0	1,170.7
Less: Imports	*−136.2*	*−176.7*	*−316.2*
Gross Domestic Product	986.8	1,246.2	1,510.8
Less: Net factor payments abroad	*−10.1*	*−9.8*	*−15.7*
Gross National Expenditure = GNP	976.7	1,236.4	1,495.1
National Income at market prices	832.7	1,136.9	1,379.7

Source: IMF, *International Financial Statistics*.

INDUSTRIAL PRODUCTION

		1971–72	1972–73	1973–74	1974–75	1975–76	
Cement	'000 tons	200.6	201.2	209.1	217.1	157.1	−27.4%
Flour	'000 tons	191.3	198.2	190.1	220.9	257.3	+ 16.5%
Sugar	'000 tons	91.2	112.6	120.6	128.7	113.9	−11.5%
Wine	'000 litres	2,955.6	3,378.4	4,307.7	4,592.9	4,607.1	+ 0.3%
Beer	'000 litres	7,713.7	8,697.7	8,579.4	9,634.3	9,579.1	−0.7%
Cigarettes	'000 kilos	522.4	489.7	567.9	514.3	894.9	+ 74.0%
Shoes	million pairs	14.7	17.7	12.1	13.3	14.4	+ 8.3%

FOREIGN INDEBTEDNESS

Source of Loan

	Outstanding as at 30 June, 1976 $ million
Arab countries and organizations	410.35
International Organizations (IBRD, African Development Bank, IMF*)	284.86
Western industrialized countries	336.00
Iran	43.65
Eastern Europe and China	25.00
Total foreign indebtedness of Government of Sudan	1,099.686

*Includes an IMF facility of 178m
Source: *African Research Bulletin*, June-July 1977.

NOTES
(Unless otherwise stated, all the references are to Khartoum publications)

1. See *Africa Contemporary Record (ACR)* 1975–76, pp. B106ff.
2. *Al-Sahafa*, 2 January 1977.
3. *Al-Ayam*, 7 January 1977.
4. For details, see *ACR* 1976–77, p. B111.
5. *Al-Ayam*, 12 February 1977.
6. *Al-Hawadith*, Beirut; 29 April 1977.
7. *Ibid.*
8. *Al-Sahafa*, 12 February 1977.
9. Sudan News Agency (SUNA), *Daily Bulletin*, 21 April 1977.
10. *Al-Sahafa*, 26 May 1977.
11. *Al-Sayyād*, Beirut; No. 1702, 2–9 June 1977.
12. *Al-Ayam*, 19 July 1977.
13. *Africa*, London; September 1977.
14. The Central Committee of the Sudan Communist Party, *Democracy is the Key to the Solution of the Political Crisis*, August 1977.
15. *Ibid.*
16. *Al-Ayam*, 8 August 1977.
17. *Al-Sahafa*, 14 August 1977. Communist underground publications, however, claimed that while Right-wing political prisoners were being released, Left-wing prisoners, especially trade unionists, were still being detained.
18. *Sudanow*, 8 August 1977.
19. *Al-Sahafa*, 10 August 1977. Hassan al-Turabi is al-Mahdi's brother-in-law.
20. *Al-Ayam*, 16 August 1977.
21. *Ibid.*
22. *Africa*, September 1977.
23. See *ACR* 1972–73, pp. B97ff.
24. *Africa*, September 1977.
25. *Al-Sahafa*, 11 September 1977.
26. Interview with Colin Legum in London, 26 September 1977.
27. *Al-Ayam*, 28 September 1977.
28. Interview with Italian journalist, Fulvio Grimaldi, in *The Middle East,* London; December 1977.
29. *Ibid.*
30. *Ibid.*
31. *Sudanow*, October 1977.
32. *Sudanow*, November 1977.
33. *The Middle East*, December 1977.
34. See *ACR* 1972–73, pp. B97ff.
35. For a review of developments in the South, see *ACR* 1973–74, 1974–75, 1975–76 and 1976–77.
36. *Voice*, London; 29 September 1977.
37. Quoted by David Ottaway in *The Guardian*, Manchester; 17 April 1977.
38. *Sudanow*, August 1977.
39. *Ibid*, November 1977.
40. *The Military Balance* 1977–78 (London: International Institute for Strategic Studies).
41. David Greig in *Sudanow*, September 1977.
42. *Sudanow*, December 1977.
43. *Ibid.*
44. *Al-Sahafa*, 2 January 1977.
45. SUNA, *Daily Bulletin*, 9 January 1977.
46. See *ACR* 1976–77, p. B116.
47. *Al-Ayam*, 11 January 1977.
48. SUNA, *Daily Bulletin*, 29 February 1977.
49. *Africa*, April 1977.
50. *Ibid.*
51. *Sudanow*, April 1977.
52. *Ibid*, May 1977.
53. SUNA, *Daily Bulletin*, 13 April 1977.
54. *Ibid*, 17 April 1977.
55. *Al-Ayam*, 22 May 1977.
56. *Sudanow*, November 1977.
57. *The Observer*, London; 27 March 1977.

58. *Al-Ayam*, 6 July 1977.
59. *Sudanow*, 8 August 1977.
60. For Resolution, see Documents section: International Relations.
61. *Africa*, September 1977.
62. *Sudanow*, December 1977.
63. *Al-Ahram*, Cairo; 15 November 1977.
64. *The Times*, London; 16 November 1977. Also see Documents section: Political Issues (The Horn of Africa).
65. *Ibid*, 14 December 1977.
66. *Al-Sahafa*, 22 December 1977.
67. *International Herald Tribune*, Paris; 23 November 1977.
68. *The Middle East*, December 1977.
69. *Ibid*.
70. *Al-Midan*, No. 691, December 1977.
71. *Africa Research Bulletin*, Vol. 14, No. 12, January 1978.
72. *Sudanow*, August 1977.
73. *Sudanow*, September 1977.
74. See *ACR* 1974–75, p. B114; 1975–76, p. B129.
75. Sudan Ministry of Finance, Planning and National Economy, *Development Perspective of the Sudan* (Khartoum, September 1976), pp. 14–15.
76. For report of the conference, see Documents section: Economic Developments.
77. For earlier developments, see *ACR* 1976–77, p. B116; 1975–76, p. B126; 1974–75, p. B110.
78. *Africa Guide*, London; 1977.
79. Sudan Ministry of National Planning, *The Six Year Planning of Economic and Social Development, 1977/78– 1982/83*, Vol. 2 (Khartoum, April 1977), p. 31.
80. *Ibid*.
81. SUNA, *Daily Bulletin*, 17 April 1977.
82. *The Guardian Weekly*, Manchester; 13 February 1977.
83. *Ibid*.
84. See *ACR* 1976–77, p. B121.
85. *Sudanow*, August 1977.
86. *Ibid*, May 1977.
87. *Ibid*, August 1977.
88. *Ibid*, May 1977.
89. *Ibid*.

PART TWO

Cuba: The New Communist
Power in Africa

Cuba: The New Communist Power in Africa*

Cuba's credibility as a genuine Third World ally of Africa to which it offers unselfish brotherly assistance (with the sole motive of establishing the 'international solidarity of the Cuban people with the struggle of the African people against colonialism, neo-colonialism and imperialism') has become accepted by an increasing number of OAU member-states who, if they have not openly endorsed Cuba's military role both in Angola and Ethiopia, have also not condemned it.[1]

Cuba appears to have succeeded in convincing its African friends that despite its close ties with the Soviet Union, it is not Moscow's puppet; nor does it act on orders from the Kremlin.[2] While Cuban leaders concede the necessity of consultations with their friends (after all, it is Moscow which pays Havana's military bills and helps sustain its economy), they resolutely maintain that theirs is a sovereign and independent country which decides its own African policy. Thus when Fidel Castro proudly proclaims that 'the one country of this underdeveloped world of this hemisphere that the imperialists will never be able to buy or manipulate . . . is the Government of Cuba',[3] his words imply that nobody else can manipulate or buy Cuba either. This independence is stressed by Cuban diplomats in their conversations with Africans; Castro does not have to say it out loud.

There can be no doubt that the Soviet African policy-makers in the secretariat of the Central Committee of the Communist Party of the Soviet Union (where policy is made and left for the Soviet Foreign Ministry to execute), would like to use Cuba to enhance their interests in the Third World in the same way they use Comecon member-countries. Clearly, as is shown by the experience in Angola and Ethiopia, they can count on the Cubans in situations where Cuban and Russian interests happen to coincide. For example, it was the Cubans and not the Russians who opened the way for their successful joint intervention in Angola; both Castro and Che Guevara supported the MPLA and PAIGC in their anti-Portuguese struggle at a time when Moscow's aid was limited and its relations with Dr Agostinho Neto often strained.[4]

There is no reason to disbelieve the version of Cuba's initial involvement in Angola which was given by its Vice-President, Carlos Rafael Rodriguez, to Hugh O'Shaugnessy in February 1978: 'Look, its obvious that we have a close relationship with the Russians. But when we first sent troops to Angola we did not rely on a possible Soviet participation in the operation. We started it in a risky, almost improbable fashion, with a group of people packed in a ship and in those British Britannia aircraft of ours.' Eventually, the operation was co-ordinated with the Russians, who were beginning to send military supplies to help President Agostinho's MPLA Government in Angola. 'But,' he insisted 'the thing started off as a purely Cuban operation.'[5]

Therefore, to see Cuba as merely a surrogate of the Soviet Union in furthering Moscow's interests in the Third World fails to take account of hidden tensions in their relationship. The Cubans make no secret of their displeasure with aspects of Soviet policy in Angola—and especially over the behaviour of Russian military advisers. They speak freely to African and some Western diplomats about the inability of Russians to deal with people of the Third World as equals.

*The authors would like to acknowledge the research assistance of Roland Stanbridge, currently attached to the Scandinavian Institute of African Studies.

As a kindred Third World country many of whose people are black, Cuba represents to many Africans an alternative to the heavy-handed and often all-too-demanding super-powers who inevitably pursue their own global interests. Thus from Washington's viewpoint, the Cubans are seen as even more 'dangerous' than the Russians because they are more acceptable—and therefore more effective—in promoting Marxist-Leninist ideas in Africa and in stirring up feelings against 'US imperialism'. The same applies to China: the Cubans, whom Peking describes as 'Russian mercenaries', are perhaps Moscow's most effective weapon in the Third World against 'the revisionism' of Peking.

Cuba shows no interest in obtaining military facilities abroad because it has no strategic need for them. A small nation of limited military outreach and manpower, it poses no threat to the all-too-vulnerable sovereignty of most African countries. Nor do the Cubans seek economic advantage from their military and technical assistance—as do most other countries. On the contrary, when President Neto offered Cubans a gift of Angolan coffee, Castro proudly refused it. This act made a very deep impression on many Africans.

The view that Cuba should not be seen simply as a satrap of the Russians, but rather as a country using its Moscow links to fulfil a national psychological need (born out of its own peculiar historical circumstances) to become the 'revolutionary leader of the Third World' is supported by Sir Herbert Marchant, who was Britain's ambassador in Havana from 1960–63. While supporting the view that 'it is always agreeable for one country to promote or defend its special cause to the last drop of the blood of soldiers of another country, especially when it [the USSR] has been subsidizing that country to the tune of some $2m a day for the past 15 years,' Marchant added: 'This does not mean, however, that Cuba is operating in Africa solely under the strict direction and control of the Soviet Union, or even that the partners are in full accord in their assessments, targets and priorities. Castro has maintained a rugged independence of spirit and action in all his dealings with the Soviets. He is liable to accept their roubles with one hand and thumb his nose at them with the other. But there is clearly sufficient Soviet-Cuban agreement over general objectives to give cause for concern to those of us who remember how this unusual partnership brought the world to the brink of nuclear destruction with the missile crisis of 1962—and racial tensions in black Africa can in their own way be as destructive as any nuclear weapon.'[6]

Changing African perceptions about Cuba's role were exemplified by a report in *Africa*, the magazine with the largest circulation in the continent and an estimated 1m readers. Commenting on Castro's tour in Africa in its May 1977 issue, it wrote:

None can doubt that the eyes of the world followed the chief of the Cuban revolution, nor that millions in the Third World and especially in Africa, listened intently to his pronouncements. The small Caribbean island of only 9m people occupies a unique position among the developing nations and those not yet free. Perhaps it is something of an irony that Fidel Castro's stature as a world leader has been so overtly accepted in much of Africa rather than on his own continent. The Cuban leader's African safari should not, however, be seen as simply a symbolic and ceremonial one. The lengthy visit has underlined in no uncertain terms Cuba's presence and influence in Africa, served to reinforce its support for the continent's growing number of socialist-orientated states, emphasized its commitment to the national liberation movements, and strengthened relations between Cuba and the countries concerned. Neither can Cuba be dismissed as an island of 'bearded revolutionaries' whose Marxist rhetoric, high ideals, cigars and gun-barrels have little relevance to the needy and hungry. It is precisely because Cuba's past (with its dependence on an external power, mono-cultural agricultural system, lack of industry, backwardness, poverty, illiteracy and disease) so mirrors the colonial legacy of the Third World that its achievements are arousing such interest today. It is a well known fact, not missed in Africa, that the Cuban people have made a considerable effort to achieve development under difficult conditions, subjected to all manner of aggression that ran from the use of mercenaries to economic blockade and the closing of Cuba's traditional markets. . . . It certainly seems as though Cuba's relations with Africa are bound to flower given the favourable conditions that are developing.

The quality of relations between Cuba and the Soviet Union in their approach to Africa was illustrated by the apparent lack of any co-ordination between the two capitals in planning the visits of the then Soviet President, Nikolai Podgorny, and Fidel Castro. The fact that they covered almost the same ground at the same time—without meeting or referring to each other—might suggest careful co-ordination. But the true position appears to be rather different. Castro had no planned itinerary and advised his intended hosts only briefly beforehand of his impending visit. For example, President Nyerere of Tanzania was informed hurriedly just 48 hours in advance that Castro wished to spend two days hunting in his country. His arrival less than a week before that of the Russian President, robbed Podgorny's visit of much of its significance and appeal. The romantic figure of Castro brought a rapturous turnout in Dar es Salaam's streets; Podgorny's reception was much less spontaneous. This was true, too, of what happened in Maputo. Soviet diplomats did not try to hide their ruffled feelings. While Podgorny confined himself to rigid schedules and to reading orthodox speeches, approved well in advance by the Central Committee of the Communist Party in Moscow, Castro dashed from place to place, talked the way he liked, and wherever he spoke, captured the audience by his charisma.

A comparison of the political effects of Podgorny's and Castro's tours of Africa confirmed that Cuba has emerged as the most immediately effective communist country now influencing Africa. It took Washington some time to fully grasp that Africa has assumed a greater priority in Cuba's foreign policy than the restoration of its relations with the US. The sagging morale of the Cuban people depressed by a succession of economic failures may not be restored by the success of their President's tour and by the new vistas opened up for the Cuban revolution in Africa with the successful export of soldiers, doctors, technicians and development personnel. The question no doubt also asked in Cuba is how a small country can afford playing the role of a middle-range power: who is paying for it all? As Castro's few statements on this subject only lay stress on the willingness of Cubans to make 'revolutionary sacrifices', the answer must be conjectural. However, if one compares the CIA's channelling of funds to those considered helpful to American interests in the Third World with what one knows about comparable Soviet practices, it is not far-fetched to assume that much of the military expenditure incurred by Cuba in the Third World is being compensated for by the Russians—directly by defraying costs of transport and by free supplies of weapons, and indirectly by larger inputs of Soviet financial aid to Castro's economy. With Moscow as banker, the only limitation to Cuba's role in Africa is its capacity to supply such large numbers of trained soldiers, professional people and skilled technicians.

The Objectives of Cuban Policy in Africa

In an interview with Barbara Walters, Fidel Castro himself described Cuba's role in Africa:

> The role of Cuba in Africa is mainly civilian, not military. For a long time we have been assisting a growing number of countries; sending them technical assistance, civilian assistance, especially doctors. We have doctors in many countries of Africa. That is, our support to African countries is a civilian type of support, within the level of our possibilities.
>
> On certain occasions they have asked us for military advisers, to help organize their armed forces. A small group of military advisers, a dozen or a few dozen. And we have sent them, at the request of these governments. The case of Angola was the first occasion in which we sent military units. [7]

However, Castro presented his policy differently in a speech he made in mid-1977. [8] 'The continent of Africa,' he said, 'is the weakest link in the chain of imperialism.' In South America, progress was impeded by the middle class—'that bastion of fascism'. Africa, however, has no middle class, and it is therefore possible for developing African peoples—'victims of capitalist imperialism'—to pass directly 'from tribalism to socialism'.

Although Castro describes Cuba's role as civilian rather than military, the figures show that there are many more military than civilian Cuban personnel in Africa. By the beginning of 1978, there were at least 19,000 Cuban troops in Angola, possibly 20,000 (according to a statement by President Carter on 14 November 1977), as against 4,000 civilian professionals and technicians; and in Ethiopia, about 3,000 military personnel as against a probable 350 civilians. According to US Intelligence reports, there were over 27,000 Cubans in Africa in February 1978, of whom more than 23,000 were military (the majority of these being regular soldiers from Cuba's 100,000 standing army). [9] On a proportionate population basis, Cuba's involvement in Angola alone was comparable to that of the US in Vietnam at the high-water mark. In fact, Ambassador Young gave the much higher figure of 50,000 Cubans in Africa, while one Cuban diplomat put the total even higher—between 60,000–100,000.

Cuba now has diplomatic relations with 31 out of a total of 49 African countires. Havana has never given an exact breakdown of its personnel in Africa, and observers cannot easily measure traffic between Havana and Africa, but a recent estimate by the US State Department gave the following figures: Algeria, 35 doctors; Libya, 100–125 military personnel; Cape Verde Islands, 15 doctors; Guinea, 300–500, mostly military advisers; Benin, 10–20 security advisers; Ethiopia, 400 military advisers, an estimated 3,000 troops and 150 civilian advisers; Guinea-Bissau, 300–400, half military advisers; Sierra Leone, 100–125 military advisers; Uganda, possibly c. 25 military advisers; Tanzania, 350–500 technical and possibly some military advisers; Sao Tomé and Principe, 80 doctors; Madagascar, 30 military advisers; Congo, 300 military advisers and 100–150 technicians; Angola, 19,000 soldiers and 5,000 civilian advisers; Mozambique, 400 civilians. In Libya, Cuban advisers are also helping Colonel Gaddafy reorganize his intelligence service and build up a special 'anti-camp' force under his personal command.

Cuba's Role in the Horn of Africa

When President Fidel Castro arrived in Addis Ababa on 14 March 1977 on one of the stopovers of his tour of seven African countries (Algeria, Libya, Ethiopia, Somalia, Tanzania, Mozambique and Angola), he was pressed by the Chairman of the ruling Ethiopian Military Council (the Dergue), Lt-Col Mengistu Haile Mariam, for military support to help consolidate his fledgling Marxist revolution and defend it from internal and external enemies which he said were mounting a major offensive. At that time, Castro was apparently still convinced that a peaceful solution between 'the two revolutionary regimes' in Addis Ababa and Mogadishu was not only desirable but possible. This was in line with the thinking frequently expressed in the Soviet Press urging a 'socialist federation' between the two countries. The day after his meeting with Castro, Mengistu gave an interview to the magazine *Granma* (official organ of the Cuban Communist Party) in which he proposed an alliance of Somalia, Ethiopia, South Yemen (PDRY) and the Afars and Issas. This, he said, would constitute a 'common anti-imperialist front'.

Fidel Castro had previously pursued the federal idea with President Siyad Barre of Somalia whom he met before going to Addis Ababa. In Mogadishu he was cheered by enthusiastic crowds and greeted by huge posters—which, like in China, have become important media for mobilizing the masses in Somalia. Outwardly the meeting between the two leaders could not have been more cordial. Siyad Barre presented Castro with the Somali Star of Courage, the highest distinction awarded to a foreigner. In his speech at the presentation, the Somali President said that Castro had been invited 'because the two countries' views are close on all current international problems and in defence of the principles of socialism'. Castro in turn promised Somalia whatever technical and economic aid his country could muster, and added: 'We are both small and poor countries and we must tackle enormous difficulties; we want to build many schools, hospitals and universities, develop agriculture and build factories. . . . Our natural resources are meagre; they are still to be uncovered and exploited, but we have revolutionary principles and we have dignity.' At Benadir stadium, Castro made a speech on the theme he subsequently reiterated in every country visited during his 1977 tour. 'Imperialism wanted to destroy the Revolution—in Palestine, Libya, Democratic Yemen, Ethiopia and other progressive countries of the Third World. It wanted to establish a neo-colonial regime in Zimbabwe, maintain domination by monopolies and racists over Namibia, and indefinitely preserve the racist regime of South Africa.' He went on: 'Revolutionary peoples must unite in struggle and expand our alliance with the world revolutionary movement and the Socialist countries, especially the great Soviet Union'.

Behind the display of cordiality in Mogadishu was a different story. President Barre was by no means hostile to Castro's federal idea: in fact, he had been the first to propose it two years earlier, when it was flatly rejected by the Dergue. However, what the Somalis meant by federation was the linking up of the two countries together with Djibouti and an independent Eritrea—but only after the Ogaden had joined Somalia or at least after the Ogadenis had been given the right to express their wishes on the issue of self-determination. How much Castro understood these complexities at the time of his visit to Mogadishu is unclear; but once he had arrived in Addis Ababa he was left in no doubt that 'Federalism' for the Ethiopians would not be acceptable with the excision of either the Ogaden or of Eritrea. The Dergue's 'Marxist-Leninists' rejected Somali and Eritrean nationalism as 'revisionist' and 'counter-revolutionary'.[10] Castro completely accepted the Ethiopian view.

He then set up a meeting in Aden with the help of the PDRY (where Cuba has a sizeable number of military and technical advisers) to which both Barre and Mengistu were invited. Castro explained to them that borders could not constitute insuperable obstacles to federalism since there could be no fundamental differences between true Marxist-Leninists. (The Sino-Soviet conflict is of course dismissed as irrelevant since the Chinese are not regarded as 'true Marxist-Leninists'.) At the Aden meeting, the Somali President spoke sharply to Castro about his failure to understand the elements of the Ogaden conflict; he also reminded him that the 'Mengistu clique', far from being Marxist-Leninists, were in fact 'fascist imperialists'. He felt betrayed by Castro in the same way as he was already beginning to feel betrayed by the Russians. [11]

At that time, Cuban advisers were already well established in Somalia, but not yet in Ethiopia. Within barely six months of Castro's visit to the Horn, the situation was completely reversed: Cuba followed the Soviet volte face by switching its support from Somalia to Ethiopia.

Ethiopia's Foreign Minister Colonel Felleke Giorgis flew to Cuba on 15 October to 'inform our Cuban comrades about the aggression against Ethiopia'. The substance of his talks with Cuba's Foreign Minister, Isidoro Malmierca Peoli, was not made public. A few days later, the Somali Government claimed that there were 15,000 Cuban troops in Ethiopia, many of them brought in from Angola. President Barre called upon the international community to request Cuba to 'immediately withdraw its troops from the area and to abstain from any involvement in the Horn of Africa's affairs'. The Cuban Foreign Ministry broadcast an immediate denial:

> The statement that there are Cuban troops in Ethiopia is an invention on the part of the Somali authorities. Cuban leaders have such credibility in world opinion that it is known that when Cuba denies something it is being entirely truthful. We not only deny that there are 15,000 Cuban soldiers in Ethiopia; we reaffirm that there is not a single Cuban combat unit there. This statement does not mean, however, that Cuba concedes to the Somali government, or to any other government, the right to challenge the Cuban government's right to reach agreements with the Ethiopian government or any other government in Africa or other parts of the world concerning technical assistance and even military cooperation in order to defend the sovereignty of those countries if they are threatened and request such co-operation. . . . For several years now Cuba has had military instructors in Somalia itself, when the country's policies—which were proper at the time and not characterized by chauvinism or by bloody adventures for the purpose of territorial expansion—were subject to imperialist threats. These military instructors were requested by Somalia and still remain in Mogadishu, although they are serving no function. They are simply waiting for the expiration of their tour of duty in that country, which was determined in agreements approved by Somalia and Cuba before the onset of the present war promoted by the Somali army's aggressions against Ethiopia. Ethiopia has an equal right to receive aid. Cuba will never renounce any of those rights which other states, large and small, exercise in that regard.

On 13 November, Somalia expelled all Soviet and Cuban staff from the country. [12] The Somali statement declared that the Cuban government had 'deliberately sent its troops to the Horn of Africa to assist colonialism and annihilate a people who are struggling for a just cause. Therefore a decision was reached to sever diplomatic relations between the Somali Democratic Republic (SDR) and Cuba whose diplomats, staff and experts in the country must leave within 48 hours.' [13]

In a speech following this statement, President Barre said that a major attack on Somalia was being planned by the Russians with the help of Cuban and other forces. 'In view of this,' he said, 'the SDR had no alternative but to withdraw from her longstanding relationship with Moscow and Havana.' Mogadishu radio (15 November) added that, knowing the high esteem in which the Somali people had held the USSR and the warm reception they had given Fidel Castro, observers were wondering what had led to the abrupt change. 'The fact was that, of late, Soviet policy had acquired a new face. The USSR had involved itself in the worst scandal of all time in the Horn of Africa and had become the worst enemy of the liberation movements fighting against the Abyssinian colonial regime. In so doing, it had contravened the principles of socialism it claimed to pursue. As for Cuba, the stooge of the USSR, its armed forces had been transformed into mercenaries hired for any war anywhere.'

By November 1977 there was no longer any doubt about the Cuban military presence in Ethiopia. US reconnaissance satellites had evidence from photographs taken by high resolution cameras capable of 'seeing' objects less than one meter in height. However, in an interview with ABC correspondent Barbara Walters in November 1977,[14] Fidel Castro still denied that there were any Cubans in Ethiopia. But he also made it clear that 'if it were necessary, if the Ethiopian government requested it and it were possible for us, we would not give up our right to send troop instructors there'.

In January 1978 there was some evidence that Cubans were engaged, if not actually as combat fighters, then as technicians in close support of the Ethiopian forces in the Ogaden fighting area. In February, the Somalis produced their first Cuban prisoners of war.

Cuba and Angola

Angola has remained the cornerstone of Cuba's African policy and thus the main obstacle for the US Administration to normalizing relations with Havana. With 19,000–20,000 soldiers and 5,000 civilians, technicians and professionals in the country, Cuba has achieved a physical presence not equalled in any Third World country even by the super-powers. The Cubans proved indispensable to the MPLA regime in 1977, probably to its survival. The failure to quell the violent opposition of the FNLA and especially of Unita, as well as the secessionist forces in Cabinda, has involved the Angolan and Cuban forces in continuous security operations and produced not inconsiderable casualties.[15] Although Cuban losses can only be estimated, US intelligence sources put the total at between 500–1,000.[16] There are over 200 Cuban military graves at one cemetery at Quifangondo, near Luanda. Cuban support was also crucial in suppressing the attempted coup against President Neto on 27 May 1977. Differences within the MPLA as well as internal security problems were discussed during the visits of Fidel Castro to Luanda in April, of Raul Castro to Angola in June, and of President Neto to Havana in August. In a speech on 12 June, Neto paid tribute to the Cubans' assistance during late May:

We have the good fortune to have genuine friends, who show their solidarity at every time of difficulty. . . . We have felt that the majority of the countries of the world are with us and ready to give their co-operation at all times. There are comrades who are criticized because of this. They are accused by imperialism. They are the comrades from the USSR and Cuba. They are accused of coming to Angola, not to contribute to this new process, the building of socialism and defence of independence, but of being here for other ends. I should like to reaffirm here, before the whole population of our country, especially that of Luanda, that the comrades of the USSR have expressed at all the difficult times in our life their feelings, but have in a practical and positive way contributed to the promotion of our army, to reducing economic difficulties, to the training of technicians, and to enable us actually to enter the phase of national reconstruction. The Cuban comrades likewise. The [forces of] reaction here in Angola, supported of course by the espionage services, make propaganda against the Cuban comrades. They have tried everything to make the Angolan people hostile to the Cuban comrades. But I simply have this to say: that if there is one people, if there is one party, if there is one government which is truly contributing to all aspects of our life here in Angola, it is the comrades from Cuba . . . contribution of the Cuban people is so wonderful that we shall never again in our national life forget it.

Hundreds of thousands of people gave Castro a tumultuous welcome when his party arrived in Luanda on 23 March 1977. He told the crowd: 'We are proud to be Angolans and Cubans, to be united. Socialism, internationalism, Marxism-Leninism tell us that we must be united. For this reason I think that the unity and brotherhood, the solidarity and co-operation between the Angolan and Cuban people are an example to the world.' He said he felt a deep satisfaction when he recalled 'that the reactionaries and imperialists were unable to occupy Luanda, that the South African racists were unable to occupy Luanda to establish oppression, exploitation, discrimination and apartheid here. The blood of brave Cubans and Angolans was able to save your joy, your smiles, your future. Our language may be different, but our hearts are identical, our revolutionary spirit is one and that is why we understand one another.'

Castro laid two wreaths at the war cemetery in Luanda—the first on the tomb of an unknown soldier, and the second on the grave of a Cuban officer, Major Raul Diaz Arguelas. Accompanied by President Agostinho Neto, he then visited the former 'northern front' of the civil war. At Quifangondo he unveiled a plaque to commemorate the battle for the strategic pumping-station which supplies water to the Angolan capital. He visited Caxito, scene of bloody clashes with FNLA troops which is again a sugar refining centre; renamed the 'Hero of Caxito', it operates with Cuban technical assistance. Later in Luanda, he visited a residential quarter where an MPLA regional committee has embarked on a housing and school building programme, again with Cuban assistance.

The biggest moment of Castro's visit was a rally in Luanda on 27 March—the anniversary of the defeat of the South African expeditionary force in Angola. Defying the US, he reaffirmed Cuba's pledge to continue military assistance: 'Our duty is to maintain military collaboration while the Angolan armed forces are organized, trained and equipped. The day will come when Angola has sufficient military units, tanks, cannon, airplanes and soldiers to confront all imperialist aggression.' Cuba, he added, felt no need to account for its actions to the West. 'The imperialists ask that Cuba withdraw its military aid to Angola. . . . How many years, how many [Cuban] soldiers will remain in Angola? We don't have to give an answer to that to the Yankee imperialists.'

Raul Castro returned to Luanda in December 1977 at the head of a Cuban delegation to address the first MPLA Congress:

We are linked to the peoples of Africa, as the first secretary of our Party, Com-rade Fidel Castro, has said many times, by an indestructible fraternity: the blood of many African peoples flows through our veins; thousands of Africans uprooted from their lands shed their blood for our independence during the last century, many of them were among the great patriots and outstanding military leaders who fought against Spanish colonialism for 30 years. Only the reac-tionaries and the imperialists are surprised by the fact that the descendants of those slaves who gave their lives for the freedom of our country have shed their blood for the freedom of their ancestors' homeland. We once again want to reaffirm from this distinguished rostrum that, as far as Cuba is concerned, principles are not negotiable. The ruling circles in the US are wasting their time by obstinately making an improvement in state relations with our country dependent on the withdrawal of the internationalist Cuban troops in Angola. The decision as to the number, makeup and length of time the Cuban troops will stay in Angola and the missions they will fulfil is the exclusive concern and depends on the sovereign will of the Governments of the People's Republic of Angola and the Republic of Cuba, the MPLA and the Communist Party of Cuba, Comrades Agostinho Neto and Fidel Castro, and nobody else.

Cuba and Zaire

When on 8 March 1977 c. 5,000 insurgents describing themselves as the Congo National Liberation Front (FNLC) invaded Zaire's province of Shaba from their camps in Angola, President Mobutu's first reaction was to blame the Angolans, the Soviets and the Cubans for backing the uprising. This view was fully shared by China. An NCNA correspondent's broadcast on radio Peking (4 May 1977) entitled 'Mercenaries—the Trojan horse of the new Tsars' commented: 'The ways and means that the social-imperialists resort to are more reckless and insidious. The mercenary troops employed by the old-time imperialists were formed with those colonialists who had lost their "paradise" and national dregs of the colonies; while the new tsars simply dictate the regular forces of a certain country to serve as their cannon-fodder. Everybody knows that the "foreign legion" of the new tsars, which had been waging sanguinary wars in Angola and later was used in training and supporting the criminal band for the invasion of Zaire, is a regular force trained and controlled by Soviet officers. Equipped with Soviet tanks and missiles and financed by the new tsars, this contingent of mercenary troops was sent to Africa by Soviet means of transportation to serve as cats' paws in their masters' moves for expansion and aggression there. The blood they shed in Africa is, in essence, used as a return for the "investments" of several billion US dollars that their masters have put in their country.'

Despite the absence of any proof that the Cubans were anywhere near the theatre of fighting, the Zaire Government decided to suspend diplomatic relations with Cuba.[17] Kinshasa radio reported on 4 April that a member of the Cuban embassy in Zaire described as an 'agent of the Cuban intelligence service' had allegedly been caught red-handed by the Zairean security service. This 'had made it clear that there was Cuban collusion in the invasion of Zaire'. The Cuban embassy staff was given 48 hours to leave, and Zairean diplomats in Havana were recalled.

However, on the following day, the Cuban Foreign Ministry described as 'totally false' the allegation of Cuban spying. 'The decision to suspend diplomatic relations . . . without a valid reason and giving as an excuse slanderous facts which do not exist, demonstrates the falsehood of a regime which is decadent and lacks the most elementary seriousness'. Fidel Castro also repeatedly denied Cuban involvement in Zaire. He said that 'accusations that Cuba is involved in the fighting in Zaire are made in order to solicit the support of imperialism'.[18] In his interview with Barbara Walters, Castro was asked whether Cuban advisers had trained troops to fight in Zaire:

No. Absolutely not. Take note of what I am going to say. During the war, Zairois citizens from the province of Katanga were together with the MPLA. During the war, there were contacts with them. Once the war ended, more than a year ago, we had no other contact with these people of Zaire. Why? Because we thought that what Angola needed was peace. And even when we knew that Zaire's government was one of the most corrupt, repressive, reactionary and bloody governments in Africa, what Angola needed was to improve relations with its neighbours. They needed peace to rebuild the country. That is why we avoided all sorts of contacts with Zairois elements which could hinder this policy. We have consistently followed that rule. That is why we have had no contact, nor has there been any training, nor weapons. Furthermore, we did not even know that those events were going to happen, because these people lived to the east of Angola. It's thousands of kilometers. There are areas that are isolated. Now, the CIA knows, the US government knows, the French government knows, and everybody knows that we Cubans have neither trained, armed nor had anything to do with that question of Zaire, because it is strictly an internal question. Everybody knows that. The rest are lies, simply to justify France's, Morocco's, Egypt's intervention with the approval of the US, to send troops to Zaire from Morocco, Egypt and other countries, with logistic support from France. [19]

However in the same interview Castro admitted for the first time that it was because of the rebellion in Shaba province, and the subsequent French and Moroccan intervention that he had stopped the withdrawal of Cuban troops from Angola 'because we have more than justified reasons to believe that behind all this there may be a further plan to attack Angola'.

Cuba's Relations with the Front-line States

Tanzania has always been careful not to have too-close ties with China and the Soviet Union, and although it has succeeded in retaining the friendship of both, it is jealous of its independent position within the Third World. President Nyerere was among the first African leaders to endorse Cuba's intervention in Angola and saw Cuba as an ally of the Front-line States in their confrontation with the white minority regimes of southern Africa. Castro's visit from 17–21 March was anticipated by an editorial in the government paper: 'Among the small countries that are opposed to imperialism, none stands out more boldly than Cuba, the first liberated territory of the Americas, whose very maximum leader, Ndugu Fidel Castro Ruiz, will arrive in Dar es Salaam this afternoon. The very mention of his name evokes very intense revolutionary sentiments. Castro and Cuba epitomize the aspirations of the poor humiliated peoples of the world.' [20] The following day the paper devoted its full front page to a report on Castro's arrival under the heading 'VIVA FIDEL'. Nyerere told his guest: 'The difference between Tanzania and Cuba is that while we talk so much of our policy of education for self-reliance, the Cubans talk less but go ahead and implement it'. Speaking of the value of Cuban personnel assistance, he added: 'Cubans have proved better and more hard-working'. Later in the year, in August, an eight-man Cuban delegation arrived in Dar es Salaam for consultations on health, agricultural and educational aid to Tanzania.

Before his departure from Tanzania, Castro sought to allay the fears of those leaders like President Kaunda that Cuba might intervene in Zimbabwe and Namibia, and thus turn the liberation struggles there into an East-West conflict. He ruled out the possibility of Cuban troops being used in either of the guerrilla wars, emphasizing that the task of liberating white-ruled southern Africa was the responsibility of the people of those countries 'because independence is not brought from abroad'. He added, however, that Cuba and other progressive countries in the world had a duty to support the southern African nationalist movements.

Although Castro by-passed Lusaka on his way from Tanzania to Mozambique, this omission did not impede the rapprochement between the two countries which followed the normalization of Zambian-Angolan relations strained by the civil war.

Kaunda had been one of the fiercest critics of the Cuban intervention in Angola in 1975. He warned at the time against 'a tiger and his cubs threatening Africa', and described the MPLA success as 'a Russian-Cuban victory'.[21] However, Kaunda joined Nyerere in praising Castro on the occasion of the visit to Lusaka on 13 November 1977 of Raul Valdes Vivo, a member of the Cuban Central Committee responsible for foreign affairs. Kaunda described Castro as a 'dynamic man' and added that he is an effective administrator, an organizer and a revolutionary whose commitment to the well being of mankind is unsurpassable. Vivo replied that Fidel Castro held Kaunda and the Zambian people in high esteem for their commitment to the liberation of southern Africa. Both called for more contacts between their two parties, governments and peoples. Vivo was repaying a visit made by Zambia's Foreign Minister to Havana in October, following which a joint Cuba-Zambia communique (31 October) appealed to the world for political, moral and material support for 'the just struggle of the peoples in southern Africa for national independence'. The two sides underlined 'the need for strengthening solidarity with African and Latin American peoples struggling for freedom and sovereignty'. They also denounced 'imperialist attempts at smashing the unity of the peoples in the Horn of Africa'.

Castro was welcomed in Maputo by President Samora Machel, who expressed his happiness at the friendship that united his people with the Cubans. He told workers that they 'were privileged to receive a delegation representing the courageous and heroic Cuban people who had always supported Mozambique's liberation struggle'. (In fact, the past history of their relations was rather different: Frelimo had resented Che Guevara's criticism of its founder-leader, Eduardo Mondlane, as a CIA agent; and there was no close co-operation during the independence struggle.) An official communique at the end of Castro's visit expressed the intention to further develop educational, cultural, scientific, economic and technical co-operation. Cuba undertook to aid Mozambique in establishing a fisheries company, to train Mozambicans in modern fisheries techniques, and to assist in setting up a marine products trading network. Both leaders expressed their support for the Patriotic Front. Machel returned Castro's visit in October, when a co-operation agreement was signed between the Cuban Communist Party and Frelimo; Castro also offered to increase the number of Cuban technicians in Mozambique.

On 6 December, following one of Rhodesia's 'hot pursuits' into Mozambique, the Cuban Foreign Ministry issued a statement which 'reiterated Cuba's unlimited support for the Government led by President Samora Machel at a time when his revolutionary firmness arouses the hatred of imperialism and international reactionary forces'.

Cuba's Relations with the Southern African Liberation Movements, 1977

During Castro's visit to Luanda, he met three African nationalist leaders—Joshua Nkomo of the Patriotic Front of Zimbabwe, Sam Nujomo of Swapo and Oliver Tambo of the ANC of SA. The Angolan Government provided a special Boeing 737 to transport them from Lusaka to Luanda on 29 March. No news was published on the talks but all three African leaders travelled to Cuba later in the year.

Joshua Nkomo visited Havana in July and again in August 1977 and was told by Castro that future supplies of equipment to the Patriotic Front 'would only be limited by availability'. Asked by journalists if Castro had offered to send Cuban troops to help his guerrillas, Nkomo replied: 'We did not request volunteers. We have to fight our own war. We can only seek equipment from our friends'. However, it is now known that Cuba agreed to train Nkomo's Zapu guerrillas in camps subsequently set up in Angola.[22]

Oliver Tambo arrived in Havana during October for talks with General Raul Castro. Tambo said he would be discussing 'what role the government, party and people of Cuba can play in support of the struggle of my people'.

Sam Nujomo paid several visits to Cuba in 1977, and Swapo opened an office in Havana on 1 November. Havana radio said this would 'provide Swapo with beneficial relations with Latin America'. Extremely close relations were forged between Nujomo, the Cubans and the Russians in Angola during 1977. Swapo guerrillas were armed with Russian weapons and trained by Cuban military instructors.[23]

Cuban-US Relations in Africa[24]

American-Cuban relations acquired a new dimension after Castro's intervention in Angola in 1975. The Ford Administration linked Angola's admission to the UN to the withdrawal of Cuban troops from the country. When assurances to this effect were conveyed to Dr Kissinger by Sweden's then Prime Minister, Olaf Palme, the US yielded and Angola became a UN member. Although the Carter Administration softened its attitude on this issue, it still continued to press for the gradual reduction of Cuban troops in Angola, making this a prerequisite for the resumption of normal relations between the two countries. In February 1977, Castro hinted that he might be ready to reduce his forces; but after July 1977, they were instead increased from c. 13,000 to over 19,000. Castro's explanation for this was the foreign intervention in Zaire over the Shaba episode (see above). In December 1977, he told visiting US journalists that while relations with the US were better than they had been for 18 years, he would not withdraw his 'military advisers' from Angola in order to improve relations with Washington.[25]

Ambassador Andrew Young tried early in 1977 to take some of the emotion out of the controversy by suggesting that the Cubans were in fact a force for 'stability' in Angola—a remark that did not go down very well with the State Department. However, after Cuba had begun both to increase its forces in Angola and to become militarily involved in the Horn of Africa, Young took a less lenient view, while at the same time trying to keep the Cuban military role in perspective. Addressing the Harvard Club in New York on 30 November 1977, Young discouraged 'panicking over the increasing numbers of Cubans or Russians sent to the African continent [because] the vastness of the continent and the perception of the African leadership make it impossible for any outside power to dominate Africa':

> Essentially what the Cubans are doing has to come under question in Ethiopia, in Guinea, in Uganda and in other places where their military role seems to be to support a repressive regime that maintains power by killing off the opposition. In almost every instance, the opposition just happens to be the most intelligent people in the country. Uganda was one of the places in Africa that had one of the best universities, one of the best civil service operations and a broader and better-trained middle class than almost any place else. The same thing was true in Ethiopia. What we are finding is that the Cuban military presence ends up becoming associated with the purging of some of the better-trained and more skilled people in Africa, and not necessarily contributing to order, stability or development. What Africans are saying—and what they are saying and understanding clearly—is that in their quest for genuine non-alignment and in their desire to develop their own population, that frankly they are better off being associated with the West in dealing with the kinds of problems that they have, than they are under the influence of small cadres of Cuban military advisers and

troops. The US didn't have a thing to do with putting the Russians out of Egypt or getting them run out of Sudan, or with having the Cubans and the Russians run out of Somalia. It was essentially an awakening of African leadership themselves that this was not a constructive presence. Now that's not true in Guinea-Bissau or in Tanzania, where there has been a presence of people running hospitals and contributing to technical assistance. But almost every place where there is a huge military component of Cubans, there's death and destruction rather than life and development.

In an interview with *Le Nouvel Observateur* at the end of December 1977, Ambassador Young said that while there was no denying that the Cubans had helped Angolans beat back invading South African forces and restored activity in the cities after the departure of the Portuguese, today the Cubans should be condemned for killing opponents of the ruling MPLA-Labour Party and for intervening militarily alongside Ethiopia in its war with Somalia. The Cubans had left 'blood and tears' in their wake, he added. He also mentioned the question of Cuban activities in Guinea and Uganda.

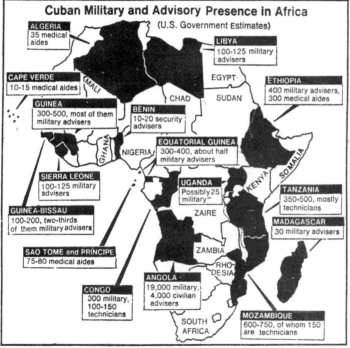

The New York Times/Nov. 17, 1977

NOTES

1. For a previous analysis of Cuba's policy in Africa see *Africa Contemporary Record (ACR)* 1976–77, pp. A84–90.
2. Also see essay, 'The Crisis in the Horn of Africa'.
3. *Daily Times,* Dar es Salaam; 15 January 1978.
4. See *ACR* 1975–76, pp. A14ff.
5. *The Observer*, London; 26 February 1978.
6. *The Times*, London; 16 August 1977.
7. From a transcript published in *Seven Days* (San Francisco: Institute for New Communications), December 1977.
8. 'Dr Castro Develops His Own Style of Gunboat Diplomacy in Africa'; *The Times*, 16 August 1977.
9. *International Herald Tribune (IHT),* Paris; 2 February 1978.
10. See chapter on Ethiopia and essay, 'The Crisis in the Horn of Africa'.
11. This information was provided by Somali diplomatic sources.
12. For full statement, see Documents section: Political Affairs (Somali-Soviet Relations).
13. BBC Summary of World Broadcasts, 15 November 1977 (ME/5667/B/7).
14. See note 7, above.
15. See chapter on Angola.
16. *IHT*, 18 November 1977.
17. Also see chapter on Zaire.
18. *The Daily News*, Dar es Salaam; 22 March 1977.
19. See note 7, above.
20. *The Daily News*, 16 March 1977.
21. See *ACR* 1975–76, pp. A26ff, B388–9.
22. See essay, 'The Crisis in Southern Africa'.
23. *Ibid.*
24. Also see essay on US policy in Africa.
25. *IHT*, 7 December 1977.

PART THREE

Documents

The Horn of Africa

Somali-Soviet Relations

Repudiation of Treaty of Friendship and Co-operation
between Somali Democratic Republic and the USSR:
Statement by President Siyad Barre
to the Central Committee of the
Somali Socialist Revolutionary Party

13 November 1977

As you all know, our country has a longstanding relationship with the USSR: such a
relationship, which dates back to the time of our accession to independence in 1960,
was neither accidental nor baseless. It was inspired by understanding, respect for
each other and mutual co-operation. As such it was founded on common principles
and on concrete material interests of the two nations.

Our co-operation in the past 18 years has covered many fields including defence,
education and training, trade and economic co-operation, which proved of great
benefit to the Somali people and for which we feel duty bound to express our deep
and sincere gratitude to the Soviet people.

At the same time, the Somali people appreciated the general stand of the Soviet
Union in support of the national liberation movements against colonialism. It was
no wonder then that the mutual understanding and co-operation of the two
countries gained momentum year after year. This took new dimensions after the 21
October Revolution. The development of these close relations with the Soviet Union
reached its pinnacle in 11 July 1974 when a Friendship Treaty between the Somali
Democratic Republic and the USSR was concluded in Mogadishu.

For some time now, a completely new situation radically affecting these friendly
relations has arisen when the Soviet Union embarked upon a new policy of all-out
support for the colonialist regime of Ethiopia at the expense of the genuine and
legitimate struggle of the liberation movements. Needless to say, the Soviet Union
like any other nation, is sovereign to adopt any policy it wishes towards other
nations. We have no claim and no right to prevent the adoption of any such policy.
Nevertheless, we have the right to protest against such political choice inasmuch as
it contravenes the spirit and letter of the Agreement between the two countries and
even endangers the security and existence of our country.

In view of these circumstances and in consonance with the friendly relations
between the two countries, we tried to explain to the USSR government to the utmost of our ability, the present and historical complexity of the situation in the
Horn of Africa. We patiently explained on various occasions and at various levels,
including my visit last August to Moscow, that the basic cause of the conflict in the
Horn of Africa is Ethiopia's colonization of other peoples. We explained the
historical background of the situation: how European colonialism in the late
nineteenth century abetted and aided the expansion of the Abyssinian Kingdom to
the presently claimed boundaries of the Ethiopian Empire; how Ethiopia was an
active participant with the European powers in the division and colonization of the
peoples of the Horn and, as such, can only be considered a colonial power; and
how, in such circumstances, the colonized peoples of that power cannot be denied
their inalienable right to self-determination and independence.

The history of colonization and domination had its echo in the continued struggle and resistance of the colonized people. Thus we patiently explained to the Soviet Government how the struggle of the people under Ethiopian colonial rule for freedom was simultaneous with similar liberation struggles against European colonialism raging in the African continent. The only difference today is that the European colonial powers bowed to the will of the people while the Ethiopian rulers, past and present, have consistently turned against the tide of history.

We also explained the already familiar position of Somalia since its independence on the question; namely, that she is fully committed to the support of the legitimate rights of all the peoples under colonial oppression, including those of western Somalia, for self-determination and independence.

The negative and intransigent attitude of the Ethiopian regime towards decolonization has all along been evident to the Soviet Union as well as the rest of the world.

The colonized peoples expected a change in the attitude of the new regime after the overthrow of the feudal monarch in Ethiopia. But the Dergue regime opted for a course of action that intensified the brutal oppression so characteristic of the previous regime. In the face of such brutality and denial of their rights, the colonized peoples had no choice but to engage in armed struggle to defend themselves and gain their freedom. The Somali Democratic Republic, under such conditions, was obliged to give its full support to the legitimate liberation struggles, just as it had always supported all other genuine liberation movements.

The Somali Democratic Republic repeatedly made representations to the Soviet leadership against this course of action which comes in direct contradiction with one of the most fundamental principles of the international community—namely, the principle of the right of all peoples to self-determination, a principle which as you know constitutes the cornerstone for human justice as well as international stability and security.

Apart from the complete disregard for these basic principles, the Soviet Union has taken actions and positions which endanger the interests and security of Somalia.

First of all, she has levelled false and baseless accusations against the Somali Democratic Republic, describing it as an aggressor.

Secondly, for the past several months she has been conducting an intensive political, diplomatic and propaganda campaign against the Somali Democratic Republic throughout the world: in Africa, the Arab world and in all international organizations of every nature.

Thirdly, as explained earlier, she is presently pouring massive and highly sophisticated quantities of armaments, unprecedented in the region, into Ethiopia— an act which can only be regarded as a prelude to an all-out invasion against the Somali Democratic Republic.

Fourthly, she has mobilized and sanctioned the commitment of Cuban and other troops on the side of Ethiopia against the liberation struggles in the area and against the Somali Democratic Republic.

Fifthly, she has pressurized the socialist countries allied to it to take a position inimical to the interests of the SDR in the present conflict in the Horn of Africa.

And, finally, she has unilaterally terminated the supply of legitimate defensive arms to the Somali Democratic Republic in direct contravention of existing agreements between the two countries.

The implication of all these actions can only be interpreted as constituting a unilateral abrogation of the Friendship Agreement of July 1974 and other agreements between our two countries both in letter and spirit. It is pertinent to quote here some relevant articles of the said Agreement.

Article 4 of the Agreement states: 'In order to strengthen the defensive capacity of the Somali Democratic Republic, the two respected sides will continue their military co-operation, in accordance with special agreements. This co-operation will be specifically concerned with the training of Somali military personnel and the supply of military equipment to the Somali Democratic Republic so as to strengthen its defensive capacity.'

Article 7 of the said Agreement states as follows: 'Believing in the principles of freedom and equality of all peoples, the two respected sides condemn imperialism and colonialism in all their forms. The two sides will continue to oppose imperialist and colonial forces, and they will co-operate with other governments in giving support to the just cause of the peoples struggling for freedom, independence and people's progress, based on the principles of equality and the people's right to self-determination as sanctioned in the UN Charter.'

And Article 10 of the same Agreement states: '**Each respected side declares that it will not enter into military pacts or alliances with other Governments, or undertake actions or measures inimical to the other side.**'

In spite of the above, the note of warning made in my October 1977 address to the nation on the natural consequences of such Soviet intervention in the conflict in the Horn of Africa has now begun to assume different dimensions. We are now fully convinced of the existence of an immediate and imminent joint Soviet-Cuban plan for an all-out military aggression from Ethiopia against the Somali Democratic Republic. Plans for this massive military invasion by Ethiopia have been drawn with the help of Soviet experts and is to be executed with the collaboration and support of Cuban troops and other military contingents.

Under these circumstances, the Somali Democratic Republic has no alternative but to review her longstanding relationship with the Governments of the USSR and Cuba. Accordingly, the Central Committee of the Somali Revolutionary Socialist Party in its meeting on 13 November 1977 took the following decisions.

1. The Friendship Agreement, already violated by the Soviet side, is from now onwards null and void; and Somalia abrogates it from its side.

2. Any facilities of a military nature hitherto available for the use of the Soviet Union in the territory and waters of the Somali Democratic Republic are withdrawn immediately.

3. All Soviet experts, military and civil, now in the Somali Democratic Republic are requested to leave the country within a week.

4. The diplomats and staff of the Soviet embassy in the Somali Democratic Republic and its subsidiaries are reduced to the same number as those in the Somali embassy in Moscow.

Furthermore, so long as the Government of Cuba had openly sent its troops to the Horn of Africa to fight for colonialism and oppression to wipe out peoples struggling for freedom, and had, in addition, used offensive language against the Somali Democratic Republic, it had been decided to sever diplomatic relations with that Government. All diplomats, staff and experts from Cuba are requested to leave the country within 48 hours.

As I have remarked in my address to the nation on 21 October 1977, we have every confidence in the determination and courage of our people and their readiness for self-sacrifice. Our people had been steeled in their long resistance to colonial domination, in their struggle for independence and emancipation and in their struggle for building the foundations of revolutionary Somalia. We have never been overawed by the power and arrogance of the enemy. The ex-colonial European powers had confronted the unbreakable mettle of our people and had, accordingly, left our shores for good. The powers that today desire to break the will of our people through suppressing the armed struggle of the liberation movements and endangering the Somali Democratic Republic are extremely mistaken.

I am fully confident that you will prove to them, and to the rest of the world, that you are a proud and courageous nation that will never submit to arrogance; that will give up everything to defend its dignity, sovereignty and unity. We are neither weak nor friendless. We are not intimidated by modern weapons and political deceit. We shall courageously build our revolution and defend our independence. Victory is ours.

Official Soviet Statement on the Withdrawal of Russian Specialists from Somalia

TASS, 15 November 1977

The Government of the Somali Democratic Republic has stated that it does not regard as necessary the further stay of the Soviet specialists in the Somali Democratic Republic and is also denouncing the Soviet-Somali Treaty of Friendship and Co-operation of 11 July 1974.

The Somali Government has taken its action unilaterally and in the conditions of the actual war which it has unleashed against neighbouring Ethiopia. In essence, what lies behind this action is dissatisfaction because the Soviet Union has not supported Somalia's territorial claims on a neighbouring state and has refused to facilitate the stirring up of fratricidal war in the Horn of Africa.

It is common knowledge that the Soviet specialists are in Somalia at the request of the Somali Government itself, which on more than one occasion has expressed gratitude for their assistance. The Somali side has also, on more than one occasion, given a high assessment of the significance for Somalia of the Treaty of Friendship and Co-operation. Judging by the present steps, chauvinist expansionist moods have prevailed over common sense inside the Somali Government.

The Soviet side has taken note of these actions of the Somali Government, the responsibility for which fully rests with the Somali side. The Soviet Government has decided to recall all Soviet specialists from Somalia to the Soviet Union.

Source: Soviet News, 22 November 1977.

Soviet Reaction to Somalia's Repudiation of Friendship Treaty

Article issued by Novosti Press Agency, *signed by*
'Observer' (usually an official Soviet Spokesman)

It may be recalled that the Treaty was signed on the initiative of Somalia. It did, beyond all doubt, correspond to the fundamental, long-term interests of both states and peoples. The most important point about it was that it served, in the first place, to strengthen Somalia's international position as a sovereign independent state. Great value was placed on this in statements by Somali government officials, including those at the top level.

The Soviet Union, under the Treaty, consistently and firmly pursued the line of promoting friendship and equitable co-operation with Somalia. The Soviet Union has always acted on the assumption that the Treaty, designed to serve peaceful objectives, cannot be used for the purposes of an unjust war.

The government of the Somali Democratic Republic knew that the Soviet Union did not support and would not support the Somali leadership's territorial claims on neighbouring countries. The only purpose of Soviet military aid was to strengthen the defences of Somalia, which was, like other progressive states, a target for imperialist expansionism. All the arms were given to the Somalis for the defence of their country and only for its defence, and not for an attack on neighbouring states. It has turned out that the Somali leaders' professions regarding their devotion to peace were at variance with their real intentions.

Egged on by the reactionary circles in Saudi Arabia and some other Arab countries and obsessed with the chauvinist idea of striving to create a greater Somalia, the leadership of the Somali Democratic Republic has plunged its peace-loving people into a murderous venture.

Under the guise of a non-existent 'Western Somalia Liberation Front', regular Somali forces have occupied a considerable portion of the territory of Ethiopia with a population of up to 15m people, of whom from 1-1.5m are Somali tribes. So what has happened has not been the 'liberation' of the Somalis living in Ethiopia, as is being claimed in Somalia today, but the seizure of other people's territory and a redrawing of the existing inter-state frontiers by violent means. This is action of a kind which the Soviet Union cannot support, out of considerations of principle. Nor has it any support from the African states, whose attitude is reflected in the resolutions of the OAU condemning the revision of frontiers by force of arms.

The war of aggrandizement against revolutionary Ethiopia has acted as a boomerang against Somalia itself. Somalia has sustained heavy losses in military hardware and human lives. The war has worsened the material conditions of the mass of the people and has placed the country in a state of dependence on the foreign forces which pushed the Somali leadership into this military gamble and did their utmost to extend this murderous and pointless conflict. It is only the imperialist and other reactionary circles whose policy is hostile to the interests of the Somali people that are interested in seeing the conflict continue.

It is common knowledge that Somalia's true friends, including the Soviet Union, did everything possible to avert this clash in the first place, and then to put an end to it so as to open the way to a settlement of the points at issue between the two countries by peaceful means.

The Somali leadership recklessly rejected the peace initiatives of the Soviet Union, Cuba, the People's Democratic Republic of Yemen, Madagascar and other countries which offered to mediate in a solution to the problem at the negotiating table. It appears that the chauvinist and expansionist trends in Somalia have prevailed over common sense, as is said in the recent *Tass* statement.

Today, imperialist circles are promising arms, money and economic aid to the Somali leadership. But this will not help Somalia to extricate itself from this disastrous military conflict, nor will it help to strengthen the independence of that young African state or to overcome the economic difficulties, which have increased since the beginning of these reckless military operations against a neighbouring country.

There is an evident lack of wisdom behind the Somali Government's decision to renounce the assistance of Soviet specialists who were in Somalia at that country's own request and who, by their selfless work, were making a worthy contribution towards promoting that country's national independence and development. It is with Soviet assistance, as everybody knows, that a deep-water sea port at Berbera, a meat-packing plant, a fish cannery, a dairy factory, a radio station, a printing establishment, two hospitals and some other projects have been built in Somalia, and an important new sector of the country's economy, a sea-fishing industry, has been created.

During a severe drought which struck most parts of the country, the Soviet Union lost no time in helping to move 120,000 nomads from the drought-stricken areas to new settlements. This operation, to quote the Somali leadership, was 'an epoch-making event in the country's history'.

It was not so long ago that President Muhammad Siyad Barre, highly praising the work of the Soviet specialists, said from the rostrum of the 25th Congress of the Communist Party of the Soviet Union: 'Full of sentiments of profound gratitude for aid and support, the Somali people have inscribed words of friendship with the Soviet people in their history in letters of gold'.

Now the Somali leadership is trying to explain its unfriendly acts against the Soviet Union by alleging that the Soviet Union, disapproving of Somalia's actions and backing Ethiopia, is 'interfering' in affairs in the Horn of Africa and thereby harming Somalia's security.

These explanations are quite obviously unfounded and far-fetched.

The Somali leadership seems to believe that it can do without the Soviet specialists and the Treaty. Small wonder that its latest actions have earned the approval of imperialist and other reactionary forces which would like to see nothing left of what has been gained as a result of good relations between the USSR and Somalia over the years.

The Soviet people have entertained and continue to entertain sentiments of friendship for the people of Somalia as well as for the peoples of other African countries who have cast off the yoke of colonialism. And this has found expression in the many-sided support which the Soviet Union has given to the young Somali state. By scrapping the Soviet-Somali Treaty, the Somali leadership puts itself in a position of dependence on the reactionary Arab regimes and imperialists who are out to turn Somalia into a tool in their own hands. But this is completely at variance with the interests of the Somali people.

Source: Soviet News, 22 November 1977.

Chinese Reaction to Somalia's
Repudiation of Friendship Treaty

*Commentary by Hsinhua, the official Chinese
News Agency, 15 November 1977*

China praised Somalia's renunciation of its Treaty of Friendship and Co-operation with the Soviet Union and called it a daring act of a dauntless people to safeguard national sovereignty and independence. At the same time, Peking warned that Moscow must be closely watched for a possible counterattack and troublemaking.

'This is a just action against hegemonism, an action of great significance taken by a third African state following Egypt's abrogation of the Egyptian-Soviet treaty last year and the expulsion of Soviet military experts by the Sudan last May.'

It was the inevitable end of a super-power's policy, characterized by 'hypocritical acts of sham aid but real plunder, sham friendship but real control'.

It recalled that the Soviet Union signed the treaty with Somalia in 1974 to serve its contention with the US for control over the Red Sea and the Indian Ocean.

Proceeding from its strategic interests of rivalry in the Horn of Africa and the Red Sea area, the Soviet Union last spring proposed a pro-Moscow confederation of four states in the area, including Somalia. But the prompt rejection by Somalia 'threw the new czars into a rage'.

'Since then the Kremlin has time and again tried hard to bring Somalia to her knees, and by making use of disputes and differences left over by history in the area, it keeps sowing dissension and adding fuel to it to sabotage unity among African states.'

Without naming Ethiopia—with which China maintains diplomatic ties— *Hsinhua* pointed out that the Soviet Union had poured vast quantities of sophisticated arms and military equipment into the Horn of Africa, greatly aggravating tension there.

China's View of Soviet's African Policy

Extracts from an article by Jen Ku-ping

Soviet social-imperialism is waiting for the chance to move in some other parts of Africa. Podgorny proclaimed while in Africa not long ago that the sea lane across the Indian Ocean linked the European part of the Soviet Union with the Soviet Far East. According to this logic, wouldn't the sea lane across the South Atlantic also serve this purpose? This is blatantly laying a big time bomb for new Soviet acts of aggression on both the east and west coasts of Africa including in the Red Sea, Indian Ocean and South Atlantic regions. This intention can only rouse the sharp vigilance of the African countries and people.

The fresh offensive by the Kremlin to expand in Africa has revealed its greed for the continent's rich resources and its ambition to dominate the whole continent. It is also a component part of its global strategy and is geared to its overall plan of contending for Europe, the key point in its strategy. Moscow's expansion south of the equator is co-ordinated with its contention for hegemony in the Red Sea. Super-power rivalry in Africa is a 'peripheral war' in contending for Europe. The Kremlin's strategic aim there is to start on the underbelly of Africa, slice horizontally across the African continent, seize control of vital coastal sections, gradually squeeze out US and other Western influence from southern Africa and control that region's strategic resources and the important strategic passageway from the Indian Ocean to Western Europe so as to cut the Western countries' vital supply line at any time, thereby getting a stranglehold on Western Europe. As a result, Soviet aggressive expansion has been opposed by numerous African countries and people and aroused anxiety in the Western world, particularly the West European countries which are gravely threatened. After the Soviet mercenaries invaded Zaire, West European countries like Belgium and France immediately gave Zaire support to fight back in resistance.

The Africa of today is no longer what it was a century ago when colonialism and imperialism began carving up the continent. Chairman Mao pointed out: 'The frantic struggles of the imperialists and reactionaries will only stimulate the peoples of African countries to sharper vigilance and stronger determination in the fight against imperialism and old and new colonialism and for the defence of national independence and the prosperity and the progress of their countries.' Having summed up both positive and negative experience, the awakening African people are becoming increasingly aware of the ferocious features and insatiable ambitions of Soviet social-imperialism which is making disturbances here today and plotting invasion there tomorrow. But the African people have buried batch after batch of overbearing colonialists and aggressors. Can Soviet social-imperialism be an exception? The initial victory won by Zaire with the support of many African countries in counterattacking the Soviet mercenaries proves that it is nothing terrifying and can be defeated.

Sharp, complex struggles are being waged on the continent of Africa—the African countries and people versus the racists; the African countries and people versus super power hegemonism; the two super-powers, the Soviet Union and the US, versus each other. Within these contradictions, the decisive factor is still the African people who, united as one, dare to struggle and are good at struggle. Their road ahead is full of twists and turns, but the future is infinitely bright. Africa's destiny is in the hands of the African people.

Source: Peking Review, No 20, 13 May 1977.

Reaction to the Conflict in the Horn

Sudan's Attitude to the Conflict in the Horn

*Text of Joint Communiqué Issued after President Numeiry's Visit
to Somalia, 17–20 March 1977*

In response to an invitation extended from HE Muhammad Siyad Barre, the Secretary-General of the Somali Revolutionary Socialist Party (SRSP) and President of the SDR, HE President Gaafar Muhammad Numeiry, President of the Democratic Republic of Sudan, made a working visit to Mogadishu from 17 to 20 March 1977.

The two Presidents held talks in a cordial atmosphere, imbued with the spirit of deep understanding and the definite desire for co-operation and co-ordination between the two fraternal countries in all bilateral, regional, continental and international fields.

With regard to bilateral relations, the two Presidents expressed their complete satisfaction at the course of relations between the two countries and renewed their true desire to develop and advance them to new horizons of co-operation on the political, economic and cultural planes, by the intensification of contacts at all levels, the exchange of experience, increase in the volume of trade, cultural and artistic exchanges, and the deepening of the present contacts existing between the two popular organizations of the two countries, the SRSP and the Sudan Socialist Union, and their popular affiliated organizations, in order to strengthen the eternal relations binding the Somali and Sudanese peoples.

The two Presidents studied the agreements so far reached between the experts of the two countries during this visit to implement the work programmes connected with bilateral co-operation. The two Presidents discussed, in detail, the situation in the Red Sea area and the need for agreement between the states in the region on a defined strategy to ensure its exclusion from international conflict and Zionist greed, bearing in mind that its security cannot be separated from the security of the two countries and the states in the region and the world as a whole.

They consider that security in the Red Sea area is linked to security in the Indian Ocean, which must remain an ocean of peace, free from nuclear and strategic weapons, in accordance with the resolutions passed in the UN General Assembly and the conferences of the non-aligned countries.

President Barre expressed his support for President Numeiry's initiatives in this regard. The two Presidents agreed to continue consultations among themselves on everything connected with this matter. The two Presidents believe that the tension existing in the Horn of Africa is a natural result of keeping the situation [stagnant] in the region since the colonialist scramble for it, without taking into consideration the national bonds and the rights of the peoples in the region to self-determination. They condemned the wrong and inhuman practices, genocidal operations and the bloody liquidations carried out against some of the peoples in the region in a manner that contradicted both the UN and the OAU Charters, as well as the world Declaration on Human Rights.

They have also condemned the policy of persecution, repression and forced movement of communities which aim at changing the demographic structure of the region. They pointed out that such wrong practices were likely to open the door to the intervention of foreign forces. The two leaders appealed to the international community and, especially OAU member-states, to condemn such acts and to take action to protect these peoples.

Source: Omdurman Radio, 20 March 1977.

Statement by President Gaafar Numeiry on Soviet Strategy in the Horn

Soviet strategy in Africa and the Middle East had completely failed and this failure should be ascribed to the incorrect information reaching Boris Ponomarev, candidate member of the CPSU Central Committee Politburo, responsible for Middle East Affairs.

The USSR is backing a loser. The USSR is not in agreement with Gaddafy, but what is of concern to it are the funds that it can obtain to implement its strategy. The same applies to Mengistu Haile Mariam, Chairman of the Ethiopian Provisional Military Administrative Council (PMAC).

Asked if he believed that the Ethiopian militia were capable of attacking Eritrea, President Numeiry said: 'The Ethiopian forces will not be able to advance an inch into the liberated Eritrean territories'. He pointed out that Mengistu's militia had no task but to protect his government.

Sudan stood by Somalia, which would ultimately triumph. If the flow of Soviet weapons into Ethiopia continued, then Somalia would find itself compelled to carry out a preventive action against Ethiopia.

Source: Radio Omdurman, 1 June 1977.

Egypt's Attitude to the Conflict in the Horn

President Anwar Sadat's Message for Africa Day
25 May 1977

We have for some time been facing a new danger to our unity, solidarity, co-operation, independence and freedom, as manifested by the fact that some powers take advantage of their relations with some of our states in order to train, arm and move some elements in these states against other neighbouring states for the purpose of overthrowing existing regimes by violent means, and in order to establish regimes which support those powers. This action takes the form of invasion in which the territories of the neighbouring states are used. Such action not only implies aggression against other states and interference in their internal affairs, but also constitutes part of the mercenary activities which we have been trying to eliminate since the end of the sixties so that our affairs and situation would stabilize, and security and democracy would be consolidated in our continent.

There is another danger which threatens our unity, solidarity and freedom. It is the desire of certain states to try and establish military bases in some of our states, exploiting disputes left over among us from previous regimes, and tempting us with arms on the pretext of confronting the ambitions of the neighbouring countries. This will involve us in the struggle among the big powers and threaten our safety and security, as well as our freedom and independence. These powers are serving their own interests in world domination and in confronting each other. . . .

Egypt wishes to draw the attention of all African peoples and states to this plot which is aimed at returning them to super-power spheres of influence which serve the economic interests and political and military considerations of those super-powers. Therefore, I call on all African peoples and states to forget their differences and to solve their problems among themselves or with the help of the other African states, without any interference from countries outside the continent. . . .

Our continent is so rich that it has become the target of economic designs. Our continent occupies a central position in the world and the various powers are struggling to secure influence or military bases in it, with which to confront one another. This is detrimental to our interests. Therefore let us unite in the face of any plot aimed at dividing or fragmenting us geographically, racially or ideologically.

Source: Radio Cairo, 25 May 1977

US Policy on the Conflict in the Horn

Statement by White House Spokesman Hodding Carter III
14 November 1977

Washington will 'abide by a decision not to supply arms' to either Somalia or Ethiopia in their dispute over the Ogaden region of eastern Ethiopia. The Somali action of ousting Soviet advisers and ending the Soviet use of naval facilities puts Somalia 'in a far better position to pursue a truly non-aligned foreign policy. We believe that much of the present problem within the Horn of Africa has been the result of the Soviet decision to provide Somalia with a great amount of military supplies, and then, in search of further strategic advantage, to inaugurate a massive military relationship with Ethiopia.'

The US position is that 'African problems should be settled by the Africans themselves'. The US supports the 'full territorial integrity of Ethiopia [and] that includes the Ogaden' region that Somalia claims.

No outside powers should 'take steps which would . . . enlarge the scope of that conflict' in the Ogaden. The 'peacemaking process by the OAU should be supported by everyone'.

Mr Carter expressed American 'concern' about the 'sharp increase in Cuban strength that has apparently occurred' in Ethiopia 'during the past few weeks'. The 'growing presence' of Cuba 'is detrimental to finding an African solution to the Horn of Africa dispute. . . . We continue to express our concern to the Cubans about their actions in Africa.'

The presence of Cuban troops in Africa 'is a detriment to the improvement' of US relations with the Government of Fidel Castro.

Eritrea

Ethiopian Statement on the Status of the Red Sea

Comments made by a Spokesman of the Ethiopian
Ministry of Foreign Affairs on 1 March 1977
in reply to the declaration in Khartoum by
the leaders of Egypt, Sudan and Syria

What the three leaders said about the Red Sea being an Arab sea and that they would collaborate to guarantee the security of the Red Sea area was indicative of a feeling of superiority and readiness to interfere. Since Ethiopia had sea coasts, it would keenly follow all events in the region and would not stand idly by if countries made decisions affecting the Ethiopian part of the Red Sea area.

Ethiopia had had full control over the Red Sea coast in its region until the colonialists arrived in Africa, and it had clearly demonstrated this by waging several battles to safeguard its independence. The Red Sea should by no means be regarded as an Arab sea.

It was surprising and alarming that a statement had been issued declaring the Red Sea to be an Arab sea on the eve of the opening of the Afro-Arab conference. The statements released in Khartoum were good indications for African leaders who will participate in the conference of the sort of co-operation some Arab governments seek with Africans.

Source: Addis Ababa home service in Amharic, 1 March 1977.

Arab Support for Eritrea

Iraq voiced its reservations about the resolution passed by the Eighth Islamic Foreign Ministers' Conference concerning Eritrea. The resolution called on the conference participants to make every effort to seek a satisfactory solution to the Eritrean problem. The conference also recommended that its efforts be co-ordinated with those of the OAU to reach a just and fair solution to the problem. Voicing Iraq's reservation, the Iraqi delegate said that that resolution dealt with only one aspect of the problem and overlooked the essence and basis. The Eritrean problem, he added, was not one of a Muslim minority but of a people, who included Muslims and Christians, demanding their national rights.

He said that Eritrea had never been part of Ethiopia. Its present plight had been imposed on it by imperialist circles through the establishment of a federation between Eritrea and Ethiopia as a first step. This had been followed by a forced merger imposed by force of arms and imperialist pressure. The Eritrean people had been forced to declare a revolution against this aggression which had usurped their rights and their national and patriotic characteristics as an independent people.

'Because of our national, Islamic and humanitarian responsibilities, we cannot abandon our Arab people in Eritrea in their just and legitimate struggle against the oppression, terror, genocide and expulsion practised by the fascist regime in Ethiopia', he said.

The delegates of Kuwait, Palestine, Jordan, Bahrain and Tunisia also voiced their reservations on this resolution.

Source: Baghdad Radio, 22 May 1977.

Agreement in Principle on Unity:
Joint Statement by the Eritrean Liberation Front
and the People's Liberation Forces

Two delegations representing the Eritrean Liberation Front (the Revolutionary Council) and the People's Liberation Forces (ELF/PLF) held a meeting on 24 July and 25 July 1977, in the liberated territory in Eritrea. At the end of discussions, in which a spirit of mutual understanding prevailed, the two sides agreed upon the following points:

1. That the international situation surrounding our cause requires a speedy realization of national unity.

2. That a single democratic national organization be set up in the Eritrean field.

The People's Liberation Forces clarified that what they meant by immediate amalgamation with the Eritrean Liberation Front (the Revolutionary Council) was the realization of urgent unity between the two sides as early as possible, whether by means of procedures to be agreed on by the two sides, or through a unification conference in case the former alternative becomes impossible.

As regards the Popular Front for the Liberation of Eritrea, the People's Liberation Forces have reiterated their readiness to enter into a dialogue with it in order to establish a single democratic national organization.

3. With respect to the conspiracies being woven by the Ethiopian enemy against our cause, and his preparation of an armed march, it was agreed that a joint and concerted confrontation to the invasion be organized, and that the enemy's complots be frustrated.

4. That the two sides ought to create a suitable atmosphere conducive to the realization of national unity in all spheres.

Eritrean Liberation Front—the Revolutionary Council
Eritrean Liberation Front—People's Liberation Forces

Source: *The Eritrean Review*, August 1977

Eℓ 322

DATE DUE

GAYLORD			PRINTED IN U.S.A.